Beginning Jakarta EE

Enterprise Edition for Java: From Novice to Professional

Peter Späth

Apress®

Beginning Jakarta EE: Enterprise Edition for Java: From Novice to Professional

Peter Späth
Leipzig, Sachsen, Germany

ISBN-13 (pbk): 978-1-4842-5078-5   ISBN-13 (electronic): 978-1-4842-5079-2
https://doi.org/10.1007/978-1-4842-5079-2

Copyright © 2019 by Peter Späth

This work is subject to copyright. All rights are reserved by the Publisher, whether the whole or part of the material is concerned, specifically the rights of translation, reprinting, reuse of illustrations, recitation, broadcasting, reproduction on microfilms or in any other physical way, and transmission or information storage and retrieval, electronic adaptation, computer software, or by similar or dissimilar methodology now known or hereafter developed.

Trademarked names, logos, and images may appear in this book. Rather than use a trademark symbol with every occurrence of a trademarked name, logo, or image we use the names, logos, and images only in an editorial fashion and to the benefit of the trademark owner, with no intention of infringement of the trademark.

The use in this publication of trade names, trademarks, service marks, and similar terms, even if they are not identified as such, is not to be taken as an expression of opinion as to whether or not they are subject to proprietary rights.

While the advice and information in this book are believed to be true and accurate at the date of publication, neither the authors nor the editors nor the publisher can accept any legal responsibility for any errors or omissions that may be made. The publisher makes no warranty, express or implied, with respect to the material contained herein.

Managing Director, Apress Media LLC: Welmoed Spahr
Acquisitions Editor: Steve Anglin
Development Editor: Matthew Moodie
Coordinating Editor: Mark Powers

Cover designed by eStudioCalamar

Cover image by RawPixel

Distributed to the book trade worldwide by Springer Science+Business Media New York, 233 Spring Street, 6th Floor, New York, NY 10013. Phone 1-800-SPRINGER, fax (201) 348-4505, email orders-ny@springer-sbm. com, or visit www.springeronline.com. Apress Media, LLC is a California LLC and the sole member (owner) is Springer Science + Business Media Finance Inc (SSBM Finance Inc). SSBM Finance Inc is a **Delaware** corporation.

For information on translations, please email editorial@apress.com; for reprint, paperback, or audio rights, please email bookpermissions@springernature.com.

Apress titles may be purchased in bulk for academic, corporate, or promotional use. eBook versions and licenses are also available for most titles. For more information, reference our Print and eBook Bulk Sales web page at http://www.apress.com/bulk-sales.

Any source code or other supplementary material referenced by the author in this book is available to readers on GitHub via the book's product page, located at www.apress.com/9781484250785. For more detailed information, please visit http://www.apress.com/source-code.

Printed on acid-free paper

To Salome

Table of Contents

About the Author

Peter Späth graduated in 2002 as a physicist and soon afterward became an IT consultant, mainly for Java-related projects. In 2016, he decided to concentrate on writing books on various topics, but with the main focus set on software development. With two books about graphics and sound processing and two books on Android app development, the author continues his effort in writing software development–related literature.

About the Technical Reviewer

Manuel Jordan Elera is an autodidactic developer and researcher who enjoys learning new technologies for his own experiments and creating new integrations. Manuel won the Springy Award—Community Champion and Spring Champion 2013. In his little free time, he reads the Bible and composes music on his guitar. Manuel is known as dr_pompeii. He has tech reviewed numerous books for Apress, including *Pro Spring, 4th Edition* (2014), *Practical Spring LDAP* (2013), *Pro JPA 2, Second Edition* (2013), and *Pro Spring Security* (2013). Read his thirteen detailed tutorials about many Spring technologies or contact him through his blog at http://www.manueljordanelera.blogspot.com, and follow him on his Twitter account, @dr_pompeii.

Introduction

Software development is about telling computers what has to happen if some kind
of input arrives. This is the most salient quality of computer programs, from the very
beginning of computer history up to today. Other and more detailed qualities emerged
as computer programs more and more showed their ability to handle everyday
tasks. While the practical applicability of computer programs increased, two early
discriminations for different kinds of computer programs showed up: the first is the
place where data live, and the second is the place where programs get stored and run.
With the rise of networks and personal computers (PCs), developers had two options
concerning the program storage place:

- programs could be stored and run locally on PCs,

- or they could be stored and run at some central place on a network,
  with the PCs serving as mere input-gathering and presentation-
  offering units at software operators' desks.

The data soon was handled by specialized programs called *databases,* which could
be tailored to store huge amounts of data and which offered fast access to data by virtue
of specialized data-access languages.

The delegation of computer programs away from the users' desks so as to favor
central program storage at some network node led to a really powerful software
development paradigm: the *client-server architecture.* Here, clients basically are units
accessing services offered by servers running at central network nodes. In this context,
we use the term "service" in a very general manner; in modern architectures,
services often show up in combinations like web services or service-oriented
architecture, which often means specialized-access technologies. See Figure 0-1 for a
bird-view plot.

The advantage of such a client-server architecture is clear: new software versions
with updated or new service program features need to be installed at just one place.
The presumably many client program installations need to be updated only if the input

or presentation logic changes. In addition, the installation programs for different client software versions could be provisioned by the server too, such that other than the client software installation procedure, the complete program logic concerning services and client software installers could be managed at just one place—the server node in the network. In one way or another, this client-server paradigm prevailed over all other evolutionary steps in the history of IT.

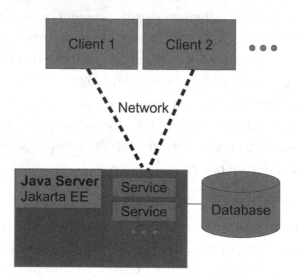

Figure 0-1. *Java client-server architecture*

Note that clients are not restricted to input and presentation units like terminals or browsers. Clients can also be other servers that, in their functioning, need to access services from a server. This frequently happens in a corporate environment, where different servers are responsible for different aspects of a business. Think of a factory, where one server could hold process instructions, another one could handle human resources, a third one would deal with invoices, a fourth one could serve the company's website, and so on.

In this book, we will be talking about such server programs. We will capitalize on Java®[1] as a programming language and the set of Java enterprise edition specifications known by *Jakarta EE* (formerly JEE or J2EE). The services in question include the following:

– **Web access**

  This comprises various formats and protocols used for browser access to resources.

– **Web services**

  These are for a standardized access to resources. They get primarily used by other servers, so web services are for machine-to-machine communication purposes.

– **Messaging services**

  These handle asynchronous processing of messages. Messaging plays an important role in large architectures where message producers can send messages to message brokers and after that can immediately resume their work, while message receivers can fetch messages after some delay.

Under the hood, several other technologies play a role. This includes access to databases, transaction control, special objects for remote access, and more.

Java enterprise server technologies are closely coupled with a specific version of the underlying constituent technologies. The target Java enterprise server version addressed in this book is Jakarta EE 8, exemplified by the open source edition of the *Glassfish* reference implementation (version 5.1). During the course of this book, we'll talk more about the details of Jakarta EE sub-technologies at use.

For development, an *integrated development environment (IDE)* comes in handy and helps with everyday development tasks. It is a program run on a developer's desktop machine (or laptop, of course), and it can be used to build Jakarta EE programs, which can be run both locally on the developer's machine or be transported to a real server somewhere in the network. We will be using the *Eclipse* IDE, which is freely available and free to use for any development stage, including production.

---

[1]Both Java and Oracle are trademarks or registered trademarks of Oracle Inc. The author is independent of Oracle Inc.

> **Note** The Java programming language, the underlying Java runtime engine, and its enterprise variant form just one option for a computer language and technology capable of running servers. There are many more. The reason we talk about Java is that it is modern and quite versatile, can be freely used, has Oracle as a big supporting company, and is widely adopted by a huge community of developers.

The Book's Targeted Audience

This book is for beginning enterprise software developers with knowledge of Java standard edition version 8 or later programming. Profound Java programming is surely helpful, but the author tries to explain advanced language constructs wherever necessary. Also, online Java documentation is available, including tutorials, which can help to fill in knowledge deficiencies.

As a development platform, the Linux operating system gets used, although Windows instructions will be presented as well, and Java can run on several platforms, which can be used interchangeably without major adaptions. This book does not talk about hardware issues, except for maybe some cases where hardware performance has a noticeable impact on the software.

The readers will in the end be able to develop and run Jakarta EE 8 programs of beginning to mid-level complexity.

Source Code

This book's source code can be accessed by clicking the Download Source Code link located at www.apress.com/9781484250785.

How to Read This Book

Reading this book sequentially from the beginning to the end gives you the maximum benefit. If you already have some basic enterprise Java development knowledge, you can skip sections and chapters at will, and you can of course always take a step back and reread sections and chapters while you are advancing inside the book.

CHAPTER 1

Java Development, Enterprise Needs

In a corporate environment, a programming language and software platform like Java has to fulfill a couple of needs that are important to running a business. It has to be able to connect to one or more databases, reliably establish communication with other IT-based systems in the same company or connected businesses, and be powerful enough to consistently handle input and perform calculations based on both input and database data, as well as present the appropriate output to clients. As a cross-concern, security also plays an important role: an authentication process needs to be established that forces users to identify themselves, and an authorization needs to be achieved to limit the amount of resources a particular user is allowed to access. In addition, activities need to be logged for technical maintenance and audit purposes, and the platform should be able to present monitoring data for technical sanity checks and performance-related investigations.

For all of these elements to work in a desired way, a language and platform must be stable with respect to future changes and enhancements. This has to happen such that new language and platform versions can be appropriately handled by the IT staff. Jakarta EE follows this trail and by that largely augments its usefulness for corporate environments.

In this chapter, we will talk about standardization issues that help Jakarta EE to achieve its goals. And we will deal with licensing and the relationship of Jakarta EE to other technology stacks. The chapter closes with a short survey about Java 8 as a platform and as a programming language.

© Peter Späth 2019

P. Späth, *Beginning Jakarta EE*, https://doi.org/10.1007/978-1-4842-5079-2_1

Standardized Specifications

Specifications are important—they tell us what a software can do and how it does it, and they keep track of new versions. The main specification we use in this book reads Jakarta EE 8, and it includes sub-technologies also closely described by exact version numbers. We give a list here and a short description of what each technology does. If you don't understand it yet, don't worry. We will give thorough introductions to most of them in the course of this book. Note that the list is not exhaustive—it does not include some more advanced APIs, which we won't cover in this beginning Jakarta EE book.

– **Enterprise Java Beans (EJB)—Version 3.2**

EJBs represent entry points for business logic. Each EJB plays the role of a *component* in an overall Jakarta EE architecture and signs itself responsible for a dedicated business task. EJBs allow one to add security, transactional features, JPA features for communication with databases, and web services functionality, and they can also be entry points for messaging (JMS; see later bullet item).

– **Java Server Faces (JSF)—Version 2.3**

JSF is the dedicated web front-end technology to be used for browser access. It superseded JSPs (Java Server Pages), although the latter is still part of the Jakarta EE specification. In this book, we will concentrate on JSF for front-end work. JSFs usually communicate over EJBs with the business logic.

– **Unified Expression Language (EL)—Version 3.0**

An important means for JSF pages to communicate with the application logic.

– **RESTful Web Services (JAX-RS)—Version 2.1**

REST (REpresentational State Transfer) is about the original HTTP protocol, which defines reading and writing resources. It recently gained increased attention for single-page web applications, where the front-end page flow gets completely handled by JavaScript running in the browser.

– **JSON Processing (JSON-P)—Version 1.1**

JSON (JavaScript Object Notation) is a lean data format that is particularly useful if a considerable amount of the presentation logic gets handled by JavaScript running in the browser.

– **JSON Binding (JSON-B)—Version 1.0**

This technology simplifies the mapping between JSON data and Java classes.

– **Web Sockets—Version 1.1**

Provides a full-duplex communication between web clients (browsers) and the Jakarta EE server. Other than "normal" access via HTTP, web sockets allow the server to send messages to a browser client as well!

– **JPA—Version 2.2**

The Java Persistence API. Provides high-level access to databases.

– **Java EE Security API—Version 1.0**

A new security API that didn't exist prior to Jakarta EE 8. It includes an HTTP authentication mechanism and an identity store abstraction for validating user credentials and group memberships, and also provides a security-context API to programmatically handle security.

– **Java Messaging Service (JMS)—Version 2.0**

This is about messaging, which means messages can be produced and consumed asynchronously. A message sender produces and issues a message and can instantaneously continue its work even when the message gets consumed later.

– **Java Transaction API (JTA)—Version 1.2**

JTA makes sure that processes that combine several worksteps acting as a unit can be committed or rolled back as a whole. This can become tricky if distributed partners are involved. JTA helps a lot here to ensure transactionality, even for more complex systems.

- **Servlets—Version 4.0**

  Servlets are the underlying technology for server–browser communication. You usually configure them only once at the beginning of a project. We describe servlets where necessary to get other technologies to run.

- **Context and Dependency Injection (CDI)—Version 2.0**

  CDI allows one to bind contexts to elements that are governed by a dedicated lifecycle. In addition, it injects dependencies into objects, which simplifies class associations. We will use CDI to connect JSF elements to the application logic.

- **JavaMail—Version 1.6**

  This provides facilities for reading and sending email. This is just an API; for an implementation, you can, for example, use Oracle's reference implementation: `https://javaee.github.io/javamail/`.

- **Bean Validation—Version 2.0**

  This allows for restricting method call parameters to comply with certain value predicates.

- **Interceptors—Version 1.2**

  Interceptors allow you to wrap method calls into invocations of interceptor classes. While this can be done by programmatic method calls as well, interceptors allow you to do that in a declarative way. You usually use interceptors for crosscutting concerns, like logging, security issues, monitoring, and the like.

- **Batch Processing—Version 1.0**

  This handles jobs that need to be started based on some scheduling.

- **Java Server Pages (JSP)—Version 2.3**

  JSPs can be used to establish a page flow in a server–browser communication. JSP is an older technology, but you still can use it if you like. You should, however, favor JSFs over JSPs, and in this book we don't handle JSPs.

– **JSP Standard Tag Library (JSTL)—Version 1.2**

This is used in conjunction with JSPs for page elements. You *could* use it for JSFs as well, but you should avoid it, since confusing side effects are likely to show up if you combine them. In this book, we won't talk a lot about JSTL.

Jakarta EE runs on top of the Java Standard Edition (SE), so you can always use any classes and interfaces of the Java SE if you program for Jakarta EE. A couple of technologies included within the Java SE, however, play a prominent role in Jakarta EE, as follows:

– **JDBC—Version 4.0**

An access API for databases. All major database vendors provide JDBC drivers for their product. You *could* use it, but you shouldn't. Use the higher-level JPA technology instead. You'll get in contact once in a while, because JPA uses JDBC under the hood.

– **Java Naming and Directory Interface (JNDI)**

In a Jakarta EE 8 environment, objects will be accessed by other objects in a rather loose way. In modern enterprise edition applications, this usually happens via CDI, more precisely via dependency injection. Under the hood, however, a lookup service plays a role, governed by JNDI. In former times, you'd have to directly use JNDI interfaces to programmatically fetch dependent objects. You could use JNDI also for Jakarta EE 8, but you normally don't have to.

– **Java API for XML Processing (JAXP)—Version 1.6**

This is a general-purpose XML processing API. You can access XML data either via DOM (complete XML tree in memory), SAX (event-based XML parsing), or StAX (see the following bulleted item). This is just an API; normally you'd have to also add an implementation, but the Jakarta EE server does this automatically for you.

– **Streaming API for XML (StAX)—Version 1.0**

This is used for streaming access to XML data. *Streaming* here means you serially access XML elements on explicit demand (pull parsing).

– **Java XML Binding (JAXB)—Version 2.2**

JAXB is for connecting XML elements to Java classes.

– **XML Web Services (JAX-WS)—Version 2.2**

Web services are for remotely connecting components using XML as a messaging format.

– **JMX—Version 2.0**

JMX is a communication technology you can use to monitor components of a running Jakarta EE application. It is up to the server implementation as to which information gets available for JMX monitoring, but you can add monitoring capabilities to your own components.

The specifications get handled by a community process, and there will be tests that have to be passed if a vendor wants to be allowed to say its server product conforms to a certain version of Jakarta EE (or one of its predecessors, JEE or J2EE). It is not necessary to study this process if you want to understand Jakarta EE to the level we cover in this book, but if you are interested, the corresponding online resources give you much information about it. As a start, enter "java community process jcp" or "java eclipse ee.next working group" in your favorite search engine.

Multi-tiered Applications

In a corporate environment especially, it is common practice to modularize applications. On a higher level, the modules usually get called *layers,* and if there is more than one layer the application architecture is referred to as multi-layered or multi-tiered architecture.

So far, we've been talking about the client–server model, which is the most common example of a two-tiered architecture. For web applications and applications with dedicated client applications instead of browsers, it is, however, more appropriate to consider a three-tier architecture, which consists of the following elements:

- **Client applications**

  Browsers or specialized programs running on client machines and
  containing only input and presentation logic.

- **Application server**

  A server like Jakarta EE responsible for calculating and delivering
  data to the presentation layer.

- **Data source**

  A layer that holds the data. Most probably this is a database.

In a multi-tiered or multi-layered model, each layer depends only on the layer
underneath it. So, in a three-tiered model the application tier depends on the data tier,
and the presentation tier depends on the application tier. See Figure 1-1.

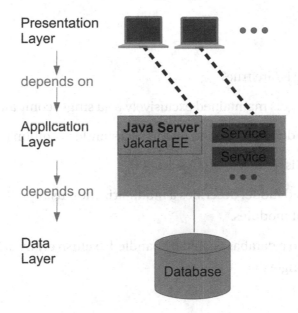

Figure 1-1. *Three-tiered model*

There are other models with a different tier demarcation, or even four and more
tiers. For our aim, it is best to think of a three-tiered model as just stated.

Why Jakarta EE?

The Java enterprise edition was initially developed by Sun Microsystems and had the name J2EE. In 2006, the naming and versioning schema was changed to JEE, and after J2EE version 1.4 came JEE version 5. Since then, major updates have happened, and versions JEE 6, JEE 7, and JEE 8 were released. In 2010, Sun Microsystems was acquired by Oracle Corp. Under Oracle Corp., the versions JEE 7 and JEE 8 were released. In 2017, Oracle Corp. submitted Java EE to the Eclipse Foundation, and there the name of JEE 8 was changed to Jakarta EE 8.

In the beginning of 2019, the transition from JEE 8 to Jakarta EE 8 was still ongoing. So, depending on when you read this book, it could be that for online research on Jakarta EE 8 you have to consult pages about both JEE 8 and Jakarta EE 8. This is something you should keep in mind. To not complicate things in this book, we will only talk about Jakarta EE.

Exercise 1

Which of the following is/are true?

1. Jakarta EE 8 gets maintained exclusively by a single company.

2. Jakarta EE 8 does not depend on the Java standard edition (JSE).

3. Jakarta EE 8 is a successor of Jakarta EE7.

4. A multi-tiered model describes a modularization using independent modules.

5. The access to a database could be handled exclusively by a dedicated single tier.

Jakarta EE Servers and Licensing

When this book was written, there were not many Jakarta EE 8 servers released. There are basically the following:

- Glassfish Server, Open Source Edition, from Oracle Corp.

- WildFly Server, from Red Hat

- JBoss Enterprise Application Platform, from Red Hat

- Websphere Application Server Liberty, from IBM

- Open Liberty, from IBM

These servers have different licensing models. Glassfish, WildFly, and Open Liberty are free. This means you can use them without charge both for development purposes and production. To run the JBoss Enterprise Application Platform a subscription is required, although the sources are open. Websphere Application Server Liberty is proprietary.

In this book, we will talk about the Glassfish server, open source edition, version 5.1. Due to the nature of Jakarta EE 8, a transition to other servers is always possible, although you would have to spend a considerable amount of time changing the administration workflow.

Note   If you target a proprietary server, it is generally not recommended to start development with a different product from a different vendor. You should at least try to develop with a free variant of the same server, or try to get a developer license. To learn Jakarta EE 8, using Glassfish first and only later switching to a different product or vendor is a reasonable approach.

Excursion to Microservices

Microservices are currently en vogue. They describe an architecture model where each module is responsible for just a single fine-grained task. While it is not this book's goal to introduce microservices, nothing prevents us from following microservice architecture paradigms, as follows:

- Each microservice handles just one identifiable and easy-to-grasp business task.

- Microservices are loosely coupled. Each microservice may easily be replaced by a new version.

- When releasing a new version of a microservice, the old version should be made available for some time to allow for transition.

- Microservices must be well isolated from other microservices. That means each microservice should be functional as independently from other microservices as possible.

- Each microservice may provide its own user interface. This could be a web front end, for example.

- Communication between different microservices should happen in a lean message format, like, for example, JSON.

- Microservices should be stateless to avoid complex state handling.

- If combined with Jakarta EE, each microservice gets deployed using its own deployment artifact. Under certain circumstances, a single microservice might be running in its own server instance. It could be possible, for example, to run microservices all in one server instance, or to scatter them over many different servers running on different network nodes.

- Microservices often use lean REST interfaces for communicating with other microservices.

We won't describe microservices explicitly in this book, but if it fits your purpose you can tailor your Jakarta EE application to adhere to these microservices paradigms.

Jakarta EE Applications and the Cloud

There is an ongoing discussion about whether enterprise applications should be running on something that is considered a monolithic Jakarta EE server, or in a cloud environment, which basically means following a microservices architecture and having the infrastructure for running applications get outsourced to a cloud. If you consider them opposite poles, there are good reasons to favor one over the other. Some of the reasons are technical, some stem from marketing perspectives, and some target licensing and maintenance issues. Instead of contributing to this almost religious discussion, I leave the final decision to the reader. A couple of points that could be taken into account are as follows:

- A cloud is not utterly new from a technical perspective; the services infrastructure gets handled by a cloud product, which could be run by a third-party company. It still follows the venerable client–server paradigm.

- Jakarta EE servers are nowadays more lightweight than they used to be a single instance has an infrastructure overhead of less than 100 MB of memory. This is small compared to what modern servers can provide. A RAM of 64 GB capacity, common today, allows for hundreds of Jakarta EE instances to run on one computer, and it is even possible to switch off certain unneeded parts of a Jakarta EE server to further reduce the memory footprint.

- Cloud applications presumably are better scalable compared to monolithic Jakarta EE applications.

- If you rely on cloud infrastructures provided by other companies, you have to be aware that your business data get handled by foreign companies. This requires a big amount of trust, and in the worst case you lose control over valuable business resources.

- If you use clouds provided by other companies, you outsource technical know-how. This is an advantage since you don't have to provide appropriate human resources yourself, but you also give away control and risk a vendor lock-in.

If control over your own applications and your own data is important, having your own Jakarta EE infrastructure might be the way to go. You could even consider running your own company cloud either with or without the participation of Jakarta EE. In this book, we won't cover cloud issues, but you are free to tailor your applications to mimic cloud-like behavior from an infrastructure perspective.

Exercise 2

True or false?

1. Jakarta EE 8 follows a microservices architecture.

2. To run Jakarta EE 8 you need cloud access.

The Java Standard Edition JSE 8

In this book, we talk about the Jakarta EE 8 server, which entirely runs on and depends on Java. Java was invented in 1991 but was first publicly released under version 1.0 by Sun Microsystems in the year 1996. Over the twenty-three years since then, Java has played an important role as both a language and a runtime environment or platform. There are several reasons why Java became so successful, as follows:

- The same Java program can run on different operating systems.

- Java runs in a sandboxed environment. This improves execution security.

- Java can be easily extended by custom libraries.

- The Java language was extended only slowly. While a slow evolution means new and helpful language constructs are often missing from the most current language version, it helps developers to easily keep track of new features and thoroughly perform transitions to new Java versions in longer-running projects. Furthermore, with only a small number of exceptions, Java versions were backward-compatible.

- Java includes a garbage collector, which automatically cleans up unused memory.

Since 1998 and the major rebranding as Java2, the platform was made available in different configurations, as follows:

- The standard edition J2SE for running on a desktop. Further separated into JRE (Java runtime environment) for just running Java, and JDK (Java development kit) for compiling and running Java.

- The micro edition J2ME for mobile and embedded devices

- The enterprise edition J2EE with enterprise features added to J2SE. Each J2EE configuration includes a complete J2SE installation.

For marketing purposes, the "2" was removed in 2006, and the configurations since then got named JSE (or JDK, which is JSE plus development tools), JME, and JEE, respectively. In 2018, JEE was moved to the Eclipse Foundation and renamed Jakarta EE. The Java language substantially changed in the transition from Java 7 to Java 8. We will be using all modern features of Java 8 for our explanations and code examples.

So, if we talk about Jakarta EE, a complete set of the standard edition is included. Knowledge of the SE is a requirement for this book; the author, however, tries to explain complicated constructs.

Java, of course, gets developed further. While the latest version of Jakarta EE was 8 while writing this book, and the underlying Java standard edition version was 8 as well, the latest Java SE (JSE) version you could download was 11. We won't be talking about Java SE versions 9 or higher in this book.

The Java 8 Language

While knowledge of the Java standard edition (JSE) version 8 is considered a prerequisite for this book, for readers who are only partly familiar with Java 8, the following new features are worth investigating before moving on to the next chapters:

- Functional interfaces

- Lambda calculus (unnamed functions)

- The streams API for working with collections and maps

- The new date and time API

We will be using these where appropriate for the examples we are going to describe in this book.

Exercise 3

True or false?

1. Jakarta EE 8 can be run with Java exchanged by C++.

2. Java is a language, *and* it is a platform.

3. Jakarta EE 8 applications can be developed with a programming language other than Java.

CHAPTER 2

Getting a Jakarta EE Server to Work

This chapter is about getting a Glassfish Jakarta EE 8 open source edition server to work. For the operating system, you can choose either Linux or Windows, as I will describe running the server on each of them.

First, we need to have a Java SE8 SDK. Download and install it from Oracle's home page. Let us abbreviate the installation path as SDK_INST. You can choose any path you like.

Note Sometimes paths with spaces in them lead to problems. So if you get an error, such as some component XYZ cannot be found, try to move the JDK to a folder with no spaces in the path.

To check whether Java starts up correctly, open a CMD interpreter for Windows or a shell terminal for Linux, and enter the following:

```
REM Windows:
JDK_INST\bin\java -version
```

```
# Linux:
JDK_INST/bin/java -version
```

where for JDK_INST you substitute the path of your JDK installation. The output should look like this:

```
java version "1.8.0_60"
Java(TM) SE Runtime Environment (build 1.8.0_60-b27)
Java HotSpot(TM) 64-Bit Server VM (build 25.60-b23, mixed mode)
```

© Peter Späth 2019
P. Späth, *Beginning Jakarta EE*, https://doi.org/10.1007/978-1-4842-5079-2_2

Of course, the version numbers may differ if you choose a later build of the JDK. What's important is the "1.8" in the version number.

Getting and Installing Glassfish

Now it is time to download the Glassfish server, version 5.1. As of early 2019, you can get it at: `https://projects.eclipse.org/projects/ee4j.glassfish/downloads` (one line). If the link is broken, enter "glassfish 5.1 download eclipse" in your favorite search engine. Choose the standard (full) version, not the "web profile" version.

Note By the time this book is published and you are reading it, there will probably be more current versions of Glassfish available. You might try versions greater than 5.1, and maybe you won't have any problems installing and using it for this book, but to avoid issues it will always be possible to get an archived Glassfish 5.1 installer.

Extract the archive to any place in your file system. Again, it might not be an issue, but to avoid problems it is best to choose a file system path without spaces in it. We will abbreviate the Glassfish server installation directory as `GLASSFISH_INST`.

Next, we tell the Glassfish server where to find the Java JDK. The server scripts try to find the JDK folder themselves, but to be on the safe side it is better to explicitly configure the server to use the JDK we recently installed. To do so, open the following file:

```
REM Windows:
GLASSFISH_INST\glassfish\config\asenv.bat

# Linux:
GLASSFISH_INST/glassfish/config/asenv.conf
```

and add the following line:

```
REM Windows:
REM Note, if the JDK_INST contains spaces, wrap it
REM inside "..."
set AS_JAVA=JDK_INST
```

```
# Linux:
AS_JAVA="JDK_INST"
```

where for JDK_INST you substitute the installation folder path of your JDK installation.

To see whether the Glassfish server starts up correctly, use the bin/asadmin (Linux) or bin\asadmin.bat script and write the following:

```
cd GLASSFISH_INST
```

```
REM Windows:
bin\asadmin start-domain
```

```
# Linux:
bin/asadmin start-domain
```

where for GLASSFISH_INST you substitute the path of your Glassfish server installation directory. The output should read as follows:

```
Waiting for domain1 to start ..........
Successfully started the domain : domain1
domain  Location: [...]
Log File: [...]
Admin Port: 4848
Command start-domain executed successfully.
```

Once you see that the server started up correctly, you can stop it if you like. To do so, enter the following:

```
REM Windows:
bin\asadmin stop-domain
```

```
# Linux:
bin/asadmin stop-domain
```

Note   For the rest of this chapter, we will assume that you entered cd GLASSFISH_INST to change to the Glassfish installation directory. I will also stop distinguishing between Windows and Linux and write bin/asadmin, which on Windows always transcribes to bin\asadmin.bat.

The Glassfish server has three administrative front ends:

- a shell (or Windows command prompt) front end,

- a GUI front end for browser access, and a

- a REST HTTP front end.

We will talk about these three front ends in the subsequent sections.

Glassfish Shell Administration

The shell front end works via the `bin/asadmin` script, which you can call from a shell (or a Windows command prompt). This command is extremely powerful, as it comprises hundreds of options and sub-commands. We do not list them all here; for complete online documentation, enter "oracle glassfish server administration guide" in your favorite search engine.

As a starting point, the `asadmin` command also provides a "help" functionality. To see it, enter one of the following:

```
bin/asadmin help
bin/asadmin -?
```

where the first variant opens a MORE page. To list all sub-commands, enter the following:

```
# Note: server must be running!
bin/asadmin list-commands
```

And to see the help for a particular sub-command, you can write one of the following:

```
bin/asadmin help <SUB-COMMAND>
bin/asadmin -? <SUB-COMMAND>
```

where for `<SUB-COMMAND>` you substitute the name of the sub-command.

Note   For many sub-commands to run properly, the server must be running as well. In the following, we assume that the server has started before you issue sub-commands.

Multi-mode Sessions

There is also a *multi-mode* session, where a special sub-shell gets opened. In this sub-shell you can enter sub-commands directly without prepending bin/asadmin. To start a multi-mode session, enter

```
bin/asadmin
```

without arguments. You can also use the sub-command multimode to start a multi-mode session:

```
bin/asadmin multimode
```

The sub-command allows for an optional --file <FILE_NAME> as argument, which causes the specified file to be read in as a list of sub-commands to be executed sequentially, as follows:

```
bin/asadmin multimode --file commands_file.txt
```

where the file path is relative to the current working directory.

In the following paragraphs, we show a non-exhaustive list of the most useful options and sub-commands.

General Options

The most useful general options are shown in Table 2-1. You add them as in bin/asadmin --host 192.168.1.37 list-applications.

Table 2-1. *General Options*

Option	Description
--host <HOST>	Specifies the host where the server is running. If you don't specify it, localhost will be taken.
--port <PORT>	The administration port. Default is 4848.
--user <USER_NAME>	Use the specified user for authenticating to the server. Use this if you restricted access to the asadmin utility. The default is the admin user.
--passwordfile <FILE_NAME>	If you restricted access to the asadmin utility, and you want to prevent a user password from being prompted, you can specify a file with password information instead. For details, see the output of bin/asadmin -?.

For a complete list of the options you can add to the `asadmin` command, see the output of `bin/asadmin -?`.

Inquiring After Information

Sub-commands to inquire after various information data from the server are shown in Table 2-2. You enter them as in `bin/asadmin list-applications`.

Table 2-2. *Inquiring After Information*

Sub-command	Description
`version`	Outputs the Glassfish server version.
`list-applications`	Use this to list all applications deployed and running on the server.
`list-containers`	Containers embrace components (modules, if you like) of a certain type. Use this sub-command to list all the containers running in the server.
`list-modules`	Use this to list all OSGi (Open Services Gateway Initiative) modules running in the server. We won't be talking about OSGi in this beginner's book, but in case you are interested: Glassfish incorporates an *Apache Felix* OSGi module management system. You can administer Glassfish components also via an OSGi shell named "Gogo," which needs more configuration work in order to run.
`list-commands`	List all sub-commands. If you add `--localonly` the server need not be running, and only those sub-commands will show that can be issued without the server running.
`list-timers`	Use this to show all timers. We don't talk about timers in this book.
`list-domains`	List all domains. In this book, we will be using the pre-installed default domain "domain1," so this will be the only entry showing up here.

Setting and Changing the Admin-Password

After you perform the installation of the Glassfish server, there will be one administration user named "admin" without a password. Not having a password makes administrative tasks easy, but it will also leave your server insecure. To remedy that and give the `admin` user a password, enter the following:

```
bin/asadmin change-admin-password
```

You will then be asked for the actual password, which is empty, so just press ENTER, and type in the new password twice.

Once the admin user has a password, you will have to enter the password for most asadmin sub-commands.

Domain Administration

To start a domain means to start the Glassfish server. We could have several domains in one Glassfish server, but a multi-domain setup is best left for a more advanced Jakarta EE book. We will go with the single "domain1" domain, which gets installed by default.

To start, stop, or restart the Glassfish server, enter one of the following commands:

```
bin/asadmin start-domain
bin/asadmin stop-domain
bin/asadmin restart-domain
```

All three sub-commands take an optional domain name as a parameter (for example, "domain1" or "domain2"), but since we have only one default domain, it can be left off here.

To see the uptime of the server, which more precisely is the time that has elapsed since the default domain started, enter the following:

```
bin/asadmin uptime
```

Administering the Built-In Database

The Jakarta EE Glassfish server comes with a built-in database. This comes in handy for development purposes, although you probably won't use this database for production setups.

This database is a JavaDB (or Derby, which is the same but just an older name) database. It does not run by default when the Glassfish server gets started; instead, to start and stop the database, enter the following:

```
bin/asadmin start-database
bin/asadmin stop-database
```

where the database port by default reads 1527.

Glassfish GUI Administration

After you start the Glassfish server, a GUI console is provided and can be accessed by opening the following URL in a browser:

```
http://localhost:4848
```

The GUI will then show up, as seen in Figure 2-1.

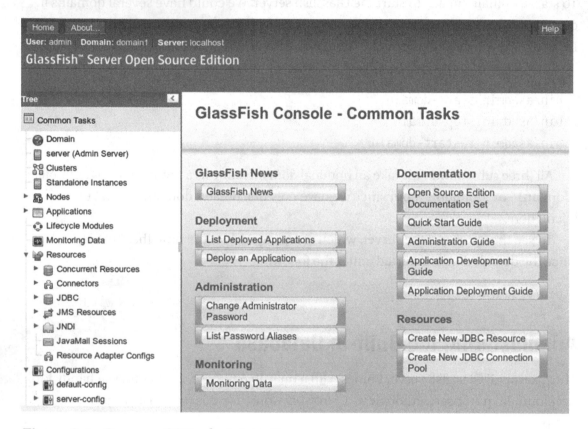

Figure 2-1. *Browser GUI administration*

We won't talk about details of the GUI administration at this time. We will, however, use and describe it once in a while, and the help button at the top-right corner is a good starting point for your own experiments and investigations.

Note   Many `asadmin` operations that you can enter in a terminal have their counterparts in the admin GUI.

Glassfish REST Interface Administration

The Glassfish Jakarta EE 8 server provides a REST interface that you can use to investigate and control the server. You can issue, for example, the following:

```
curl -X GET -H "Accept: application/json" \
http://localhost:4848/monitoring/domain/view-log/details
```

to see the domain logs via REST.

Note   For this to work, the curl utility must be installed on your system. Alternatively, you can use any other REST client (Firefox REST-client add-on, REST Client for Eclipse, and others).

We will investigate a couple of examples. To find more in-depth information about this interface, enter "rest interface administer glassfish" in your favorite search engine. Also, we will use the jq tool to provide nicely formatted output of the generated JSON data. For jq there are installers available for both Linux and Windows.

The administrative REST interface is sub-divided into two parts for configuration and monitoring:

```
http://host:port/management/domain/[path]
http://host:port/monitoring/domain/[path]
```

where for a vanilla Glassfish installation host = "localhost" and port = "4848." For [path] you must substitute a resource identifier. For example, to see the log entries you enter the following:

```
curl -X GET -H "Accept: application/json" \
http://localhost:4848/management/domain/view-log
```

(remove the backslash if you enter this in one line).

The REST interface is very extensive. You can query a lot of properties using REST's GET verb, and you can alter resources using POST or PUT. As a starting point, you can investigate the verbose output of REST capabilities you get once you enter the following:

```
curl -X GET -H "Accept: application/json" \
http://localhost:4848/management/domain
```

The output will, for example, include the following:

```
"commands": [
  ...
  {
    "path": "list-commands",
    "method": "GET",
    "command": "list-commands"
  },
  {
    "path": "restart-domain",
    "method": "POST",
    "command": "restart-domain"
  },
  {
    "path": "uptime",
    "method": "GET",
    "command": "uptime"
  },
  {
    "path": "version",
    "method": "GET",
    "command": "version"
  }
  ...
]
```

and lots of others. So, to see version and uptime you enter the following:

```
curl -X GET -H "Accept: application/json" \
   http://localhost:4848/management/domain/version | jq .
curl -X GET -H "Accept: application/json" \
   http://localhost:4848/management/domain/uptime | jq .
```

If you use a browser and enter REST URLs there, you can get more information about REST resources. If you open a browser and enter `http://localhost:4848/management/domain/version` as the URL, you will get an HTML variant of the preceding CURL output. Both also tell us about child resources.

So, for example,

```
curl -X GET -H "Accept: application/json" \
  http://localhost:4848/management/domain/applications | jq .
```

shows us about commands that refer to an installed application. It tells us that for the actual list we have to enter the following:

```
curl -X GET -H "Accept: application/json" \
  http://localhost:4848/management/domain/applications/
  list-applications | jq .
```

(no line break after `applications/`). And it tells us about attributes. To get a more verbose output, we can add a `?long=true`, as in the following:

```
curl -X GET -H "Accept: application/json" \
  http://localhost:4848/management/domain/applications/
  list-applications?long=true | jq .
```

CHAPTER 3

Setting Up an IDE

Integrated Development Environments or IDEs are graphical desktop applications that help to both develop and test Jakarta EE applications. Several IDE products exist; in this book, we will be using the Eclipse IDE, which is free to install and use, even for commercial purposes. Installers exist for Linux, Windows, and MacOS.

In this chapter, we will discover how to get and install Eclipse, and we will develop a first simple Jakarta EE application.

Installing Eclipse for Jakarta EE Development

Eclipse comes in several variants. Go to the download page at `https://www.eclipse.org/downloads/packages/` and download "Eclipse IDE for Enterprise Java Developers" for your operating system. If the link is broken, enter "eclipse download packages" in your favorite search engine.

Note   In this book, we will use Eclipse version "2019-03." Later versions might be OK, but you should not use an earlier version. Downloading the exact version "2019-03" will always be possible using an archived installer.

Perform the basic installation as described on the Eclipse installation site. For everything to work correctly, you must make sure Eclipse gets started using a Java JDK8 installation. To find out which Java gets used by the IDE, start Eclipse, then navigate to Help ➤ About Eclipse IDE ➤ Installation Details ➤ "Configuration" tab.

© Peter Späth 2019
P. Späth, *Beginning Jakarta EE*, https://doi.org/10.1007/978-1-4842-5079-2_3

Note   When you start Eclipse, it asks you for a *workspace.* This is a folder that can hold several distinct or interrelated projects. It is up to you if you want to choose an existing workspace or use a fresh new folder for an empty workspace.

In the pane, find the line that starts with `java.runtime.version=...`. The version behind the "=" sign should show at least 1.8.0. If this is not the case, close Eclipse, navigate to the

```
ECLIPSE_INST_DIR/eclipse.ini
```

file, open it in an editor, and add

```
-vm PATH_TO_YOUR_JDK8_JAVA
```

directly underneath the line with `openFile`. Replace `PATH_TO_YOUR_JDK8_JAVA` with the path to the Java executable inside your JDK8 installation directory. The executable reads `java` for Linux and `javaw.exe` for Windows, and you can find it inside the `bin` folder of the JDK installation. If, inside the file `eclipse.ini`, there are two lines starting with `openFile`, you can use either of them.

Note   The folder structure on MacOS is slightly different, but the file name is the same, so it is easy to find.

So, for Linux you would have something like the following:

```
...
openFile
-vm
/path/to/jdk8/bin/java
...
```

And for Windows:

```
...
openFile
-vm
C:\path\to\jdk8\bin\javaw.exe
...
```

Restart Eclipse and check again for the correct version.

As a next preparatory step, we need to make sure Eclipse also uses a Java JDK8 for new projects. To do so, go to Window ➤ Preferences (or the corresponding place on MacOS). In the dialog, navigate to Java ➤ Installed JREs and make sure that the JDK8 is the checked default Java in the list. If it is missing, click the "Add..." button and register your JDK8. See Figure 3-1.

Figure 3-1. *JRE setting in Eclipse*

The Eclipse IDE for enterprise Java developers already contains a toolset for Jakarta EE 8 development. But one thing is missing—we need to add a plugin that provides the capabilities to handle a Glassfish version 5 or 5.1 server. To install that plugin, go to Help ➤ Install New Software…. Click on the "Add…" button at the top of the dialog window that then appears. Enter "Oracle Enterprise Pack" in the "Name" field and "`http://download.oracle.com/otn_software/oepe/12.2.1.9/photon/repository/dependencies/`" in the "Location" field. See Figure 3-2.

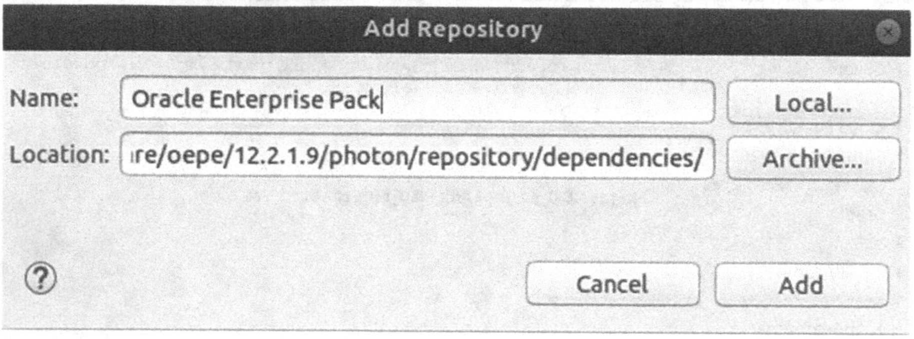

Figure 3-2. *Oracle Enterprise Pack*

Note   There might be a more recent version available for the Oracle Enterprise Pack. Go to `https://www.oracle.com/technetwork/developer-tools/eclipse/downloads/index.html` and check for new versions.

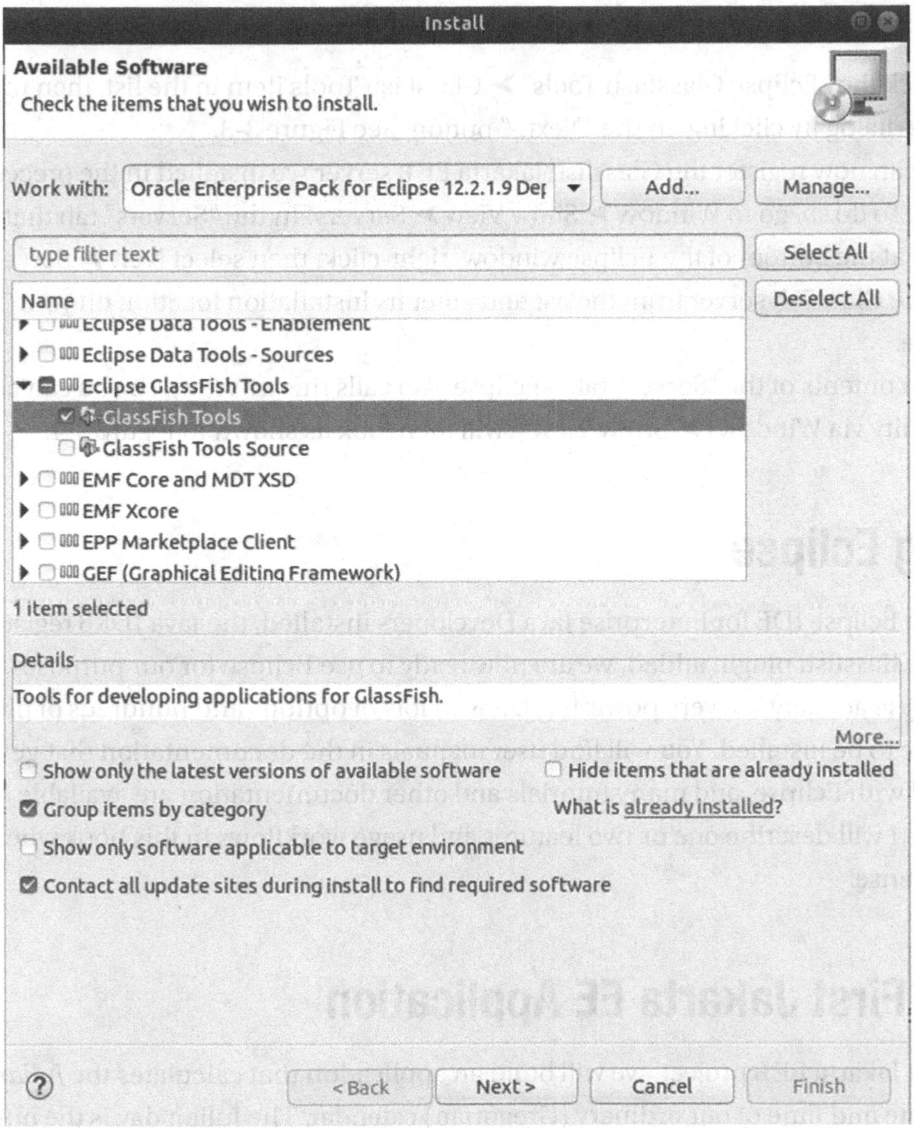

Figure 3-3. Glassfish Tools installation

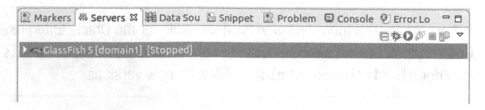

Figure 3-4. Eclipse Servers view

Check the "Eclipse GlassFish Tools" ➤ GlassFish Tools item in the list, then proceed with the dialog by clicking on the "Next>" button. See Figure 3-3.

We can now register the Glassfish Jakarta EE 8 server we installed in the preceding chapter. To do so, go to Window ➤ Show View ➤ Servers. In the "Servers" tab that appears at the bottom of the Eclipse window, right-click, then select New ➤ Server. Select the Glassfish server from the list and enter its installation location on your machine.

The contents of the "Server" tab—Eclipse also calls this a "View," so you can control its visibility via Windows ➤ Show View—will then look as shown in Figure 3-4.

Using Eclipse

With the Eclipse IDE for Enterprise Java Developers installed, the Java JDK8 registered, and the Glassfish plugin added, we are now ready to use Eclipse for our purposes.

Eclipse actually is a very powerful IDE with lots of options and hundreds of plugins available to be installed. You will find user manuals in the documentation that gets shipped with Eclipse, and many tutorials and other documentation are available on the internet. I will describe one or two features and usage workflows in this book where it makes sense.

Your First Jakarta EE Application

As a first Jakarta EE 8 project, we will build an application that calculates the *Julian* day given date and time of our ordinary (Gregorian) calendar. The Julian day is the number of days since noon UTC 4317 years before Christ.

The application consists of two layers: a front-end part for communication with the user for acquiring the input date and returning the Julian day, and a back-end part for the calculation. For this simple application, we don't need a database layer.

We separate the two layers into two Eclipse projects. For the front end we'll use JSF pages, and for the back end a RESTful service for the calculation. The purpose of this chapter is not to give you a detailed introduction to Java enterprise application development; instead, we want to build a first, non-trivial Jakarta EE 8 project so as to get acquainted with the Java enterprise features and to start learning how to use Eclipse.

The Julian Calendar Back End

To start the back-end project, open Eclipse with the workspace of your choice.

Then, in the Project Explorer pane on the left side of the Eclipse window, right-click and select New ➤ Project... and then select Maven ➤ Maven Project. Press the "Next>" button twice, then choose "maven-archetype-quickstart" from the archetypes catalog and enter the following project data:

```
Group-Id:    book.jakarta8
Artifact-Id: julian
Version:     0.0.1-SNAPSHOT
```

With the wizard finished, the new project "julian" will appear in the Project Explorer.

Note   Because of the way Eclipse handles the Maven "quickstart" archetype, it will create a first Java package, "book.jakarta8.julian." This is just for convenience; for our Java classes we can use any package name we like. We will deviate from this auto-suggestion from time to time, but for the current project the suggestion is fine.

For the project to work in a Jakarta EE 8 environment, we must add a special library to it. To this aim, open the pom.xml file and in the dependencies section add the following:

```
<dependency>
    <groupId>javax</groupId>
    <artifactId>javaee-api</artifactId>
    <version>8.0</version>
</dependency>
```

In the same file, change the packaging to `<packaging>war</packaging>`. Right-click on the project name in the Project Explorer and select Maven ➤ Update Project.... Make sure "Update project configuration from pom.xml" is checked and press "OK."

Ensure version 8 of the Java JDK gets used. To do so, right-click on the project in the Project Explorer, then select "Properties." Navigate to "Java Build Path" ➤ "Libraries" tab. Make sure the correct JRE system library is shown. If not, remove it, then click on the "Add Library..." button, select "JRE System Library," make sure "Workspace default JRE" is checked, and then press "Finish". Press "Apply and Close."

To make sure the Maven build tool uses the correct Java version, open `pom.xml`. Check that it contains the following, or add it:

```
<project ...>
    ...
    <build>
      <plugins>
        <plugin>
          <artifactId>maven-compiler-plugin</artifactId>
          <configuration>
            <source>1.8</source>
            <target>1.8</target>
          </configuration>
        </plugin>
      </plugins>
    </build>
</project>
```

The `<build>` element can, for example, be placed underneath the closing `</dependencies>` in that file. If you changed something in the `pom.xml` file, right-click on the project, then invoke Maven ➤ Update Project....

Caution   Under some circumstances the project might use the wrong compiler level. To check that, right-click on the project in the Project Explorer, then select "Properties." At "Java Compiler" make sure the "Enable project specific settings" checkbox is *not* checked.

Next, we must convert the project to a *faceted* project, which allows us to later add Jakarta EE 8 capabilities. To do so, right-click on the project in the Project Explorer, then select Configure ➤ Convert to Faceted Form.... If this menu entry does not exist, the project is already faceted. In the facets dialog, which you can see after you click "Convert to Faceted Form..." or by right-clicking on the project name ➤ Properties ➤ Project Facets, check and enter the following:

```
Dynamic Web Module 4.0
Java 1.8
JavaScript 1.0
JAX-RS (REST Web Services) 2.1
```

If it is not possible to change the version, remove the check, click "Apply and Close," and open the dialog again. Then you can recheck and select the desired version.

In the Project Explorer, if there exists a new "WebContent" folder, move it to the "src/main" folder and rename it "webapp." The "WebContent" folder gets created by the facets wizard, but in a Maven project it is better to have it inside the "src/main" folder.

Make sure the following files exist in the "src/main/webapp/WEB-INF" folder (if the folder doesn't exist, create it): beans.xml, web.xml, and glassfishweb.xml.

If it does not yet exist, create the file src/main/webapp/WEB-INF/glassfish-web.xml. Let its contents read as follows:

```
<?xml version="1.0" encoding="UTF-8"?>
<!DOCTYPE glassfish-web-app PUBLIC
    "-//GlassFish.org//DTD GlassFish Application Server
    3.1 Servlet 3.0//EN"
    "http://glassfish.org/dtds/glassfish-web-app_3_0-1.dtd">
<glassfish-web-app error-url="">
    <class-loader delegate="true"/>
</glassfish-web-app>
```

(The DOCTYPE element in one line, one space after PUBLIC, just one space in front of "3.1", and one space before the "http...".) This file is a Glassfish-specific addition. It is not part of the Jakarta EE 8 specification, but the server uses it for some configuration settings.

The file src/main/webapp/WEB-INF/beans.xml can be empty for now (but do not delete it!).

The file `src/main/webapp/WEB-INF/web.xml` must contain the following lines:

```xml
<?xml version="1.0" encoding="UTF-8"?>
<web-app xmlns:xsi=
    "http://www.w3.org/2001/XMLSchema-instance"
  xmlns="http://xmlns.jcp.org/xml/ns/javaee"
  xsi:schemaLocation="http://xmlns.jcp.org/xml/ns/javaee
    http://xmlns.jcp.org/xml/ns/javaee/web-app_4_0.xsd"
  id="WebApp_ID" version="4.0">

  <display-name>julian</display-name>
  <servlet>
    <servlet-name>
      javax.ws.rs.core.Application
    </servlet-name>
  </servlet>
  <servlet-mapping>
    <servlet-name>
      javax.ws.rs.core.Application
    </servlet-name>
    <url-pattern>/webapi/*</url-pattern>
  </servlet-mapping>
</web-app>
```

This file is responsible for mapping URL requests starting with "/webapi/" to a REST processing engine.

So much for the preparation. Later, in your everyday work, you will realize that in a Jakarta EE environment you will spend a lot of time preparing a fluent development workflow. There is nothing wrong with that, and always keep in mind that a thorough preparation helps to speed up the actual implementation and get it stable.

For the implementation in this back end, all that is left to do is create a class that handles REST requests. Let us call it `Julian`, and let us put it into the package `book.jakarta8.julian`. After you create the class, replace its contents with the following:

```java
package book.jakarta8.julian;

import java.util.function.Function;

import javax.ws.rs.GET;
import javax.ws.rs.Path;
import javax.ws.rs.PathParam;
import javax.ws.rs.Produces;

/**
 * REST Web Service
 */
@Path("/")
public class Julian {
    @GET
    @Produces("text/plain")
    @Path("convert/{inDate : .*}")
    public String convert(
            @PathParam("inDate") String inDate) {

        Function<Double,Integer> trunc = (d) ->
            d.intValuc();

        // yyyy-MM-dd-HH-mm-ss
        int inYear = Integer.parseInt(
          inDate.substring(0, 4));
        int inMonth = Integer.parseInt(
          inDate.substring(5, 7));
        int inDay = Integer.parseInt(
          inDate.substring(8, 10));
        int inHour = Integer.parseInt(
          inDate.substring(11, 13));
        int inMinute = Integer.parseInt(
          inDate.substring(14, 16));

        double jd = 367 * inYear
          - trunc.apply(  7.0 * (
              inYear + trunc.apply((inMonth+9.0)/12)
```

```
                              ) / 4   )
        + trunc.apply(275.0 * inMonth / 9)
        + inDay
        + 1721013.5
        + 1.0 * (inHour + inMinute / 60.0) / 24
        - 0.5*Math.signum(100*inYear + inMonth -190002.5)
        + 0.5;

    return "" + jd;
  }
}
```

This class installs a REST interface by virtue of the @Path and @GET annotations.

After you save the file, we want to tell Eclipse to start the server and deploy the calculation back end. For this aim, right-click on the project in the Project Explorer and select Run As ➤ Run on Server. Select the Glassfish server and click the "Finish" button. See Figure 3-5.

Eclipse then starts the server, unless it is already running, and builds and deploys the application. When this is done, Eclipse by default tries to load a web page, which, however, leads to an error. Ignore this—we don't have a user interface for the back-end application.

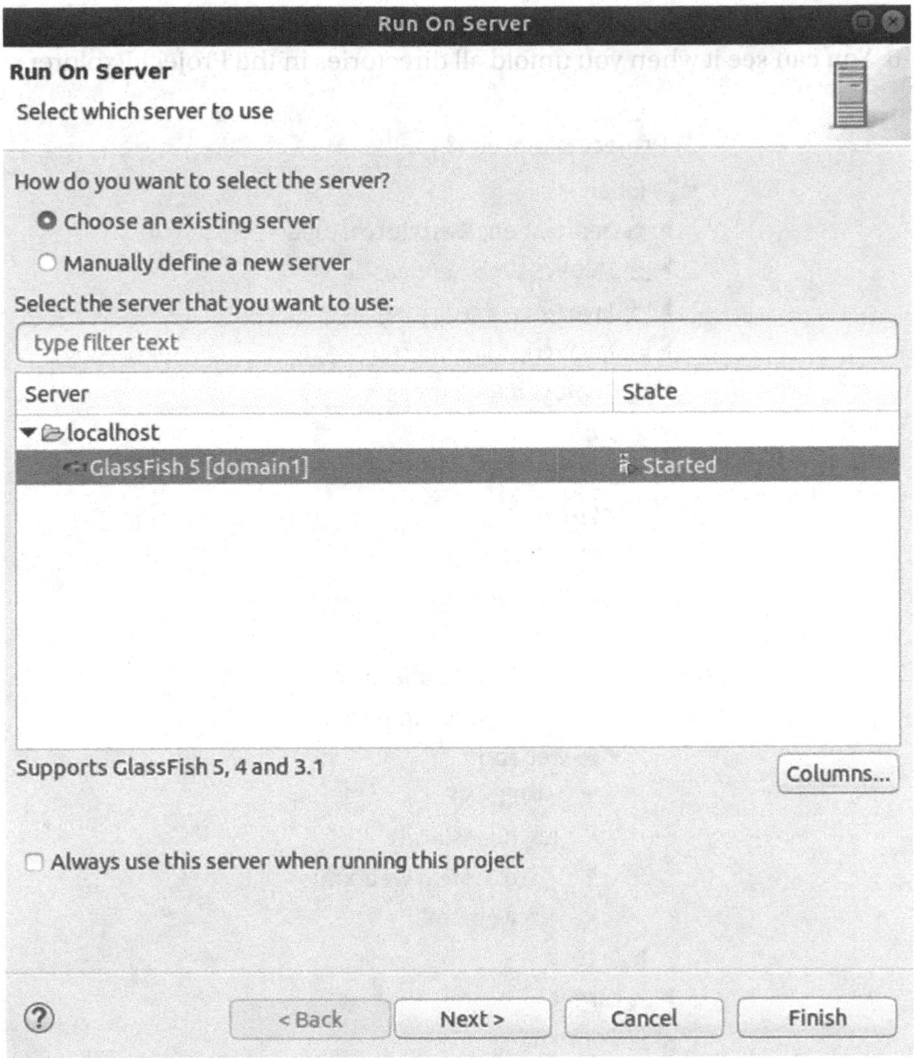

Figure 3-5. *Deploy the back-end application*

To see whether the back end works as expected, we need a program that can emit REST requests. There are several options—try to find a REST client on the internet (there are, for example, several REST add-ons for the Firefox web browser). Or you can use the `curl` command (you might first have to install it on your operating system) as follows:

```
curl -X GET
http://localhost:8080/julian/webapi/convert/2000-01-01-12-00-00
```

(write it on one line, with no spaces after 8080/). The output should read `2451545.0`.

An overview of all the files that participate in the back-end application is shown in Figure 3-6. You can see it when you unfold all directories in the Project Explorer.

Figure 3-6. *Back-end files*

The Julian Calendar Front End

The front-end application, whose responsibility is to provide browser-based access to the Julian day-conversion REST service, exists in its own Eclipse project. First, open Eclipse using the same workspace you chose for the back-end project. In the Project Explorer pane, right-click and select New ➤ Project.... Choose Maven ➤ Maven project, select "maven-archetype-quickstart" from the archetypes catalog after two "Next>" clicks, and enter the following project data after another "Next>" click:

```
Group-Id:    book.jakarta8
Artifact-Id: julian-gui
Version:     0.0.1-SNAPSHOT
Package:     book.jakarta8.juliangui
```

Click on the "Finish" button. In the Project Explorer pane, the new project "julian-gui" appears.

In the Maven build file pom.xml, change the packaging to war and add the same dependencies and build configuration as were used for the back-end project:

```
<project ...>
    ...
    <dependencies>
        ...
        <dependency>
          <groupId>javax</groupId>
          <artifactId>javaee-api</artifactId>
          <version>8.0</version>
        </dependency>
    </dependencies>

    <build>
      ...
      <plugins>
        ...
        <plugin>
          <artifactId>maven-compiler-plugin</artifactId>
          <configuration>
            <source>1.8</source>
            <target>1.8</target>
          </configuration>
        </plugin>
      </plugins>
    </build>
</project>
```

Make sure the project uses Java JDK version 8; use the same procedure as described for the back-end project (project JRE library and compiler level). Also, convert the project to a faceted project and add the same features as for the back end, plus

```
Java Server Faces 2.3
```

but with "JAX-RS (REST Web Service)" unchecked. If the dialog tells you that further configuration is required (see Figure 3-7), click on the message text (blue in the figure) and in the dialogs that appear check the checkbox for "Generate web.xml deployment descriptor." Also make sure that in the appropriate places "Disable Library Configuration" is selected. Click "Apply and Close."

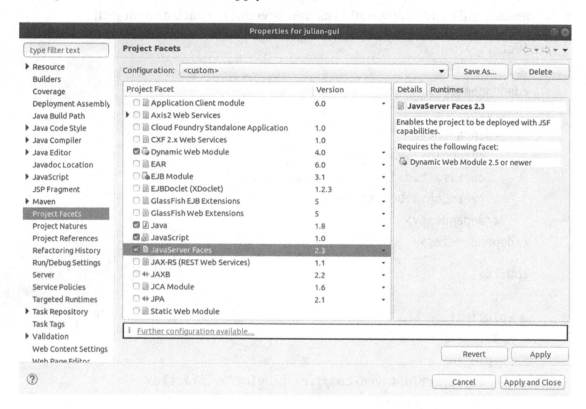

Figure 3-7. *Front-end project facets*

If a new folder "WebContent" appears, move it to "src/main" and rename it "webapp." If it does not exist yet, create a folder "src/main/webapp/WEB-INF." Copy the files beans.xml, web.xml, and glassfish-web.xml from the back-end project to this folder. This is not supposed to tell you they are related, but the copying might save some keyboard work.

If it does not exist yet, create a file called `src/main/webapp/WEB-INF/facesconfig.xml`. Let it read as follows:

```xml
<?xml version="1.0" encoding="UTF-8"?>
<faces-config
  xmlns="http://xmlns.jcp.org/xml/ns/javaee"
  xmlns:xsi="http://www.w3.org/2001/XMLSchema-instance"
  xsi:schemaLocation="http://xmlns.jcp.org/xml/ns/javaee
  http://xmlns.jcp.org/xml/ns/javaee/
        web-facesconfig_2_3.xsd"
    version="2.3">

    <application>
      <resource-bundle>
        <base-name>
          julian.web.WebMessages
        </base-name>
        <var>bundle</var>
      </resource-bundle>
      <locale-config>
        <default-locale>en</default-locale>
        <!--  <supported-locale>es</supported-locale> -->
      </locale-config>
    </application>
</faces-config>
```

(Remove the line break after `javaee/` and leave no space after it).

Replace the contents of `src/main/webapp/WEB-INF/web.xml` with the following lines:

```xml
<?xml version="1.0" encoding="UTF-8"?>
<web-app xmlns:xsi=
  "http://www.w3.org/2001/XMLSchema-instance"
  xmlns="http://xmlns.jcp.org/xml/ns/javaee"
  xsi:schemaLocation="http://xmlns.jcp.org/xml/ns/javaee
  http://xmlns.jcp.org/xml/ns/javaee/web-app_4_0.xsd"
  id="WebApp_ID" version="4.0">
```

43

```
<display-name>julian-gui</display-name>
<welcome-file-list>
  <welcome-file>greeting.xhtml</welcome-file>
</welcome-file-list>
<servlet>
  <servlet-name>Faces Servlet</servlet-name>
  <servlet-class>
    javax.faces.webapp.FacesServlet
  </servlet-class>
  <load-on-startup>1</load-on-startup>
</servlet>
<servlet-mapping>
  <servlet-name>Faces Servlet</servlet-name>
  <url-pattern>*.xhtml</url-pattern>
</servlet-mapping>
</web-app>
```

We now must create two JSF pages for the front end. The first goes to `src/main/webapp/greeting.xhtml` and is the entry point for the web app. Create the file and let it read as follows:

```
<!DOCTYPE html>
<html xmlns:h="http://xmlns.jcp.org/jsf/html"
      xmlns:f="http://xmlns.jcp.org/jsf/core"
      xmlns:pt="http://xmlns.jcp.org/jsf/passthrough">
<h:head><title>Julian Converter</title></h:head>
<h:body>
  <h:form id="form">
    <h2>
        <h:outputText value="#{bundle.welcome}"/>
    </h2>
    <h:outputText value="#{bundle.instructions}"/>
    <p/>
    <h:outputText
        value="#{bundle.label_gregorianDate} "/>
    <h:inputText id="getdate"
        value="#{julian.dateIn}">
```

```
    <f:convertDateTime
        pattern="yyyy-MM-dd HH:mm:ss" />
  </h:inputText>
  <h:message for="getdate" style="color:red" />
  <p/>
  <h:commandButton value="#{bundle.submit}"
                  action="#{julian.convert}"/>
 </h:form>
</h:body>
</html>
```

Note   The file is not XHTML in a strict sense—actually, it is an HTML 5 page with non-standard namespaces. We use the .xhtml ending so Eclipse will provide a suitable editor for such files. In the rest of this chapter we use the term *template file*.

This template file uses a resource bundle; you can see this from the #{bundle. WHATSOEVER} expressions. This refers to strings from a localized resource we must now create. To do so, create a file called src/main/resources/julian/web/WebMessages. properties and as its contents write the following:

```
welcome=This is a Gregorian date to Julian day converter.
instructions=Enter a Gregorian UTC date in the form \
    yyyy-mm-dd hh:mm:ss (use 24hr format), then submit.
label_gregorianDate=Gregorian Date:
label_response=The Julian Day Reads:
submit=Submit
back=Back
```

We must tell JSF to use this bundle. This happens in the file src/main/webapp/WEB-INF/faces-config.xml, which we added earlier. Type the following:

```
<?xml version="1.0" encoding="UTF-8"?>
<faces-config ...>
    <application>
        <resource-bundle>
```

```
            <base-name>julian.web.WebMessages</base-name>
            <var>bundle</var>
        </resource-bundle>
        <locale-config>
            <default-locale>en</default-locale>
            <!-- <supported-locale>es</supported-locale> -->
        </locale-config>
    </application>
</faces-config>
```

For our simple example, we only use the default resource. If we, for example, wanted to add Spanish text, we'd provide the translation in the `WebMessages_es.properties` file in the same folder, and we'd uncomment the `<supportedlocale>` element from `faces-config.xml`.

We must now tell the web app to use this `greetings` page as a landing page. This happens inside `src/main/webapp/WEB-INF/web.xml`, where we write the following:

```
...
<welcome-file-list>
        <welcome-file>greeting.xhtml</welcome-file>
</welcome-file-list>
...
```

You can remove any other elements inside `<welcome-file-list>`, as we don't need them.

We then create a second template file for the response, `src/main/webapp/response.xhtml`, with the following contents:

```
<!DOCTYPE html>
<html xmlns:h="http://xmlns.jcp.org/jsf/html"
    xmlns:f="http://xmlns.jcp.org/jsf/core"
    xmlns:pt="http://xmlns.jcp.org/jsf/passthrough">
    <h:head>
        <title>Julian Response Page</title>
    </h:head>
    <h:body>
        <h:form>
            <h:outputText
```

```
            value="#{bundle.label_response}"/>
        <p/>
        <h:outputText
            value="#{julian.gd} -> "/>
        <h:outputText
            value="#{julian.jd}"/>
        <p/>
        <h:commandButton id="back"
            value="#{bundle.back}"
            action="greeting"/>
        </h:form>
    </h:body>
</html>
```

This represents the response page after a submission from the greetings page. JSF knows to navigate to this page because of the string the class Julian returns when its convert() method gets called (see following code section for the class code).

We still need to write a Java class for holding variables that we can access from the JSF pages, and for reacting to button presses and performing the calculation. We call this class Julian, and it goes to package book.jakarta8.juliangui. Create this class and replace its contents with the following:

```
package book.jakarta8.juliangui;

import java.io.Serializable;
import java.time.LocalDateTime;
import java.time.ZoneId;
import java.time.format.DateTimeFormatter;
import java.util.Date;

import javax.enterprise.context.SessionScoped;
import javax.faces.application.FacesMessage;
import javax.faces.context.FacesContext;
import javax.inject.Named;
import javax.ws.rs.client.Client;
import javax.ws.rs.client.ClientBuilder;
import javax.ws.rs.client.WebTarget;
```

```java
/**
 * A CDI managed bean.
 */
@Named
@SessionScoped
public class Julian implements Serializable {
  private static final long serialVersionUID =
      -1110733631543658209L;

  private Date dateIn;
  private String jd;

  public String convert() {
    try {
      Client client = ClientBuilder.newClient();
      String gdStr = getGd().replace(" ", "-").
          replace(":", "-");
      String q =
          "http://localhost:8080/julian/webapi/convert/" +
          gdStr;
      WebTarget target = client.target(q);
      jd = target.request().get(String.class);
    } catch (Exception e) {
      FacesContext.getCurrentInstance().
          addMessage("myform:getdate",
          new FacesMessage("Exception " + e,
              "Exception " + e));
      jd = "0.0";
      return null;
    }
    return "/response.xhtml";
  }

  public Date getDateIn() {
    return dateIn;
  }
```

```
public void setDateIn(Date dateIn) {
  this.dateIn = dateIn;
}

public String getGd() {
  LocalDateTime ldt = LocalDateTime.ofInstant(
      dateIn.toInstant(), ZoneId.of("UTC"));
  return ldt.format(DateTimeFormatter.ofPattern(
      "yyyy-MM-dd HH:mm:ss"));
}

public String getJd() {
  return jd;
}
}
```

The front-end project is now ready for deployment. In the Project Explorer, right-click on the project and select Run As ➤ Run on Server. Choose the Glassfish server. Once running, in a browser, open the following URL:

```
http://localhost:8080/julian-gui
```

You will then see the greetings page (see Figure 3-8).

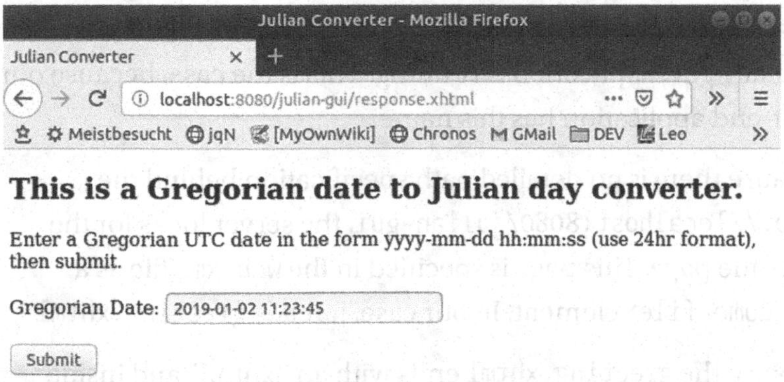

Figure 3-8. *Greetings page*

Enter a date like "2019-01-02 11:23:45," then click the "Submit" button. The output should look like that shown in Figure 3-9.

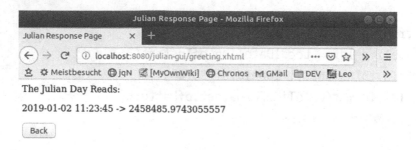

Figure 3-9. *Response page*

Summing Up: The Julian Day Calendar

With both projects "julian" and "julian-gui" running, we now have our first little "Hello World"–style Jakarta EE 8 application. Don't worry if you don't fully understand it yet; we will talk about the details later in the book. However, you should be aware of a few characteristics of the sample application so as to get you started improving your knowledge about Java enterprise applications. Let us investigate what happens:

1. Once the browser sends the `http://localhost:8080/julian-gui` request, the Jakarta EE 8 server, with an HTTP connector running under port `8080` (this is the default, and we didn't change it in the Glassfish configuration) receives the request and checks whether a "julian-gui" application is running. This is the case, because our front-end application has this name.

2. Because there is no detailed path specification behind the `http://localhost:8080/julian-gui`, the server looks for the welcome page. This page is specified in the `web.xml` file as a `<welcome-file>` element. In our case, it reads `greeting.xhtml`.

3. Because the `greeting.xhtml` ends with an ".xhtml" and inside `web.xml` we specified a servlet mapping with such an ending to initiate a JSF request, the file `greeting.xhtml` gets transformed by the JSF template handler.

4. Because of the "julian.web.WebMessages" specified as a resource
    bundle in file `faces-config.xml`, the files `src/resources/`
    `julian/web/WebMessages.properties` and `src/resources/`
    `julian/web/WebMessages_{LANG}.properties` get used as
    localized front-end element text files. Because of the `<var>`
    element in `faces-config.xml` the localized text is available to the
    JSF files via expressions #{`bundle.SOMETHING`}.

5. Because of the `@Named` annotation of the `Julian` class, JSF provides
    an instance of this class to its pages under #{`julian.SOMETHING`}
    (the first letter of the class name just lowercased).

6. The "Submit" button gets connected to the method `convert()` of
    the `Julian` class via `action="#{julian.convert}"`. Because this
    method returns `/response.xhtml`, JSF forwards the page flow to
    the `response.xhtml` page.

7. The `convert` method accesses the back-end component to
    perform the calculation.

8. The response page uses the same approach to access the `Julian`
    object as the `greeting.xhtml` page did.

9. Because of the `action="greeting"` attribute for the "Back" button
    in the response, upon pressing the "Back" button JSF forwards you
    to the greeting page (it just adds ".xhtml" to "greeting").

An overview of all the files that make up the front-end application is shown in
Figure 3-10. You can see these when you unfold all directories in the Project Explorer.

In case something goes wrong, you'll find the server logs inside the Glassfish
installation folder under the following:

`GLASSFISH_INST/glassfish/domains/domain1/logs/server.log`

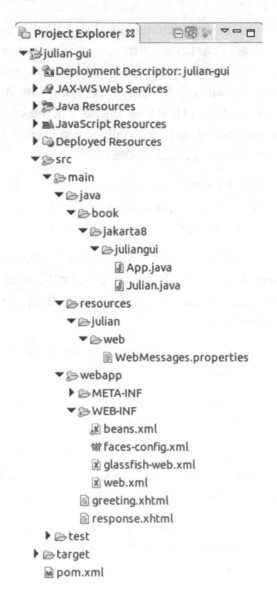

Figure 3-10. *Front-end files*

CHAPTER 4

Building Page-Flow Web Applications with JSF

Java Server Faces (JSF) is the dedicated front-end technology for establishing page-flow web applications running in a Jakarta EE 8 environment. By *page flow* we mean several interrelated web pages, including a user-initiated navigation.

> **Note** If you instead want to create a single-page web application with the page control and data flow performed by JavaScript and REST, you should use RESTful web applications with JAX-RS. We'll talk about JAX-RS in a later chapter.

Servlets and JSF Pages

On a lower technical level, the communication between browsers and a Jakarta EE server gets controlled by *servlets*. A servlet is an instance of the javax.servlet.Servlet interface. The generation of servlet instances and the mapping from URL patterns to appropriate servlets gets controlled by the src/main/webapp/WEB-INF/web.xml file.

The detailed structure of a web.xml file for Jakarta EE 8 gets described in the "Servlet 4.0" specification. For JSF to work, at a bare minimum we use a web.xml file with the following contents:

```
<?xml version="1.0" encoding="UTF-8"?>
<web-app xmlns:xsi=
  "http://www.w3.org/2001/XMLSchema-instance"
  xmlns="http://xmlns.jcp.org/xml/ns/javaee"
```

© Peter Späth 2019
P. Späth, *Beginning Jakarta EE*, https://doi.org/10.1007/978-1-4842-5079-2_4

```
xsi:schemaLocation="http://xmlns.jcp.org/xml/ns/javaee
http://xmlns.jcp.org/xml/ns/javaee/web-app_4_0.xsd"
id="WebApp_ID" version="4.0">

<display-name>Name of my App</display-name>
<welcome-file-list>
  <welcome-file>greeting.xhtml</welcome-file>
</welcome-file-list>
<servlet>
  <servlet-name>Faces Servlet</servlet-name>
  <servlet-class>
    javax.faces.webapp.FacesServlet
  </servlet-class>
  <load-on-startup>1</load-on-startup>
</servlet>
<servlet-mapping>
  <servlet-name>Faces Servlet</servlet-name>
  <url-pattern>*.xhtml</url-pattern>
</servlet-mapping>
</web-app>
```

This file specifies a welcome file, greeting.xhtml, which gets used if in the URL the path ends with the context root and no specific page gets specified. And it also registers the JSF servlet and a mapping that identifies any file ending with ".xhtml" as a JSF page.

Note   The specification says that the web.xml file is optional and an automatic mapping of some URL patterns will occur instead. It is, however, recommended to explicitly provide a web.xml file to keep such magic automatisms at this place at a minimum. After all, not specifying a web.xml makes the URL mapping, hidden somewhere in the depths of the Jakarta EE server, appear kind of random.

There could be several <url-pattern> elements inside the mapping, and patterns also could use paths instead of file-name endings. In this book, we will always let .xhtml files designate JSF pages, so apart from the welcome page and maybe a <display-name> element, and unless otherwise noted, the web.xml files will all look the same.

A Sample JSF Application

As a sample JSF application, we will create a simple household accounting web application. We will start with a page where the user can enter her or his name, a date, and per-day expenses. At the beginning, there will only be a single page; we will add more features as we advance through the book.

Preparing the JSF Application

To start the JSF application development, open Eclipse and select File ➤ New ➤ Project.... From the list, select Maven ➤ Maven Project, make sure "Create a simple project (skip archetype selection)" is *not* checked, and choose "maven-archetype-quickstart." As Maven project coordinates, enter the following:

```
Group-Id:    book.jakarta8
Artifact-Id: hacc-jsfgui
Version:     0.0.1-SNAPSHOT
```

As the package name, use "book.jakarta8.hacc.jsfgui." Eclipse will automatically name the project according to the artifact-id. In this case, it will be `hacc-jsfgui`.

Make sure the process uses the Java JRE 8 libraries and compiler level 1.8. You'll find the settings in the project properties at Java Build Path ➤ Libraries and at "Java Compiler." Open the file `pom.xml`, change `<packaging>jar</packaging>` to `<packaging>war</packaging>`, and add the following:

```
<dependency>
  <groupId>javax</groupId>
  <artifactId>javaee-api</artifactId>
  <version>8.0</version>
</dependency>
```

inside the dependencies section. Then, add the following:

```
<build>
  <plugins>
    <plugin>
      <artifactId>maven-compiler-plugin</artifactId>
```

```
        <configuration>
          <source>1.8</source>
          <target>1.8</target>
        </configuration>
      </plugin>
    </plugins>
  </build>
```

after `</dependencies>`. Press CTRL+SHIFT-F to reformat the file, then right-click (on project) and select Maven ➤ Update Project....

If the project is not already faceted, right-click (on project) and select Configure ➤ Convert to Faceted Form.... Then, or inside Properties ➤ Project Facets, check and enter the following:

```
Dynamic Web Module 4.0
Java 1.8
JavaScript 1.0
Java Server Faces 2.3
```

If it is not possible to change a version, remove the check, click "Apply and Close," and open the dialog again. Then you can recheck and select the desired version.

Make sure folder "src/main/webapp/WEB-INF" exists, and if necessary add a file web.xml to this folder. Let it read as follows:

```
<?xml version="1.0" encoding="UTF-8"?>
<web-app xmlns:xsi=
  "http://www.w3.org/2001/XMLSchema-instance"
  xmlns="http://xmlns.jcp.org/xml/ns/javaee"
  xsi:schemaLocation="http://xmlns.jcp.org/xml/ns/javaee
  http://xmlns.jcp.org/xml/ns/javaee/web-app_4_0.xsd"
  id="WebApp_ID" version="4.0">

<display-name>Household Accounting JSF-GUI</display-name>
<welcome-file-list>
  <welcome-file>main.xhtml</welcome-file>
</welcome-file-list>
<servlet>
  <servlet-name>Faces Servlet</servlet-name>
```

```
    <servlet-class>
      javax.faces.webapp.FacesServlet
    </servlet-class>
    <load-on-startup>1</load-on-startup>
  </servlet>
  <servlet-mapping>
    <servlet-name>Faces Servlet</servlet-name>
    <url-pattern>*.xhtml</url-pattern>
  </servlet-mapping>
</web-app>
```

Make an empty file called `src/main/webapp/WEB-INF/beans.xml`. Make a file called `src/main/webapp/WEB-INF/glassfish-web.xml` and let it read as follows:

```
<?xml version="1.0" encoding="UTF-8"?>
<!DOCTYPE glassfish-web-app PUBLIC
  "-//GlassFish.org//DTD GlassFish Application Server
  3.1 Servlet 3.0//EN"
  "http://glassfish.org/dtds/glassfish-web-app_3_0-1.dtd">
<glassfish-web-app error-url="">
    <class-loader delegate="true"/>
</glassfish-web-app>
```

If it does not already exist, make a file called `src/main/webapp/WEB-INF/faces-config.xml` and let it read as follows:

```
<?xml version="1.0" encoding="UTF-8"?>
<faces-config
xmlns="http://xmlns.jcp.org/xml/ns/javaee"
xmlns:xsi="http://www.w3.org/2001/XMLSchema-instance"
xsi:schemaLocation="http://xmlns.jcp.org/xml/ns/javaee
http://xmlns.jcp.org/xml/ns/javaee/web-facesconfig_2_3.xsd"
version="2.3">

    <application>
      <resource-bundle>
        <base-name>
          hacc.web.WebMessages</base-name>
```

```
      <var>bundle</var>
    </resource-bundle>
    <locale-config>
      <default-locale>en</default-locale>
      <!--  <supported-locale>es</supported-locale> -->
    </locale-config>
  </application>
</faces-config>
```

Add a folder called "src/main/resources" and a file named src/main/resources/
hacc/web/WebMessages.properties, including sub-folders, and leave it empty for now.

The Household Accounting JSF Application

Once the preparational steps from the previous section are complete, we can create the
first template file. Right-click on "src/main/webapp" and select New ➤ File create main.
xhtml, and let it read as follows:

```
<!DOCTYPE html>
<html xmlns:h="http://xmlns.jcp.org/jsf/html"
      xmlns:f="http://xmlns.jcp.org/jsf/core"
      xmlns:ui = "http://java.sun.com/jsf/facelets"
      xmlns:pt="http://xmlns.jcp.org/jsf/passthrough">
<h:head>
  <title>Household Accounting</title>
  <h:outputStylesheet library="css" name="style.css"/>
</h:head>
<h:body>
  <h:form id="form">
    <h:outputText styleClass="formLabel"
        value="#{bundle.label_enterYourName}"/>
    <h:inputText id="name"
        value="#{accounting.name}"/>
    <div class="clearfloat"/>
    <h:outputText styleClass="formLabel"
        value="#{bundle.label_enterTheDate}"/>
```

```
    <h:inputText id="date"
       value="#{accounting.date}">
      <f:convertDateTime
            type="localDate"
            pattern="yyyy-MM-dd" />
    </h:inputText>
    <div class="clearfloat"/>
    <h:commandButton value="#{bundle.submit}"
                       action="#{accounting.register}"/>
  </h:form>
  <h:messages/>
</h:body>
</html>
```

This file starts with a `<!DOCTYPE html>`, which seems to identify it as an HTML 5 file. But there are differences in the HTML 5 specification, as follows:

- We have the namespaces "http://xmlns.jcp.org/jsf/html," "http://xmlns.jcp.org/jsf/core," "http://java.sun.com/ jsf/facelets," and "http://xmlns.jcp.org/jsf/passthrough," identified by h:, f:, ui:, and pt:. These namespaces tell JSF that it has to replace the corresponding elements with something it calculates.

- We have a couple of elements without namespaces, like `<title>` and `<div>`. JSF will just return them unchanged.

- In some attributes we have strings of the form #{ ... }. Those belong to *expression language* or EL expressions. JSF will replace them with calculated strings. But some of them will also handle user inputs from inside forms and make the entered data available to the application.

JSF will use this file to generate an HTML 5 document, which it then sends to the browser. But hold on—if it translates to an HTML 5 file and starts with an HTML 5 DOCTYPE declaration, why does it have a `.xhtml` ending? There are two reasons: first, JSF just doesn't care. It is happy with any DOCTYPE and just looks at those elements with namespaces belonging to JSF tag libraries. Second, it simplifies editing in Eclipse if it has a `.xhtml` ending. So, despite the `.xhtml` ending, consider them HTML 5 template files.

From the ‹h:outputStylesheet ... /› in the listing we can see that we need a stylesheet. To this aim, create a file called src/main/webapp/resources/css/style.css and inside it write the following:

```
.clearfloat { clear: both; }
```

From the #{bundle.SOMETHING} expressions in some attributes and the entry in faces-config.xml—

```
<resource-bundle>
  <base-name>
    hacc.web.WebMessages</base-name>
  <var>bundle</var>
</resource-bundle>
```

—we can see that the page accesses text resources from the file src/main/resources/hacc/web/WebMessages.properties. We add all the entries we need, which leads to the file's containing the following:

```
label_enterYourName = Enter your name:
label_enterTheDate = Enter the date (yyyy-MM-dd):
submit = Submit
```

Likewise, in the attributes of some of the elements you can find the three #{accounting.SOMETHING} expressions, as follows:

```
<h:inputText id="name" value="#{accounting.name}"/>
<h:inputText id="date" value="#{accounting.date}">

  ...
</h:inputText>
<h:commandButton ...
    action="#{accounting.register}"/>
```

This is where the binding of the JSF template page to a Java class happens. We capitalize the first letter of "accounting" and create a class, book.jakarta8.hacc.jsfgui.Accounting. We add two getters and two setters, getName(), getDate(), setName(), and setDate(), which by virtue of their names, have "Name" and "Date" directly correspond to #{accounting.name} and #{accounting.date} as follows:

```
#{accounting.name} ->  Accounting.getName() and
                       Accounting.setName()
#{accounting.date} ->  Accounting.getDate() and
                       Accounting.setDate()
```

This is why this kind of expression—(#{accounting.name} and #{accounting. date})—also gets called a *value expression*.

Note   It is the attribute's responsibility to prescribe whether the #{something} belongs to a *value* expression. Because the #{accounting.something} shows up in a value="..." attribute, we do have value expressions here.

The action="#{accounting.register}" expression is different. It corresponds to a method, as follows:

```
#{accounting.register} ->  Accounting.register()
```

and the #{accounting.register} therefore gets called a *method expression*.

With these getters, setters, and methods added, the Accounting class reads as follows:

```
package book.jakarta8.hacc.jsfgui;

import java.io.Serializable;
import java.time.LocalDate;

import javax.enterprise.context.SessionScoped;
import javax.inject.Named;

@Named
@SessionScoped
public class Accounting implements Serializable {
  private static final long serialVersionUID =
      -1110733631123456L;

  private LocalDate date;
  private String name;
```

```
public String register() {
  return null;
}

public LocalDate getDate() {
  return date;
}

public void setDate(LocalDate date) {
  this.date = date;
}

public String getName() {
  return name;
}

public void setName(String name) {
  this.name = name;
}
}
```

This class does not do anything interesting yet, so we let method `register()` return a null, which means it will return to the same page. What is interesting is the @Named annotation—this is where the mapping from class `Accounting` to the "accounting" in expressions #{accounting.SOMETHING} happens! The other annotation, `SessionScoped`, will keep the instance of this class valid as long as the browser sessions holds.

You can now run the JSF application. Right-click on the project, then select Run As ➤ Run on Server. Open `http://localhost:8080/hacc-jsfgui/main.xhtml` in your browser, and the form should show up (see Figure 4-1).

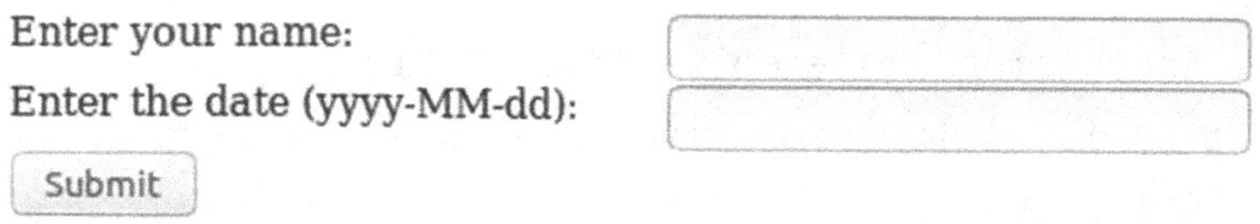

Enter your name:
Enter the date (yyyy-MM-dd):
Submit

Figure 4-1. *Household accounting*

The output that gets generated by JSF and is then sent to the browser for rendering the page will be similar to the following:

```
<!DOCTYPE html>
<html><head id="j_idt2">
  <title>Household Accounting</title>
  <link rel="stylesheet" type="text/css"
      href="/hacc-jsfgui/javax.faces.resource/
            style.css.xhtml?ln=css"/>
</head>
<body>
<form id="form" name="form" method="post"
      action="/hacc-jsfgui/main.xhtml;
        jsessionid=cba85228d2b781870d3c7643f805"
      enctype="application/x-www-form-urlencoded">
    <input type="hidden" name="form" value="form" />
    <span class="formLabel">
        Enter your name:</span>
    <input id="form:name" type="text" name="form:name" />
    <div class="clearfloat"></div>
    <span class="formLabel">
        Enter the date (yyyy-MM-dd):</span>
    <input id="form:date" type="text" name="form:date" />
    <div class="clearfloat"></div>
    <input type="submit" name="form:j_idt9"
        value="Submit" />
    <input type="hidden" name="javax.faces.ViewState"
        id="j_id1:javax.faces.ViewState:0"
        value="4202037120618133945:-331235588411554674"
        autocomplete="off" />
</form>
</body>
</html>
```

You can see that the `<h:form id="form">` from the template file gets translated to the following:

```
<form id="form" name="form" method="post"
  action="/hacc-jsfgui/main.xhtml;
        jsessionid=cba85228d2b781870d3c7643f805"
  enctype="application/x-www-form-urlencoded">
```

The `jsessionid` value here is important: because HTTP by design is stateless but our application needs to maintain a state (the instance of the `Accounting` class), the form must specify to which session it belongs. And this happens by transmitting the `jsessionid`. Because in JSF state holding is not limited to the session ID, but also includes a view ID, the form also has this special hidden input added at the end. The other input elements belong to `<h:inputText>` template page elements. In the case of the date input, we need to specify a converter, `<f:convertDateTime>`, so JSF knows that the text needs to be translated to a `LocalDate` typed class field. The `<h:commandButton>` corresponds to `<input type="submit">` for submitting the form. Upon the user's clicking on the "Submit" button, JSF takes care of translating and possibly validating the input fields, performing any activities that are important for the application, and possibly forwarding to other pages. We will talk about this lifecycle in more detail in a later section.

About JavaBean Classes

In an enterprise Java environment, and especially for JSF, often Java classes of a special kind get used: JavaBean classes. These are classes that serve as simple components with the main purpose of providing standardized access to its properties. This sounds much more complicated than it actually is. Consider the following `Person` class:

```
public class Person {
  private String lastName;
  private String firstName;
  private int age;
  private boolean smoker;
}
```

What is missing is access to the properties. For the Person class to become a JavaBean, all we need is to provide *getters* and *setters*. To this aim, we provide methods starting with "get" ("is" for Boolean properties) for getters and "set" for setters, and then we append the property name with the first letter capitalized, as follows:

```java
public class Person {
    private String lastName;
    private String firstName;
    private boolean smoker;
    private int age;

    public String getFirstName() {
        return firstName;
    }
    public void setFirstName(String firstName) {
        this.firstName = firstName;
    }

    public String getLastName() {
        return lastName;
    }
    public void setLastName(String lastName) {
        this.lastName = lastName;
    }

    public int getAge() {
        return age;
    }
    public void setAge(int age) {
        this.age = age;
    }

    public boolean isSmoker() {
        return smoker;
    }
    public void setSmoker(boolean smoker) {
        this.smoker = smoker;
    }
}
```

That is it! Because this way of providing getters and setters is so standardized and is actually easy to understand, in this book we often will omit the getters and setters for class properties and just write a hint like "+ getters/setters," like in the following example:

```
public class Person {
  private String lastName;   // + getter/setter
  private String firstName;  // + getter/setter
  private int age;           // + getter/setter
  private boolean smoker;    // + getter/setter
}
```

Expression Language in JSF Pages

In our household accounting application from the previous example, we used constructs like #{something} to draw a connection between the template file and an injected Java class, as follows:

```
...
<h:inputText id="name" value="#{accounting.name}"/>
...
```

In JSF such #{...} constructs are called *expressions*, or, more precisely, *expression language* (EL) constructs, and they are of central importance to the templating's working. Not only that, but they also build an interface between the template files and the business logic of your application by connecting template files to Java methods and fields (via getters and setters); they also allow you to write expressions in your pages.

Note   There exists another variant of expressions that use a slightly different syntax ${ ... }. Such expressions using curly braces are called *immediate evaluation syntax expressions*, while #{ ... } expressions get named *deferred evaluation syntax expressions*. While the use of immediate evaluation is allowed in JSF pages, this somewhat shortcuts JSF functionalities and leads to unexpected behavior. In this book we therefore only use the deferred syntax.

In the following paragraphs we will talk more about things we can achieve using expression language constructs.

Value and Method Expressions

A vital distinction we need to understand first in order to get acquainted with EL is the one between expressions that are used as values and expressions that denote class methods, as follows:

- **Value Expressions**

    Value expressions can show up everywhere in the template file, although in the majority of cases you will use them inside XML element attributes, as in `<h:inputText value = "#{accounting.name}"/>`. They can use fields of injected classes, and they can perform calculations. The outcome of a value expression gets used at the discretion of the component where the value expression describes an attribute, or its `toString()` representation gets printed at the place of their declaration if used outside component attributes. Wherever a component expects a value expression, you can use a literal string, which then gets handled as if it were the outcome of the expression evaluation.

- **Method Expressions**

    Method expressions directly point to method names of injected classes. You will use method expressions only inside component attributes, and you will exclusively do that only for such component attributes where the component explicitly demands a method expression. A prominent example we already used for the household accounting application is the "action" attribute inside component `<h:commandButton>`, where we wrote `#{accounting.register}` to designate the `public String register()` method from the `Accounting` class. It is also possible to pass arguments to the method invocations, but we will talk about that a little later. If a component expects a method expression for an attribute you can instead provide a literal string, as in `<h:commandButton value="Go" action="handle"/>`.

Note   Whether a method expression points to a method that returns something or not (the `public String register()` versus a `public void register()`) depends on what the method gets used for by JSF. In this case, the button click possibly navigates to a new page, so we need the method to return a string indicating where to go. The `null` returned so far just leads to reloading the actual page.

For both method and value expressions, for attributes that demand an expression you can always also write literal strings, as in `<h:commandButton value="Go" action="handle"/>`. The "Go" here will be treated as if it were the outcome of the value expression expected, and for the `"handle"` the method execution gets bypassed and the provided value gets treated as if it were the outcome of the method invocation. For `<h:commandButton value="Go" action="handle"/>` the string "Go" will get used as the button text, and a forwarding to page `handle.xhtml` will happen.

We said that we can use value expressions inside attributes and at any other place on the page. If they get used for attributes, it lies at the discretion of the component what to do with them. If found anywhere else on the page, they will be output as-is. With the component `<h:outputText>`, which writes the expression evaluation outcome value of its "value" attribute to the page, at first sight it seems that we could use either of the following:

```
<h:outputText styleClass="formLabel"
    value="#{bundle.label_enterYourName}"/>
```

... or ...

```
#{bundle.label_enterYourName}
```

to write something on the page. It seems tempting to use the latter one because it is shorter. There is an important difference though: the first one creates a component in the document tree, while the latter one represents just flat text. This difference reveals itself if we include presentation logic on the page. Consider, for example, the `<h:panelGroup>` component, which just draws a bracket around its children. If we include a decision as to whether to output it or not, this could read as follows:

```
<h:panelGroup rendered="#{accounting.renderName}">
  <h:outputText styleClass="formLabel"
      value="#{bundle.label_enterYourName}"/>
  ...
</h:panelGrid>
```

Everything will work as expected: both the panel group and all children only get rendered if the `isRenderName()` method of `Accounting` returns `true`. But if we instead use the following:

```
<h:panelGrid rendered="#{accounting.renderName}">
    #{bundle.label_enterYourName}
</h:panelGrid>
```

the label will be written, no matter what the outcome of `isRenderName()` is. So, as a bit of advice, in most cases you can avoid trouble if you never use the direct syntax and use expressions only in component attributes.

Accessing Objects from JSF Pages

In the household accounting sample application, we've already seen how to connect Java classes for handling the application logic with the template pages. The procedure is part of the *context and dependency injection* (CDI), which is why we used the term *injection* already a couple of times.

Note   In earlier JSF versions, the connection of JSF pages to the application logic was handled by something called *managed beans*. This implied additional configuration steps, like registering classes in appropriate XML configuration files. In the JSF version 2.3 we use, CDI gets used for that purpose, and the use of managed beans is deprecated. You'll still find managed beans in many introductions and tutorials on the web, but we consider them outdated, and for that reason we don't use managed beans in this book.

The procedure for connecting application logic to JSF template pages via CDI goes as follows:

- For Java classes that serve as interfaces for accessing the application logic, you add the @Named annotation (`javax.inject.Named`) to the class. If you don't add a parameter to the annotation, a @Named `public class TheClass { ... }` will lead to an object `theClass` (the first letter lowercase) being made available to EL. If you, however, add a parameter to the annotation, as in @Named(`"foo"`) `public class TheClass { ... }`, the parameter will get used as the name for the injected object.

- Let the same class implement the `java.io.Serializable` interface. JSF needs it for class state handling.

- The @Named annotation will lead to an instance of the class being injected into the JSF pages. However, the lifecycle of this instance is still unclear. For this reason, we add another annotation for the lifecycle characterization. We have several options here, as follows:

  - **@SessionScoped**

    From package `javax.enterprise.context`. This scope probably gets used most often. The injected object will be valid as long as the browser session lives. Fields of the instance will have their states maintained for the whole lifetime of the session, and the instantiation of the Java class will happen at most once per session.

  - **@RequestScoped**

    From package `javax.enterprise.context`. The instance of the injected class will be made void once the request has finished. Using this scope makes sense if state is unimportant. Also, if you use request-scoped injections the risk of unused objects hanging around in the memory is minimized.

– **@ViewScoped**

From package `javax.faces.view`. The injected instance will be valid as long as the JSF page is not left. If action methods return `null` or return to the same page, the same page gets reloaded, the view gets maintained, and view-scoped beans will be reused. You use this scope if state needs to be maintained only as long as the same page is not left.

– **@ApplicationScoped**

From package `javax.enterprise.context`. The injected instance will be valid as long as the application lives. Use with care to avoid memory leaks.

– **@FlowScoped**

From package `javax.faces.flow`. The injected instance will be valid as long as the current flow is not left. We don't handle flows in this beginner's book.

- If you need fields of the injected class for output value expressions (so-called *rvalues*), you must provide a getter. For some field `fieldName` the getter must read `getFieldName()` (or `isFieldName()` for Boolean values). You then access the field in value expressions via `className.fieldName`. In fact, the field need not even exist in the Java class; if there is a getter method `getFieldName()`, you can use `className.fieldName` in rvalue expressions.

- If you need fields of the injected class for input value expressions (so-called *lvalues*), you must provide a getter and a setter. For some field `fieldName` the getter must read `getFieldName()` (or `isFieldName()` for Boolean values), and for the setter you must write `setFieldName(...)`. You then access the field in lvalue expressions via `className.fieldName`. As for rvalues, the field need not actually exist in the Java class; if there are methods `getFieldName()` and `setFieldName(...)`, you can use `className.fieldName` in lvalue expressions.

- To access a method methodName of an injected class instance, you
  write #{className.methodName} for no parameters, or className.
  methodName(par1, par2, ...) if the method invocation requires
  parameters (for string parameters you can use single quotation marks).
  For example, someAttr = "#{className.methodName(37, 'Hello')}".

The following example shows some constructs for object access from inside JSF
template pages:

```
<h:outputText
    styleClass="formLabel" <!-- literal rvalue -->
    value="#{xyz.abc}"/>   <!-- rvalue getter -->

<h:commandButton
    value="#{'Go ' + xyz.submit}"  <!-- rvalue -->
    action="#{xyz.go}"/>   <!-- go() method -->

<h:inputText
    value="#{xyz.name}" />
<!-- rvalue + lvalue, getter + setter -->
```

A corresponding injected class would read as follows:

```
@Named
@SessionScoped
public class Xyz implements Serializable {
  private static final long serialVersionUID =
      -1110733631123456L;

  private String abc = "Hello";
  private String submit = "Submit";
  private String name;

  public String getName() { return name; }
  public void setName(String name) {
      this.name = name; }

  public String getAbc() { return abc; }
  public void setAbc(String abc) {
      this.abc = abc; }
```

```
public String getSubmit() { return submit; }
public void setSubmit(String submit) {
    this.submit = submit; }

public String go() {
  ...
  return null;
}
}
```

Implicit Objects

JSF by default injects a couple of objects into the page that you can use without further action. The list is as follows:

- **facesContext**

  The FacesContext object from package javax.faces.context contains detailed information about the currently active HTTP request and allows you to fetch messages related to validation.

- **application**

  The ServletContext object from package javax.servlet allows you to access the web application as a whole, including configuration information.

- **initParam**

  A map containing initialization parameters. Includes values you wrote inside <context-param> elements in file web.xml.

- **session**

  The HttpSession from package javax.servlet.http. It contains the session information for the current servlet context. Here you can, for example, query the session creation time or last accessed time, as follows:

  #{ session.creationTime } and #{ session.lastAccessedTime }.

- **view**

    The current UIViewRoot (package javax.faces.component) for
    this view. Represents the root of the component tree.

- **component**

    The currently processed component. This allows you to access
    fields and functions of the component that are not directly
    accessible otherwise; for example, the client ID: <h:outputText
    value = "Client-ID: #{component.clientId} " /> (you could
    use it from JavaScript code).

- **cc**

    The currently processed top-level composite component (only if it
    exists).

- **request**

    The HttpServletRequest from package javax.servlet.http.
    Allows for accessing interesting properties like cookies, HTTP
    headers, the context path, the URL, HTTP request parameters,
    querying user roles, and more.

- **Scoped attributes**

    Use applicationScope, sessionScope, viewScope, requestScope,
    or flowScope for attribute maps from the various scopes.

- **flash**

    A map that allows you to access flash-scope objects. The flash-
    scope variables survive a redirect you need for the post/redirect/
    get design pattern (you add ?faces-redirect = true to URLs
    returned from action methods).

- **param**

    A map of HTTP request parameters. Because URLs
    allow you to define parameters several times, like in
    ...?name=Peter&name=Paul, a request parameter actually is an

array. Practically, arrays don't get used often, so it is common practice to just return the first value for each parameter. This param object only takes the first value for each name.

– **paramValues**

A map of HTTP request parameters—a String[ ] per name.

– **header**

A map of HTTP header parameters. Similar to the param object, HTTP header parameters can show up several times, and this header object takes only the first value for each name (which normally suffices).

– **headerValues**

A map of HTTP header parameters—a String[ ] per name.

– **cookie**

A map of cookie name ➤ cookie value.

– **pageContext**

The PageContext from package javax.servlet.jsp contains useful page-related context information.

These objects come in handy for development purposes or for advanced expression use cases.

Literals

Inside EL expressions, you can enter literals as follows:

– **Strings**

To write strings, you can use single or double quotation marks: #{ 'Hi' + "there" } (watch out for XML attribute syntax—in most cases you'll end up writing single quotation marks, as in value = "#{ 'Hi' + 'there' }"). Use a backslash to escape: "\"", '\', and use \\ for a backslash.

- **Numbers**

  Enter numbers as usual: -37, 123.45.

- **Booleans**

  Write true and false.

- **Null**

  Use null for the null value.

Operators in Expressions

For the unary minus operator, use the conventional minus sign in front of the number: -234. The arithmetic operators + - * / % do the usual things (plus, minus, times, divided by, modulus); for / you can also write div, and instead of % you can use mod if you like. The ternary operator A ? B : C does the usual thing: if A is true, evaluate to B, otherwise to C.

To concatenate two strings, write += (no, this is not an assignment operator as in other languages!). For example, 'Hello' += ' ' += 'World' (gives 'Hello World').

The relational operators < > <= >= == != do the usual things. You can also write (surrounded by spaces) lt gt le ge eq ne respectively instead.

For logical operations you can use && ||, or and or, for AND and OR. For a negation you prepend an exclamation mark ! or a not.

To check whether a value is null or if a collection or array is empty, write empty X.

The semicolon operator A;B acts as follows: evaluate A, then discard the evaluation result. Then evaluate B and return its result.

Unless you use round brackets for grouping, the operator precedence is: (highest to lowest, left to right)

- [ ].(indexed access, dereferencing)
- •( )
- - (unary) not ! empty
- * / div % mod
- •+ –
- •+=

Using Collections Inside Expressions

The EL allows you to create and use sets, lists, and maps. It can also handle arrays, but there is no way to construct arrays from inside EL. This is not a real disadvantage, since with constructed lists you can do the same thing. To construct a set, list, or map you write the following:

```
{1,2,3}                  (a set)
[1, 27, ['Hi', 7]]       (a list)
{1:'Mark', 2:'Linda'}    (a map)
```

As an example, we use a special looping tag, <ui:repeat>, which we are going to describe in detail later. An example is written as follows:

```
<!DOCTYPE html>
<html xmlns:h="http://xmlns.jcp.org/jsf/html"
  xmlns:f="http://xmlns.jcp.org/jsf/core"
  xmlns:ui="http://java.sun.com/jsf/facelets"
  xmlns:pt="http://xmlns.jcp.org/jsf/passthrough">
<h:head>
  <title>Title</title>
</h:head>
<h:body>
  <ui:repeat value="#{['Banana','Apple','Orange']}"
      var="v">
    <h:outputText escape="false" value="#{v} <p/>"/>
  </ui:repeat>
</h:body>
</html>
```

The output will be a list of the three fruits. Note that we had to add escape = "false" and write <p/> instead of <p/> to output the paragraph delimiter so as to avoid clashes with some tag-related HTML security restrictions—the "<" with a special meaning in HTML gets some increased attention with respect to security.

For an indexed access to lists and arrays you use the usual [ ] operator. For map access, the same operator gets used, as follows:

```
#{['Mark','Linda'][1]}                    -> 'Linda'
#{{7:'Banana',2:'Apple',3:'Orange'}[7]}  -> 'Banana'
```

For operations on collections, the EL provides a set of built-in functions for filtering, transformation, and aggregation. We don't describe them all here; for a complete description have a look at the EL specification (enter "jsf expression language specification 3.0" or "jsr 341" in your favorite search engine). As an example, we extract items of lengths greater than four from a list as follows:

```
<ui:repeat value="#{['Linda', 'Ted', 'John', 'Marcus']
    .stream().filter(itm->itm.length()>4).toList()}"
    var="v">
  <h:outputText escape="false" value="#{v} <p/>"/>
</ui:repeat>
```

This generates a stream from a list, applies a filter using a lambda function (we'll talk about lambda functions next), converts a list from the resulting stream, and then iterates over the new list.

Exercise 1

Given an injected bean b and a collection b.list, write an <h:outputText> that produces one of the following strings: "The list contains 1 item" or "The list contains N items," where N gets replaced by the size, depending on the list size. Use literal strings, not resource bundle keys.

Lambda Expressions

The EL allows the use of lambda functions, which are function literals without a name, similar to the lambda function in Java SE8. The syntax variants are as follows:

```
x -> [some expression with x]
x -> x*x - 7                 (an example)
() -> [some expression]
() -> 'Hello World'          (an example)
```

```
(x,y) -> [some expr. with x and y]
(x,y) -> x + y                        (an example)
```

where x and y are just formal parameters—you can use any names you like for them.

Lambda functions can be passed as parameters to functions that support lambdas. The collection functions for filtering, transforming, and aggregating sets, lists, or maps often support lambda functions. To apply them directly you can write the following:

```
x -> x*x - 7              (the lambda)
(x -> x*x - 7)(3)         (applying it, gives 2)
```

Localized Resources

Text on web pages could, on the template side, be written literally, as follows:

```
Please enter your name:
<h:inputText ... />
```

or you could utilize attributes, as in the following:

```
<h:outputText value="Please enter your name:" />
<h:inputText ... />
```

In both cases, we have the issue that users from other countries might prefer to read the page in their own language. For this reason, JSF introduces *language bundles*. There is a procedure to internationalize your text.

First, we tell JSF that we want to use language bundles. You do this inside the src/main/webapp/WEB-INF/faces-config.xml file, where you add a <resource-bundle> and a <locale-config> element, as follows:

```
<?xml version="1.0" encoding="UTF-8"?>
<faces-config
xmlns="http://xmlns.jcp.org/xml/ns/javaee"
xmlns:xsi="http://www.w3.org/2001/XMLSchema-instance"
xsi:schemaLocation="http://xmlns.jcp.org/xml/ns/javaee
http://xmlns.jcp.org/xml/ns/javaee/web-facesconfig_2_3.xsd"
version="2.3">
```

```
<application>
  <resource-bundle>
    <base-name>
      hacc.web.WebMessages</base-name>
    <var>bundle</var>
  </resource-bundle>
  <locale-config>
    <default-locale>en</default-locale>
    <supported-locale>es</supported-locale>
    ...more of them...
  </locale-config>
</application>
</faces-config>
```

In this example, inside the element <base-name> we specify that the language resource bundles can be found in the folder called "src/main/resources/hacc/web." Instead of "hacc/web" you can write any path that best suits your needs—just update the string in <base-name> accordingly, replacing the file path separators with dots. The "bundle" inside the <var> element specifies the variable name under which the language bundle can be addressed from JSF template files. Again, you can use anything you like here, but if you change it later you will have to update all template files! In this book, we always use "bundle" as the bundle variable name.

Inside the element locale-config you list all locales you want to support. We wrote two locales here: "en," which stands for English and is marked as the default locale, and another locale, "es," for Spanish. You can add any number of supported locales, but obviously there can be only one default locale. It is also possible to distinguish between different countries using variants of the same language. So you can have

```
<locale-config>
  <default-locale>en</default-locale>
  <supported-locale>en_GB</supported-locale>
  <supported-locale>es</supported-locale>
</locale-config>
```

to express English's being the default language, but also have language files for British English in case this is the language–country pair the user agent (browser) asks for. Or you can even write

```
<locale-config>
    <default-locale>en</default-locale>
    <supported-locale>en_US</supported-locale>
    <supported-locale>en_GB</supported-locale>
    <supported-locale>es</supported-locale>
</locale-config>
```

to use a standard English language file as the default locale, and add two files for language texts different in US and British English. Which languages and countries are supported is defined by the Java SDK—a list can be obtained if you enter "java 8 supported locales" in your favorite search engine.

Now, for the localized texts themselves, you add a file, WebMessages.properties, inside the "src/main/resources/hacc/web/" folder (or whatever you specified in faces-config.xml as file name and path). This will be the default locale file, and it will correspond to the <default-locale> setting. Inside the file, you write key–value pairs as follows:

```
label_enterYourName = Enter your name:
label_enterTheDate = Enter the date (yyyy-MM-dd):
submit = Submit
label_noExpenses = No expenses
```

Each key will then be usable from inside JSF template files, and it will be replaced by the value, for which the matching locale file will be determined automatically. For the other supported locale files, you have to use file names like WebMessages_xx.properties or WebMessages_xx_XX.properties for each of the supported locales. The "xx" is then language code and the "XX" the optional country code. Inside the files, you use the same keys but add translated values, as follows:

```
label_enterYourName = Inserte su nombre:
label_enterTheDate = Inserte el día (yyyy-MM-dd):
submit = Transmitir
label_noExpenses = No expensas
```

for a locale file WebMessages_es.properties.

With the configuration adapted and the locale files added, we can now use the localized text inside the JSF template files, as follows:

```
#{bundle.label_enterYourName}
<h:inputText ... />

...or...
<h:outputText value="#{label_enterYourName}" />
<h:inputText ... />
```

Here, it is important to realize that in template files you never specify any language or country. That gets handled by JSF automatically!

Note   In such properties files, you frequently will see keys like `label.name` with dots as separators. You can do that, but it is then not possible to write `#{bundle.label.name}` inside your template file, because the dot there signifies a property accessor, not an integral part of a key name. You still can use this different notation, but then you have to write `bundle['label.name']` in the template files. It is up to you. In this book, however, dots in property keys are avoided for resource bundles.

Exercise 2

Add a Spanish translation to the household accounting application. The translations read: `label_enterYourName` ➤ "Inserte su nombre:", `label_enterTheDate` ➤ "Inserte el día (yyyy-MM-dd):", `submit` ➤ "Transmitir", `label_noExpenses` ➤ "No expensas."

JSF Tag Libraries

The three tag library namespaces are as follows:

```
xmlns:h = "http://xmlns.jcp.org/jsf/html"
xmlns:f = "http://xmlns.jcp.org/jsf/core"
xmlns:ui = "http://java.sun.com/jsf/facelets"
```

They correspond to the *Standard HTML RenderKit* tag library, the *Core* tag library, and the *Facelets* templating tag library, respectively. In our household accounting example, we used the following:

```
<h:head>
<h:outputStylesheet>
<h:body>
<h:form>
<h:outputText>
<h:inputText>
<h:commandButton>
<f:convertDateTime>
```

However, there are more. In the following paragraphs we will talk about the HTML RenderKit tags. Subsequent sections will handle the presentation language independent core tags for JSF 2.3 that you can use.

Standard HTML RenderKit Tags

The Standard HTML RenderKit tags directly correspond to elements in the generated HTML pages. We have tags for generating top-level elements, like <head> and <body>; tags for including script files and stylesheets; tags for forms and form elements, like text input, checkboxes, option lists, menus, and buttons; and tags for text output, images, and data tables.

As tag attributes, you can write literal strings—as, for example, for the styleClass attribute in the following text output tag:

```
<h:outputText ...
    styleClass="output-name" />
```

However, as we have seen, in many cases you can connect the attributes to injected classes via value expressions. We already did that for the household accounting example earlier in this chapter. Depending on the attribute type and if it is allowed for the attribute in question, this can be applied either for just output or for both output and input. The styleClass attribute is such an output-only attribute, and here we can also write

```
<h:outputText ...
    styleClass="#{person.nameStyle}" />
```

which means that the connected class, probably named Person, needs a public String getNameStyle() method. If the attribute allows for input, we also need a setter, as in the following text-input component:

```
<h:inputText ...
    value="#{person.name}" />
```

This requires getters and setters for the value attribute, as follows:

```
@Named
@SessionScoped
public class Person {
    ...
    public String getName() {
        return ...
    }
    public void setName(String name) {
        ...
    }
    ...
}
```

Because of the Named annotation the expression language knows that it needs person (the "P" from the class name lowercased) to address the injected instance.

In the following paragraphs of this section we will give an overview of the tags and show some examples. All the tags and their attributes are listed in the appendix in the "Standard HTML RenderKit Tags" section.

HTML Top-Level Tags

Top-level tags are for the `<!DOCTYPE>` declaration at the top of an HTML file, and for the head and the body tags. There seems to be a bug if you try to use the `<h:doctype>` tag for generating a DOCTYPE, but you usually write it literally on top of an XHTML file, so the tag is not needed anyway. Just don't use it. For the two others, write the following:

```
<!DOCTYPE html>
<html xmlns:h="http://xmlns.jcp.org/jsf/html"
      xmlns:f="http://xmlns.jcp.org/jsf/core"
      xmlns:ui = "http://java.sun.com/jsf/facelets"
      xmlns:pt="http://xmlns.jcp.org/jsf/passthrough">
<h:head>
      <title>The Title</title>
      [ ... import scripts and styles ]
</h:head>
<h:body>
    [ ... ]
</h:body>
</html>
```

For details and all possible attributes, see the "Standard HTML RenderKit Tags" section of the appendix.

HTML Header Elements

Inside the `<head>` element of the target HTML output, you usually want to have stylesheet files and JavaScript files included. The HTML RenderKit tag library allows us to use tags for it, so you can write the following:

```
...
<h:head>
<title>Household Accounting</title>
  <h:outputStylesheet library = "css" name = "style.css" />
  [... more like that ...]
```

```
<h:outputScript library = "js" name = "myScript.js"  />
[... more like that ...]
</h:head>
...
```

to read scripts and stylesheets from "src/main/webapp/resources/js" and "src/main/webapp/resources/css," respectively.

For details and all possible attributes, see the "Standard HTML RenderKit Tags" section of the appendix.

HTML Forms

Forms get used to transmit user data from the front end (browser) to the server. As is usually the case for input elements in the target HTML, for JSF too all input elements must be placed somewhere inside a <h:form> element. You write the following:

```
...
<h:form>
    [... form elements ...]
</h:form>
...
```

to render a form. You *must* use this instead of <form>, because otherwise JSF wouldn't be able to recognize the input elements on your page.

For details and all possible attributes, see the "Standard HTML RenderKit Tags" section of the appendix.

HTML Text Input and Output

As is usually the case for input elements in HTML, for JSF too text-input elements must be placed somewhere inside a <h:form> element, as follows:

```
<!DOCTYPE html>
<html xmlns:h="http://xmlns.jcp.org/jsf/html"
      xmlns:f="http://xmlns.jcp.org/jsf/core"
      xmlns:pt="http://xmlns.jcp.org/jsf/passthrough">
```

```
<h:head>
  <title>Page Title</title>
</h:head>
<h:body>
  <h:form id="form">
    <h:inputText id="name" value="#{accounting.name}"/>
    <!--  <- connects to getName() and setName()
          in an injected Java bean class
          'Accounting'                             -->
  </h:form>
</h:body>
</html>
```

On the other hand, the text-output tags can be placed anywhere on the page—they don't need a surrounding <h:form>. See the following:

```
<!DOCTYPE html>
<html xmlns:h="http://xmlns.jcp.org/jsf/html"
      xmlns:f="http://xmlns.jcp.org/jsf/core"
      xmlns:pt="http://xmlns.jcp.org/jsf/passthrough">
<h:head>
  <title>Page Title</title>
</h:head>
<h:body>
  <h:outputText value="Hello World!"/>

  <h:form id="form">
    [ ... ]
  </h:form>
</h:body>
</html>
```

For details and all possible attributes, see the "Standard HTML RenderKit Tags" section of the appendix.

HTML Selectables

Selectables include checkboxes, radio buttons, option lists, and menus with selectable entries. The HTML RenderKit provides quite a few tags for selectables, as follows:

```
...
<h:form id="form">

  <!-- A boolean checkbox. 'chk' must point to a  -->
  <!-- getter and setter in class 'SomeClass':    -->
  <!--   public boolean isChk() { return ...; }  -->
  <!--   public void setChk(boolean chk) { ... } -->
  <h:selectBooleanCheckbox value="#{someClass.chk}"/>
  <p/>

  <!-- A bunch of related checkboxes. 'checks1'   -->
  <!-- refers to a String[] or Collection<String> -->
  <!-- value                                       -->
  <h:selectManyCheckbox value="#{someClass.checks1}">
    <f:selectItem itemValue="v1" itemLabel="Item 1" />
    <f:selectItem itemValue="v2" itemLabel="Item 2" />
    <f:selectItem itemValue="v3" itemLabel="Item 3" />
  </h:selectManyCheckbox>
  <p/>

  <!-- The same, but more dynamic. This time we    -->
  <!-- provide a Map<String, String> for all       -->
  <!-- possible items.                             -->
  <h:selectManyCheckbox value="#{someClass.checks1}">
    <f:selectItems value="#{someClass.smcbItems}" />
  </h:selectManyCheckbox>
  <p/>

  <!-- A list with multiply selectable items       -->
  <h:selectManyListbox  value="#{someClass.checks1}">
    <f:selectItems value="#{someClass.smcbItems}" />
  </h:selectManyListbox>
  <p/>
```

```
<!-- A list where only one item can be selected -->
<h:selectOneListbox value="#{someClass.checks1}">
  <f:selectItems value="#{someClass.smcbItems}" />
</h:selectOneListbox>
<p/>

<!-- Similar to selectManyListbox, but          -->
<!-- menu-style                                  -->
<h:selectManyMenu value="#{someClass.checks1}">
  <f:selectItems value="#{someClass.smcbItems}" />
</h:selectManyMenu>
<p/>

<!-- Similar, but at most one item can be        -->
<!-- selected                                     -->
<h:selectOneMenu value="#{someClass.checks1}">
  <f:selectItems value="#{someClass.smcbItems}" />
</h:selectOneMenu>
<p/>

<!-- A radio button list                          -->
<h:selectOneRadio value="#{someClass.checks1}">
  <f:selectItems value="#{someClass.smcbItems}" />
</h:selectOneRadio>
</h:form>
...
```

A corresponding injected Java class in principle looks like the following:

```
@Named
@SessionScoped
public class SomeClass implements Serializable {
  private static final long serialVersionUID = -1110734999167266L;

  private boolean check = true;
  private List<String> checks1 = new ArrayList<>();
  private Map<String,String> smcbItems = new HashMap<>();
  // ... getters and setters for these ...
```

```
public SomeClass() {
  smcbItems.put("Label1", "v1");
  smcbItems.put("Label2", "v2");
  smcbItems.put("Label3", "v3");
  smcbItems.put("Label4", "v4");
  smcbItems.put("Label5", "v5");
 }
}
```

Instead of mapping Label ➤ Value, the value to be used for all possible select options can be an array of `SelectItem`, with `SelectItem` coming from the package `javax.faces.model`.

As an example, we add a "No expenses" checkbox in our household accounting example. Inside the `main.xhtml` file, as a new child of the `<h:form>` tag, we add a `<h:selectBooleanCheckbox>` before the command button, as follows:

```
...
<h:form id="form">
  ...
  <div class="clearfloat"/>
  <h:selectBooleanCheckbox id="noExpenses"
        value="#{accounting.noExpenses}"/>
  <h:outputLabel for="noExpenses"
        value="#{bundle.label_noExpenses}" />
  <div class="clearfloat" />
  <h:commandButton value="#{bundle.submit}"
                   action="#{accounting.register}"/>
</h:form>
...
```

Next, inside the `WebMessages.properties` file we add the text for the new label: `label_noExpenses = No expenses`. Since we want to get hold of the checkbox in the `Accounting` class, we add a corresponding field there as follows:

```
...
public class Accounting {
    ...
    private boolean noExpenses;
```

```
    ...
    public boolean isNoExpenses() {
      return noExpenses;
    }
    public void setNoExpenses(boolean noExpenses) {
      this.noExpenses = noExpenses;
    }
    ...
  }
```

Republish the application on the server to see the new page with the checkbox added.

Note   To republish inside the Eclipse IDE, open the "Servers" view, click on the server, and choose "Publish" from the context menu (right-click), or press CTRL+ALT+P.

For details and all possible attributes, see the "Standard HTML RenderKit Tags" section of the appendix.

Exercise 3

Implement the household accounting application if you haven't done so already. Add a <h:selectManyListbox> with the following item labels: Food, Clothing, Car, Fun, Other. Add five <f:selectItem> children and let the item values equal the labels. In the Accounting class add a corresponding field expenseTypes of Java type java.util. ArrayList and connect it to the value attribute.

Exercise 4

From the previous exercise, replace the five <f:selectItem> children with one <f:selectItems>. Inside <f:selectItems>, let the value attribute point to a field SelectItem[] expenseTypeOptions inside class Accounting. Fill the array inside the constructor.

HTML Images

To include an image file img.jpg, you can put it into the "src/main/webapp/resources/ images" folder and then write the following:

```
...
<h:graphicImage library="images" name="img.jpg" />
...
```

Images can, of course, have other formats, like .png or .gif.

For details and all possible attributes, see the "Standard HTML RenderKit Tags" section of the appendix.

HTML Buttons and Links

Buttons and links are things a user can click on to submit a form or initiate other actions, like reloading a page or advancing to another page. It is also possible to just invoke a JavaScript function if a button gets pressed, as follows:

```
<!--  Just a link                              -->
<h:outputLink value="http://www.amnesty.org"
       target="_blank">
   This is an arbitrary link
   <!-- There could also be an image here -->
</h:outputLink>

<!-- Just some JavaScript                       -->
<h:button value="Go" onclick="window.alert('Hi')" />

<h:form>
  <!-- A link with a navigation case. The value    -->
  <!-- expression maybe returns something like 'xyz' -->
  <!-- and there is a page 'xyz.xhtml'               -->
  <h:link value="Link text" outcome="#{accounting.nav1}" />

  <!-- Similar - points to page 'main2.xhtml'        -->
  <h:link value="Link text" outcome="main2" />
```

```
[... input elements...]

<!-- A submit button. Click submits the form and      -->
<!-- calls action method Accounting.register(). This  -->
<!-- method must return a navigation case, for        -->
<!-- example 'xyz' and there exists a page 'xyz.html' -->
<!-- Or 'null' which points to the current page       -->

<h:commandButton value="#{bundle.submit}"
  action="#{accounting.register}" />

<!-- The same, but a link instead of a button         -->
<h:commandLink value="#{bundle.submit}"
  action="#{accounting.register}" />

<!-- Shortcuts the action method - instead forwards   -->
<!-- to page 'main2.xhtml'                             -->
<h:commandButton value="Button"
  action="main2" />
</h:form>
</h:body>
</html>
```

To add URL parameters to any of those, add `<f:param>` children, as in the following:

```
<h:link value="Link text" outcome="main2">
  <f:param name="param1" value="42" />
  <f:param name="param2" value="Hello" />
</h:link>
```

This will add &param1=42&param2=Hello parameters to the link.

For details and all possible attributes, see the "Standard HTML RenderKit Tags" section of the appendix.

Exercise 5

In the household accounting application, replace <h:commandButton> with
<h:commandLink> and test it. Which of the following is true? (A) The button gets replaced
by a link, which has exactly the same functionality. (B) The attributes and/or the injected
class have to be changed first, then the link will behave like the button did. (C) The link
cannot be used to submit forms.

HTML File Upload

The <h:inputFile> tag can be used to let the user upload a file from the browser to
the server. In order to read the file data, for the value attribute you will use a value
expression pointing to a Part typed field in the class injected. In the submit method of
this class, remember you specify such a method in the action attribute of a command
button, and you save the file data via the following:

```
import javax.servlet.http.Part;
...
private Part upload; // + getter/setter
...
public void theSubmit() {
  try (InputStream input = upload.getInputStream()) {
    String n = upload.getSubmittedFileName();
    String path = "..."; // where to put the file
    String name = "..."; // file name
    Files.copy(input, new File(path + File.separator +
          name).toPath());
  }catch(Exception e) {
    // Handle exception...
    // Quick and dirty, don't use in production:
    e.printStackTrace(System.err);
  }
...
}
```

This presumes you use the following `value` attribute for `<h:inputFile>` in your template file:

```
<h:inputFile value="#{injectedClass.upload}" ... />
```

Note   For the file upload to work, you need to have a form with `<h:form enctype = "multipart/form-data">`. This is not a real restriction, because you can have several forms in your document, so for the upload you can use a dedicated upload form.

For details and all possible attributes, see the "Standard HTML RenderKit Tags" section of the appendix.

HTML Grouping

In case you need a component that just draws a bracket around its children, you can use the `<h:panelGroup>` tag. This comes in handy if you use a component that allows for only one child, but you need more complex contents. A `<f:facet>` is such a case (we will talk about facets later). Another use case is a grouping you need for styling purposes.

An example of a grouping that is required in order to add an element for styling purposes would look like the following:

```
<h:panelGroup style="color:red">
  <h:outputText value=
    "This is an error: " />
  <h:outputText value=
    "The value for input field e-mail is malformed" />
</h:panelGroup>
```

This wraps the two texts into a `<span>` element. If you want a `<div>` group instead, write the following:

```
<h:panelGroup layout="block" style="color:red">
  <h:outputText value=
    "This is an error: " />
  <h:outputText value=
    "The value for input field e-mail is malformed" />
</h:panelGroup>
```

For details and all possible attributes, see the "Standard HTML RenderKit Tags" section of the appendix.

HTML Tables

Especially for enterprise web applications, the rendering of data tables given a list of items is an important task. In addition, tables sometimes get used for the laying out of a fixed number of elements.

An example of a data table without special styling options (we will talk about styling in the Attributes table in the appendix) reads as follows:

```
@Named @SessionScoped
public class SomeClass implements Serializable {
  public static class Datum implements Serializable {
    private String lastName;
    private String firstName;
    public Datum(String ln, String fn) {
      this.lastName = ln;
      this.firstName = fn;
    }
    public String getLastName() {
      return lastName;
    }
    public String getFirstName() {
      return firstName;
    }
  }
  public List<Datum> getData() {
    return Arrays.asList(new Datum("Smith","John"),
        new Datum("Karmikel","Linda"),
        new Datum("Smear","Patrick"));
  }
}
```

```
<!DOCTYPE html>
<html xmlns:h="http://xmlns.jcp.org/jsf/html"
    xmlns:f="http://xmlns.jcp.org/jsf/core"
    xmlns:ui = "http://java.sun.com/jsf/facelets"
    xmlns:pt="http://xmlns.jcp.org/jsf/passthrough">
<h:head>
    <title>Table</title>
</h:head>
<h:body>
<h:dataTable value="#{someClass.data}" var="v">
  <h:column>
    <f:facet name="header">First Name</f:facet>
    #{v.firstName}
  </h:column>
  <h:column>
    <f:facet name="header">Last Name</f:facet>
    #{v.lastName}
  </h:column>
</h:dataTable>
</h:body>
</html>
```

The output of this example will look as shown in Figure 4-2.

First Name	**Last Name**
John	Smith
Linda	Karmikel
Patrick	Smear

Figure 4-2. *Data table example*

For details and all possible attributes, see the "Standard HTML RenderKit Tags" section of the appendix.

97

Repetition and Conditional Branching

So far we haven't seen dedicated tags for conditional rendering or repetitions—
something like the following:

```
<forEach value="#{inj.someCollection}" var="i">
    <h:outputText value="Hi #{i}" />
    <if value="#{i < 10}">
        <h:outputText value="Less than 10" />
    <else/>
        <h:outputText value="10 or more" />
    </if>
</forEach}
```

The reason for this is that JSF by design tries to build a static component tree
representing a page, and therefore repetitions and conditional branching are not first-
class citizens in the JSF world. Most people tend to mix in JSTL for conditional branching
and repetitions, which introduces another templating technology. You'll often find
corresponding solutions if you look on the internet. But do yourself a favor—Try to
avoid mixing them. JSF and JSTL do not work well together. You will be able to use both,
but mixed constructs show strange side effects quite often, and the internet is full of
questions like: "If I use x from JSF and y from JSTL, why does z not work then?"

The method you should use instead for conditional branching is applying the
"rendered" attribute of HTML components to render or not render them, as follows:

```
<h:outputText rendered="#{inj.renderName}" value="Name: #{inj.name}" />
```

This example will render the text output only if the method `public boolean`
`isRenderName()` of the injected bean class returns `true`.

For loops, use the `<h:dataTable>` tag where possible. If this is not an option, there
is a dedicated looping tag from the *Facelets* tag library and the associated namespace
`xmlns:ui = "http://java.sun.com/jsf/facelets."` Facelets is a templating technology
for orchestrating and mixing page sections using several template files. We won't talk
about facelets templating in this beginning Jakarta EE book, but we can borrow its
`<ui:repeat>` tag for repetitions, as follows:

```
<ui:repeat value="#{inj.someCollection}" var="x">
    [...do something with x...]
</ui:repeat>
```

Using this `<ui:repeat>` tag makes sure everything fits well with JSF's component layout methodology.

JSF Core Tags

The core tags are presentation-format independent tags, which means they could serve output formats other than HTML. They often get used as auxiliary elements added to HTML RenderKit tags, be it optional or obligatory to add them. We already used a couple of them; for example, to specify the options in a select list box, as follows:

```
...
<html xmlns:h="http://xmlns.jcp.org/jsf/html"
    xmlns:f="http://xmlns.jcp.org/jsf/core"
    xmlns:ui = "http://java.sun.com/jsf/facelets"
    xmlns:pt="http://xmlns.jcp.org/jsf/passthrough">
...

    <h:selectManyListbox  value="#{someClass.checks1}">
      <f:selectItems value="#{someClass.smcbItems}" />
    </h:selectManyListbox>
...
```

In the following paragraphs we will review all the core tags.

General Purpose Core Tags

The following core tags get used by various components from the RenderKit:

– **<f:attribute>**

This is a way to specify an attribute as a child element instead of directly adding it to a component as an XML attribute. So instead of

```
<h:inputText id="lastName" ... />
```

you can also write

```
<h:inputText ... >
  <f:attribute name="id" value="lastName" />
</h:inputText>
```

Its own attributes are as follows:

- **name**: The name of the attribute. A value expression of type String.

- **value**: The value of the attribute. A value expression of type Object.

– **<f:param>**

  In case a component needs parameters to function, you add one or more `<f:param>` tags as children. It is up to the component whether it needs parameters and what to do with them. Its attributes are as follows:

  - **id**: An ID. A value of type String. Not a value expression!

  - **name**: The name of the parameter. A value expression of type String.

  - **value**: The value of the parameter. A value expression of type Object.

  - **disable**: Whether or not to disable this parameter. A value expression of type Boolean.

  - **binding**: A UIParameter to bind to this component. Advanced applications only. A value expression of type UIComponent.

  A prominent example is URL parameters to be added to links, as follows:

```
<h:link value="Link label" outcome="page2">
  <f:param name="urlParam1" value="someValue" />
  <!-- There could be more... -->
</h:link>
```

The parameter will go as &urlParam1=someValue to the href attribute of the generated <a>.

-   **<f:facet>**

    If specified as a child of a component, registers a sub-tree of components to the component. It is up to the component whether it needs a facet and what to do with it. Its attributes are as follows:

    -   **name**: The name of the facet. A value of type `String`. Not a value expression! Names are not free to choose—the component you add a facet to decides what name the facet must carry.

Validator Core Tags

We saw that for form input tags like `<h:inputText>` it is possible to supply a "validator" attribute that forwards to a method where a validation of the input can happen. During the method invocation the input can be checked as to whether the format complies with field input restrictions, whether a number entered lies in a certain range, and more. It is, however, also possible to perform validations via appropriate core tags you can add as children to the input component.

The following list shows the validation components you can add as depicted in

```
<h:inputText> <!-- or other input component -->
  <f:validateLongRange ... /> <!-- or other -->
</h:inputText>
```

Don't forget to add a `<h:message>` and/or `<h:messages>` tag on the page; otherwise, you won't see the validator messages if the validation fails:

```
...
<h:messages globalOnly="true"/>
<h:form id="form">
  ...
  <h:inputText id="name" value="...">
    <f:validateLongRange ... />
  </h:inputText>
  <h:message for="name"/>
  ...
</h:form>
...
```

- **<f:validator>**

  Installs a custom validator on the surrounding component. To
  write such a validator, you create a class extending `javax.faces.`
  `validator.Validator`, add a `@FacesValidator` annotation
  (package `javax.faces.validator`) to the class, add the validator
  ID to this annotation as in `@FacesValidator( "com.example.`
  `MyValidator" )`, and use the very same ID as a `validatorId`
  attribute in a `<f:validator>` tag that you add as a child to the
  component. The tag's attributes are as follows:

  - **disabled**: Whether or not this validator is disabled. A value
    expression of type `Boolean`.

  - **validatorId**: The validator ID. A value expression of type `String`.

  - **for**: You can use this to explicitly specify a component (add its
    ID here) for which the validator acts. A value expression of type
    `String`.

  - **binding**: A `javax.faces.validator.Validator` to bind to this
    component. Advanced applications only; normally you don't
    have to use it. A value expression of type `Validator`.

- **<f:validateBean>**

  Enable bean validation (version 2.0, jsr 380) on the input
  component this tag has been added to as a child. *Bean validation*
  means the injected class contains bean validation annotations like
  `@NotBlank` in the following:

  ```
  import javax.validation.constraints.NotBlank;
  ...
  public class TheClass {
      @NotBlank(message =
          "Last name must not be empty")
      private String lastName;
      ...
  }
  ```

If the message is enclosed in curly brackets like in {some.msg. key}, the some.msg.key will be used as a property key from file src/main/resources/ValidationMessages.properties or localized variants like .../ValidationMessages_xx_ XX.properties, where xx_XX specifies a language like en or en_US. The bean validation framework specifies quite a few validation annotations—see the jsr 380 specification for details (the used bean validation version reads 2.0). The tag's attributes are as follows:

- **disabled**: Whether or not this validator is disabled. A value expression of type Boolean.

- **validationGroups:** A comma-separated list of validation groups. A validation group is a fully qualified class name. A value expression of type String.

- **for**: You can use this to explicitly specify a component (add its ID here) for which the validator acts. A value expression of type String.

- **binding**: A javax.faces.validator.BeanValidator to bind to this component. Advanced applications only; normally you don't have to use it. A value expression of type BeanValidator.

- **<f:validateRequired>**

Checks whether a value was entered at all. Same as setting the required="true" attribute. The tag's attributes are as follows:

- **disabled**: Whether or not this validator is disabled. A value expression of type Boolean.

- **for**: You can use this to explicitly specify a component (add its ID here) for which the validator acts. A value expression of type String.

- **binding**: A javax.faces.validator.RequiredValidator to bind to this component. Advanced applications only; normally you don't have to use it. A value expression of type RequiredValidator.

- **<f:validateLongRange>**

  Checks whether an integer number entered lies in a certain range specified by this tag. The tag's attributes are as follows:

  - **disabled**: Whether or not this validator is disabled. A value expression of type `Boolean`.

  - **minimum**: The minimum value. A value expression of type `long`.

  - **maximum**: The maximum value. A value expression of type `long`.

  - **for**: You can use this to explicitly specify a component (add its ID here) for which the validator acts. A value expression of type `String`.

  - **binding**: A `javax.faces.validator.LongRangeValidator` to bind to this component. Advanced applications only; normally you don't have to use it. A value expression of type `LongRangeValidator`.

- **<f:validateDoubleRange>**

  Checks whether a floating point number entered lies in a certain range specified by this tag. The tag's attributes are as follows:

  - **disabled**: Whether or not this validator is disabled. A value expression of type `Boolean`.

  - **minimum**: The minimum value. A value expression of type `double`.

  - **maximum**: The maximum value. A value expression of type `double`.

  - **for**: You can use this to explicitly specify a component (add its ID here) for which the validator acts. A value expression of type `String`.

  - **binding**: A `javax.faces.validator.DoubleRangeValidator` to bind to this component. Advanced applications only; normally you don't have to use it. A value expression of type `DoubleRangeValidator`.

- **<f:validateLength>**

  Checks whether an input's length lies in a certain range. The tag's
  attributes are as follows:

  - **disabled**: Whether or not this validator is disabled. A value
    expression of type `Boolean`.

  - **minimum**: The minimum length. A value expression of type `int`.

  - **maximum**: The maximum length. A value expression of type `int`.

  - **for**: You can use this to explicitly specify a component (add its
    ID here) for which the validator acts. A value expression of type
    `String`.

  - **binding**: A `javax.faces.validator.LengthValidator` to bind to
    this component. Advanced applications only; normally you don't
    have to use it. A value expression of type `LengthValidator`.

- **<f:validateRegex>**

  A quite powerful validator via which you can use regular
  expressions to validate the input. The tag's attributes are as
  follows:

  - **disabled**: Whether or not this validator is disabled. A value
    expression of type `Boolean`.

  - **pattern**: The regular expression pattern to check against. A value
    expression of type `String`.

  - **for**: You can use this to explicitly specify a component (add its
    ID here) for which the validator acts. A value expression of type
    `String`.

  - **binding**: A `javax.faces.validator.RegexValidator` to bind to
    this component. Advanced applications only; normally you don't
    have to use it. A value expression of type `RegexValidator`.

As an example, consider a text-input component that we want to make sure is both required and evaluates to an integer between 1000 and 9999. We use the long-range check and write the following:

```
<h:inputText vale="...">
    <f:validateRequired />
    <f:validateLongRange minimum="#{1000}" maximum="#{9999}" />
</h:inputText>
```

We wrote #{1000} and #{9999} to make sure the attributes get numerical values instead of strings.

To achieve the same result, we can also use a regular expression validator, as follows:

```
<h:inputText vale="...">
    <f:validateRegex pattern="[1-9]\d{3}" />
</h:inputText>
```

Converter Core Tags

For the conversion from string objects to any other Java type, converters get used. We need such conversions because text input and output fields present or serve string values, but the value expressions connected to the fields via value expressions may represent other types. Consider, for example, the following injected class:

```
@SessionScoped
@Named
public class TheClass implements Serializable {
    private LocalDateTime date; // + getter/setter
}
```

and the following JSF template snippet:

```
<h:inputText value="#{theClass.date}" />
```

This won't work, because even though the value attribute of <h:inputText> connects to a java.lang.Object, in the end it needs a String value for rendering, and it needs a way to convert back from string input to the target LocalDateTime object.

One way of specifying such a converter is by using the `converter` attribute of the input component, but it is also possible to use nested converter child elements, as in the following:

```
<h:inputText value="#{theClass.date}">
  <f:convertDateTime pattern="yyyy-MM-dd HH:mm:ss"
      type="both"/>
<h:inputText>
```

The following is a list of converter tags you can nest inside input components:

- **<f:converter>**

  Registers a named `Converter` instance to its closest parent component. To create a named converter, build a class implementing `Converter` (package `javax.faces.convert`) and add a `@FacesConverter` (package `javax.faces.convert`) annotation to the class, specifying a converter name as the annotation parameter, as follows:

  ```
  import javax.faces.convert.*;
  ...
  @FacesConverter("com.example.MyConverter")
  public class TheConverter implements Converter {
      [...implement methods...]
  }
  ```

  You then use the converter ID inside the `<f:converter>` tag, attribute `converterId`. The following is the full list of possible attributes:

  - **converterId**: The converter ID. A value expression of type `String`.

  - **for**: You can use this to explicitly specify a component (add its ID here) for which the converter acts. A value expression of type `String`.

  - **binding**: A `javax.faces.convert.Converter` to bind to this component. Advanced applications only; normally you don't have to use it. A value expression of type `Converter`.

- **\<f:convertNumber\>**

  A specialized converter for numbers. This converter is able to handle integers, floating point numbers, percentages, and money amounts. Its attributes are the following:

  - **currencyCode**: ISO 4217 currency code for formatting currencies. A value expression of type `String`.

  - **currencySymbol**: Currency symbol used for formatting currencies. A value expression of type `String`.

  - **groupingUsed**: Whether grouping gets used for numbers. A value expression of type `Boolean`.

  - **integerOnly**: Only the integer part of a number gets rendered and parsed. A value expression of type `Boolean`.

  - **locale**: The locale to use for formatting numbers. Either a value expression evaluating to `java.util.Locale` or a string value expression usable as the first argument to the `Locale` class constructor (the second constructor parameter is set to the empty string ""). A value expression of type `Object`.

  - **maxFractionDigits**: Maximum number of fraction digits. A value expression of type `int`.

  - **minFractionDigits**: Minimum number of fraction digits. A value expression of type `int`.

  - **maxIntegerDigits**: Maximum number of integer digits. A value expression of type `int`.

  - **minIntegerDigits**: Minimum number of integer digits. A value expression of type `int`.

  - **pattern**: A custom pattern; see API documentation of `java.text.DecimalFormat`. A value expression of type `String`.

  - **type**: The number type, one of: "number" (default), "currency," "percent." A value expression of type `String`.

- **for**: You can use this to explicitly specify a component (add its ID here) for which the converter acts. A value expression of type `String`.

- **binding**: A `javax.faces.convert.NumberConverter` to bind to this component. Advanced applications only; normally you don't have to use it. A value expression of type `NumberConverter`.

– **<f:convertDateTime>**

A specialized converter for dates and times. It is able to handle both the older `java.util.Date` class and the classes from `java.time` (since Java 8). Its attributes are as follows:

- **type**: The date/time type, one of: "date," "time," or "both." Default is "date". A value expression of type `String`.

- **dateStyle**: Predefined formatting style—only if type is "date" or "both." One of: "default" (default), "short," "medium," "long," "full." A value expression of type `String`.

- **timeStyle**: Predefined formatting style—only if type is "time" or "both." One of: "default" (default), "short," "medium," "long," or "full." A value expression of type `String`.

- **pattern**: A custom pattern; see online API documentation of `java.time.format.DateTimeFormatter`. A value expression of type `String`.

- **locale**: The locale to use for formatting dates and times. Either a value expression evaluating to `java.util.Locale` or a string value expression usable as the first argument to the `Locale` class constructor (the second constructor parameter is set to ""). A value expression of type `Object`.

- **timeZone**: A `java.util.TimeZone` typed value expression, or a string value expression usable as timezone ID as described in `java.util.TimeZone.getTimeZone()`. A value expression of type `Object`.

- **for:** You can use this to explicitly specify a component (add its ID here) for which the converter acts. A value expression of type `String`.

- **binding:** A `javax.faces.convert.DateTimeConverter` to bind to this component. Advanced applications only; normally you don't have to use it. A value expression of type `DateTimeConverter`.

Exercise 6

To the household accounting application, add a new property `value` of type `double`, and add a new text-input component with label `Value (#.##):` to the JSF template page. Add a converter tag to make sure the user enters correct numbers. Add a validator to make sure no negative numbers can be entered.

Selection Items Core Tags

For the various `<select* >` components designating selectables like checkboxes, checkbox lists, menu lists, and radio buttons we need to specify the selectable items. This can be done by several `<f:selectItem>` children or one `<f:selectItems>` child, as follows:

```
<h:selectManyCheckbox value="#{theClass.checks1}">
    <f:selectItem itemValue="v1" itemLabel="Item 1" />
    <f:selectItem itemValue="v2" itemLabel="Item 2" />
    <f:selectItem itemValue="v3" itemLabel="Item 3" />
    ...
</h:selectManyCheckbox>

<h:selectManyCheckbox value="#{theClass.checks2}">
    <f:selectItems value = "#{theClass.smcbItems}" />
</h:selectManyCheckbox>
```

In detail:

- **<f:selectItem>**

  A single checkbox, checkbox list item, selectable list item, selectable menu item, or radio button. The possible attributes are as follows:

  - **id**: The ID. A `String`. Not a value expression!

  - **itemLabel**: The label to be displayed. A value expression of type `String`.

  - **escape**: A `Boolean` flag indicating whether characters in the label that are sensitive to HTML and XML are to be escaped. A value expression of type `Boolean`. Defaults to `true`.

  - **itemValue**: The value of this item. A value expression of type `String`.

  - **itemDisabled**: Whether or not this item is to be disabled. A value expression of type `Boolean`.

  - **value**: The value describing the selected state of this item. An input/output value expression of type `javax.faces.model.SelectItem`.

  - **noSelectionOption**: Whether the option created by this item represents the special "not selected" option. A value expression of type `Boolean`. Default is `false`.

  - **binding**: A `javax.faces.component.UIComponent` to bind to this component. Advanced applications only; normally you don't have to use it. A value expression of type `UIComponent`.

  - **itemDescription**: The description. Will not be used for rendering, but serves as a hint for development tools. A value expression of type `String`.

- **<f:selectItems>**

  All items from a checkbox list, selectable list, selectable menu, or radio button set. The possible attributes are as follows:

  - **id**: The ID. A `String`. Not a value expression!

  - **value**: Represents the list of all selectable items. This is a value expression pointing to a collection (`java.util.List` or `java.util.Set`), an array, or a map. If you use a collection or an array, as element type use `javax.faces.model.SelectItem` or a plain Java object (bean). If you use a Java object, you must use the `var` attribute to expose the item object and refer to it from various other attributes. Underneath this list an example gets worked out. If the value points to a map, each map member key gets used as the label and the corresponding map member value gets used as the item value.

  - **var**: The name of a formal variable each item gets assigned to. A `String`. Not a value expression!

  - **itemLabel**: The label to be displayed. Use the variable you named at `val` to refer to the item. A value expression of type `String`.

  - **itemValue**: The value of this item. Use the variable you named at `val` to refer to the item. A value expression of type `String`.

  - **itemDisabled**: Whether or not this item is to be disabled. Use the variable you named at `val` to refer to the item. A value expression of type `Boolean`.

  - **itemLabelEscaped**: A `Boolean` flag indicating whether characters in the label that are sensitive to HTML and XML are to be escaped. Use the variable you named at `val` to refer to the item. A value expression of type `Boolean`. Defaults to `true`.

  - **itemDescription**: The description. Will not be used for rendering, but serves as a hint for development tools. Use the variable you named at `val` to refer to the item. A value expression of type `String`.

- **noSelectionValue**: The element from the "value" collection, or its exact `toString()` representation, for the option created by that item to represent the special "not selected" option. A value expression of type `Object`.

- **binding**: A `javax.faces.component.UIComponent` to bind to this component. Advanced applications only; normally you don't have to use it. A value expression of type `UIComponent`.

If you use `<f:selectItems>` and use a "value" pointing to a collection or an array of `javax.faces.model.SelectItem` objects, what will be used for the label and value of each item is determined by the `SelectItem` class. In this case, you don't have to specify any of `var`, `itemLabel`, `itemValue`, `itemDisabled`, `itemLabelEscaped`, or `itemDescription`. See the following:

```
<h:selectManyCheckbox value="#{theClass.sel}">
    <f:selectItems value="#{theClass.items}" />
</h:selectManyCheckbox>
```

The class reads as follows:

```
@Named
@SessionScoped
public class TheClass implements Serializable {
    ...
    public List<SelectItem> getItems() {
        return ...
    }
}
```

If, however, the collection or array contains plain Java objects, you must manually extract the item members, as follows:

```
<h:selectManyCheckbox value="#{theClass.sel}">
    <f:selectItems
      value="#{theClass.items}"
      var="itm"
      itemLabel="#{itm.lab}"
```

```
        itemValue="#{itm.val}"
    />
</h:selectManyCheckbox>
```

where each item has a `String getLab()` and `String getVal()` method, as follows:

```
@Named
@SessionScoped
public class TheClass implements Serializable {
    public static class Itm {
        ...
        public String getLab() { return ... }
        public String getVal() { return ... }
    }
    ...
    public List<Itm> getItems() {
        return ...
    }
}
```

Listener Core Tags

Listeners are for crosscutting activities on your page. Say, for example, you have an action button that finishes a registration step a user accomplishes on some of your pages. At some later stage of the project, the stakeholders introduce statistical audits as an additional requirement, so you want to count the final registration step in both the back-end logic and the page flow. For the latter to be implemented you can add an *action listener* to the registration button. You don't have to change the existing front-end logic at all; the listener is just an additional step that does not interfere with what was already developed.

To add the listener you can add the `actionListener` attribute to `<h:commandButton>`. We described that in the HTML RenderKit description earlier in this chapter. But there are also dedicated core tags that let us write the following:

```
<h:commandButton value="#{bundle.register}"
        action="#{user.register}">
```

```
  <f:actionListener
      type="com.example.listeners.RegisterListener"
  />
</h:commandButton>
```

where `com.example.listeners.RegisterListener` points to a suitable listener class
(of course, use a decent package and class name that fit your application), as follows:

```
package com.example.listeners;

import javax.faces.event.*;

public class RegisterListener
      implements ActionListener {
  @Override
  public void processAction(ActionEvent event)
      throws AbortProcessingException {
    System.err.println("!!! ACTION !!!");
  }
}
```

There are also listeners for value changes, phase propagation (we'll talk about JSF phases
later in this chapter at "Overview of the JSF Page Flow"), and a special action listener that
directly sets properties of injected bean classes. The complete list reads as follows:

- **<f:actionListener>**

  Adds an `ActionListener` implementation to the surrounding
  action input component. The attributes are as follows:

  - **type**: The fully qualified class name of an implementation of
    `javax.faces.event.ActionListener`. A value expression of type
    `String`.

  - **for**: You can use this to explicitly specify a component (add its
    ID here) for which the action listener is responsible. A value
    expression of type `String`.

  - **binding**: A `javax.faces.event.ActionListener` to bind to this
    component. Advanced applications only; normally you don't
    have to use it. A value expression of type `ActionListener`.

- **<f:valueChangeListener>**

  Adds a `ValueChangeListener` implementation to the surrounding action input component. Fires if an input has its value changed and loses focus. The attributes are as follows:

  - **type**: The fully qualified class name of an implementation of `javax.faces.event.ValueChangeListener`. A value expression of type `String`.

  - **for**: You can use this to explicitly specify a component (add its ID here) for which the value change listener is responsible. A value expression of type `String`.

  - **binding**: A `javax.faces.event.ValueChangeListener` to bind to this component. Advanced applications only; normally you don't have to use it. A value expression of type `ValueChangeListener`.

- **<f:phaseListener>**

  Adds a `PhaseListener` implementation to the document. The attributes are as follows:

  - **type**: Fully qualified class name of an implementation of `javax.faces.event.PhaseListener`. A value expression of type `String`.

  - **binding**: A `javax.faces.event.PhaseListener` to bind to this component. Advanced applications only; normally you don't have to use it. A value expression of type `PhaseListener`.

- **<f:setPropertyActionListener>**

  Adds a special action listener that updates an injected Java object's field upon execution. The attributes are as follows:

  - **value**: The value to set. A value expression of type `Object`.

  - **target**: (required) The target field that receives the value once the listener fires. An input value expression of type `Object`.

  - **for**: You can use this to explicitly specify a component (add its ID here) for which the action listener is responsible. A value expression of type `String`.

AJAX Core Tags

AJAX is about asynchronous processing of user interactions without reloading the complete page or advancing to a completely new page. The idea of using AJAX for JSF is as follows: without reloading the whole page or advancing to a new page, take a certain set of input components, send the associated values to the server, perform some processing there, and from the outcome re-render a certain set of components on the page.

Consider, for example, a form with two inputs for a first name and a last name of the user, another input for her birthday, and an output for the combined name, as follows:

```
<h:form id="form1">
  <h:inputText id="firstName"
      value="#{ajaxBean.firstName}">
  </h:inputText>
  <h:inputText id="lastName"
      value="#{ajaxBean.lastName}">
  </h:inputText>
  <h:inputText id="birthday"
      value="#{ajaxBean.birthday}">
    <f:convertDateTime pattern="yyyy-MM-dd"
        type="date"/>
  </h:inputText>

  <h:outputText id="combinedName"
        value="#{ajaxBean.combinedName}">
  </h:outputText>

  <h:commandButton value="#{bundle.submit}"
        action="#{ajaxBean.submit}">
  </h:commandButton>
</h:form>
```

The corresponding injected Java class reads:

```
import java.io.Serializable;
import java.time.LocalDate;
import javax.enterprise.context.SessionScoped;
import javax.inject.Named;
```

117

```
@SessionScoped
@Named
public class AjaxBean implements Serializable {
  private String firstName = ""; // + getter/setter
  private String lastName = "";  // + getter/setter
  private LocalDate birthday;    // + getter/setter

  public String submit() {
    System.err.println("submit: " + firstName +
        " " + lastName);
    return null;
  }

  public String getCombinedName() {
    return firstName + " " + lastName;
  }
}
```

This page is fully functional—once you enter values for the name inputs and press the "Submit" button, the method submit() gets called, the same page gets loaded again, and the combined name gets written to the text-output component. No miracle so far. What we want to change to streamline the communication with the server is to send first and last name to the server and only update the combined name, with no reloading of the complete page. This is where the core tag <f:ajax> can help us, as in the following:

```
...
<h:commandButton value="#{bundle.submit}"
      action="#{ajaxBean.submit}">
    <f:ajax event="action"
          execute="firstName lastName"
          render="combinedName"/>
</h:commandButton>
...
```

The rest of the template file stays unchanged. A click on the "Submit" button now changes its behavior as follows:

- Because of the event="action" in the AJAX tag, AJAX now will take care of the submit action. Since "action" is the default event for submit buttons, this attribute could also have been left away here.

- The firstName lastName in the execute attribute tells which data need to be sent to the server. We want to update the combined name, so here we add the IDs of the corresponding input fields.

- The combinedName in the render attribute tells which fields to update as a result of the AJAX call. This could also be a space-delimited list of IDs.

To make it a little bit easier to gather the components you need as input for the AJAX call, you can create a container for them using <h:panelGroup>, as follows:

```
<h:panelGroup id="ajaxGroup">
  <h:inputText id="firstName"
    value="#{ajaxBean.firstName}">
  </h:inputText>
  <h:inputText id="lastName"
    value="#{ajaxBean.lastName}">
  </h:inputText>
</h:panelGroup>
...
<h:commandButton value="#{bundle.submit}"
    action="#{ajaxBean.submit}">
    <f:ajax event="action"
            execute="ajaxGroup"
            render="combinedName"/>
</h:commandButton>
</h:form>
```

But AJAX can do more than just interfere with button clicks. Consider the following code:

```
<h:form id="form1">
  <h:panelGroup id="ajaxGroup">
    <h:inputText id="firstName"
          value="#{ajaxBean.firstName}">
      <f:ajax execute="ajaxGroup" render="combinedName"/>
    </h:inputText>
    <h:inputText id="lastName"
          value="#{ajaxBean.lastName}">
      <f:ajax execute="ajaxGroup" render="combinedName"/>
    </h:inputText>
  </h:panelGroup>
  <h:inputText id="birthday" value="#{ajaxBean.birthday}">
      <f:convertDateTime pattern="yyyy-MM-dd" type="date"/>
  </h:inputText>
  <h:outputText id="combinedName"
        value="#{ajaxBean.combinedName}">
  </h:outputText>
  <h:commandButton value="#{bundle.submit}"
        action="#{ajaxBean.submit}" />
</h:form>
```

Here, I removed the AJAX tag from the button and instead added two AJAX tags to the two name input components. First of all, you'll notice that these two AJAX tags don't have an event attribute. This means we revert to the default events for the input components, which happen to be valueChange for all text input components. A valueChange gets fired when the component's value is altered *and* it loses the focus. Now if you enter something in one of the input fields and exit the focus (press TAB or click somewhere else), AJAX will start working, and the combined name will be updated.

The same thing happens if we shorten this a little bit and let the AJAX tag surround the two input components, as follows:

```
<h:form id="form1">
  <f:ajax render="combinedName">
    <h:inputText id="firstName" value="#{ajaxBean.firstName}">
    </h:inputText>
```

```
    <h:inputText id="lastName" value="#{ajaxBean.lastName}">
    </h:inputText>
</f:ajax>
<h:inputText id="birthday" value="#{ajaxBean.birthday}">
  <f:convertDateTime pattern="yyyy-MM-dd" type="date"/>
</h:inputText>
<h:outputText id="combinedName" value="#{ajaxBean.combinedName}">
</h:outputText>
<h:commandButton value="#{bundle.submit}"
    action="#{ajaxBean.submit}">
</h:commandButton>
</h:form>
```

Because the panel group's sole purpose was to gather input components and the container spanned up by the AJAX tag now does this job, the panel group could also be removed. A surrounding <f:ajax> tag without an event specification always acts this way: it adds an AJAX handler to all AJAX-capable components from the complete subtree contained, using each component's default event.

Note   The command buttons and command links have action (pressed) as the default AJAX event, while all text-input components (texts, text areas, passwords) and all select components have valueChange (value changed and focus lost) as their default AJAX event.

The details of the AJAX tag read as follows:

- **<f:ajax>**

  Enables AJAX for the parent component, or recursively for all children components. The attributes are as follows:

  - **disabled**: Whether or not the AJAX tag is disabled. A value expression of type Boolean.

  - **event**: Tells which event triggers the AJAX communication. One of: action (for command buttons and links), valueChange (value changed and focus lost), or xyz if onxyz is a valid JavaScript event for the component. If unspecified, the default event for the component gets chosen. A value expression of type String.

- **execute**: A value expression of type `Collection<String>`, or a literal space-delimited list of IDs. The expression is supposed to evaluate to the IDs of the components that participate as input components for executing the AJAX request, or that serve as containers for such input components (for example, `<h:panelGroup>` containers). Inside the list, you may add elements `@this` (current component), `@form` (all of the current form), `@all`, and `@none`. If unspecified, `@this` is assumed.

- **render**: A value expression of type `Collection<String>`, or a literal space-delimited list of IDs. The expression is supposed to evaluate to the IDs of the components that should be updated as a result of the AJAX request, or that serve as containers for such components (for example, `<h:panelGroup>` containers). Inside the list, you may add elements `@this` (current component), `@form` (all of the current form), `@all`, and `@none`. If unspecified, `@none` is assumed.

- **immediate**: If `true`, events are broadcast during the "Apply Request Values" phase. Otherwise, the standard "Invoke Applications" phase will be responsible for the AJAX events to happen. Default is `false`. A value expression of type `Boolean`.

- **listener**: A method expression. Must point to a method `public void theName( javax.faces.event.AjaxBehaviorEvent ) throws javax.faces.event.AbortProcessingException`. This is a method that gets invoked after the AJAX event has fired.

- **onevent**: The name of a JavaScript function for handling AJAX-related status changes. The function will get a parameter object with the following properties: `responseXML` (the response to the AJAX call, in XML format), `responseText` (the same in text format), `responseCode` (some numeric response code), `source` (the DOM source of the event), `status` (one of `begin`, `complete`, and `success`), `type` (the type of the AJAX call: "event").

- **onerror**: The name of a JavaScript function for handling AJAX-related errors. The function will get a parameter object with the following properties: `description`, `errorName`, `errorMessage`, plus the properties described earlier for the `onevent` handler (`type` will be `error`, `status` will be one of `emptyResponse`, `httpError`, `malformedXML`, or `serverError`).

Other Core Tags

There are a couple more, less often used core tags. I just list them here briefly, so you will have heard about them. For details about using them, consult the online documentation.

- **<f:verbatim>**

  Create and register a child `UIOutput` component associated with the closest parent `UIComponent` custom action, which renders nested body content. The contents of this tag output as-is, without any processing by JSF. This tag is deprecated, so do not use it! With the current JSF version you can write HTML code anywhere, or you can use the `<h:outputText>` tag.

- **<f:event>**

  Allow JSF page authors to install `ComponentSystemEventListener` instances on a component in a page.

- **<f:loadBundle>**

  Load a resource bundle localized for the locale of the current view, and expose it as a `java.util.Map` in the request attributes of the current request under the key specified by the value of the `var` attribute of this tag.

- **<f:view>**

  Container for all JSF core and custom component actions used on a page. Only needed if you want to override page locale, encoding, or content type. Normally you don't need it.

- **<f:subview>**

  Container action for all Java Server Faces core and custom component actions used on a nested page via `jsp:include` or any custom action that dynamically includes another page from the same web application, such as JSTL's `c:import`. Using `<f:subview>`, you introduce a new naming context, which under certain circumstances can help to avoid ID name clashes.

- **<f:metadata>**

  Declares the metadata facet for this view.

- **<f:viewParam>**

  Used inside of the metadata facet of a view, this tag causes a `UIViewParameter` to be attached as metadata for the current view. You can use this to read parameters that were passed over while navigating to this page.

- **<f:viewAction>**

  Used inside of the metadata facet of a view. Specifies custom actions to be executed during JSF lifecycle events.

The Pass-Through Namespace

If you look at the examples for JSF template files we have introduced so far, you'll notice that we included a namespace `xmlns:pt = "http://xmlns.jcp.org/jsf/passthrough."` This namespace does not belong to any tag library, so the question is, what is it good for? Consider the following HTML 5 example snippet:

```
<input type="text" data-category="food" />
```

This is a text-input field with an additional non-standard attribute, `data-category`, which might be used, for example, by some JavaScript included with the page. HTML 5 allows the use of such `data-*` custom attributes. The thing is, JSF doesn't know about such custom attributes, and if we use the standard HTML `<h:inputText>` tag, there is of course no such `data-*` field allowed.

But there is a tricky way to circumvent this restriction, and here comes the pass-through namespace into the game: JSF can handle attributes with the pass-through namespace, and for such attributes no restrictions apply; they will just be passed through unaltered. So if we write the following:

```
<h:inputText id="item" value="#{whatever.whatever}" pt:data-
category="food" />
```

JSF won't complain about this unknown attribute, and the rendered HTML will include exactly this custom attribute:

```
<input id="form1:item"
    type="text"
    name="form1:item"
    value=""
    data-category="food" />
```

The same procedure holds for cases where HTML 5 tags use some standard attributes that JSF for some reason does not yet know about. You can at least add such unknown attributes using the pass-through namespace, even though JSF will not use them for templating or tag processing.

Navigation Between Pages

To advance from one page to another you typically use one of the submit action components, `<h:commandButton>` or `<h:commandLink>`. Inside the `action` attribute of either of them you specify a method expression, as follows:

```
<h:commandButton ... action="#{injected.someAction}" />
  <!-- or -->
<h:commandLink ... action="#{injected.someAction}" />
```

And inside the method you return a string initiating a *navigation case*, as follows:

```
@Named @SessionScoped
public class Injected implements Serializable {
    ...
```

```
    public String someAction() {
        ... do whatever ...
        return "page2";
    }
}
```

If you don't need anything done inside the injected bean and just want to advance to a certain page, you can also circumvent the method call and directly write the following:

```
<h:commandButton ... action="page2" />
  <!-- or -->
<h:commandLink ... action="page2" />
```

In all these cases, a click on the button or link will advance to page page2.xhtml.

More precisely, you have the following options to advance to a new page or reload the current page:

- If the method returns null or you omit the action attribute altogether, the form gets processed and the current page gets reloaded.

- If the method returns some string "xyz" and the file faces-config.xml does not define a navigation rule for the processed method and the returned outcome, a so-called auto-navigation happens: JSF tries to process and load a page template file xyz.xhtml. In all the examples we have presented so far, this auto-navigation procedure was used.

- If the file faces-config.xml contains an entry like the following:

```
    <navigation-rule>
      <from-view-id>main.xhtml</from-view-id>
      <navigation-case>
        <from-action>#{injected.someAction}
            </from-action>
        <from-outcome>xyz</from-outcome>
        <to-view-id>/someOtherPage.xhtml</to-view-id>
      </navigation-case>
    </navigation-rule>
```

(remove the line break and the spaces before `</from-action>`),
a matching specified rule and navigation case will take effect
instead of auto-navigation. In this case, if we are on page
`main.xhtml`, *and* method `someAction()` was invoked, *and* its
outcome was "xyz", the form will be processed and then the page
`someOtherPage.xhtml` will be processed and rendered.

Exercise 7

In the household accounting application, create a page `response.xml` summarizing the
data entered in the form, and let the "Submit" button from the main entry page advance
to the response page. On the response page, add a `<h:button>` returning to the main
entry page.

More Injection

We know that for value and method expressions we refer to injected classes. Inside
these classes, we can have properties injected that help us to further build up various
functionalities. As an example consider the following class:

```
import javax.enterprise.context.SessionScoped;
import javax.faces.context.ExternalContext;
import javax.faces.context.FacesContext;
import javax.inject.Inject;
import javax.inject.Named;
import javax.servlet.ServletContext;
import javax.servlet.http.HttpServletRequest;
import javax.servlet.http.HttpSession;

@Named
@SessionScoped
public class Accounting implements Serializable {

    @Inject private FacesContext facesContext;
    @Inject private HttpServletRequest servletRequest;
    @Inject private ExternalContext externalContext;
```

```
    @Inject private ServletContext servletContext;
    @Inject private HttpSession httpSession;

    ...
}
```

For these properties you don't even have to provide getters and setters, as the CDI (context and dependency injection) engine takes care of initializing these properties properly. You can use them for parameter queries, context parameters, session and request characteristics, and more.

Caution   For JSF 2.3, some kind of compatibility mode gets used and so the faces context cannot be injected by default. To be able to use it, add class `import javax.faces.annotation.FacesConfig; @FacesConfig(version = FacesConfig.Version.JSF_2_3) public class ConfigurationBean {  }` (yes, it is empty) anywhere in your package hierarchy.

It is also possible to hook in the instance creation and destruction procedure by annotating methods (arbitrary names) with the @PostConstruct and @PreDestroy annotations (both from package `javax.annotation`), as follows:

```
@Named
@SessionScoped
public class Accounting implements Serializable {
    ...
    @PostConstruct public void constr() {
        ...
    }
    @PreDestroy public void destr() {
        ...
    }
}
```

You can use this for preparing or cleaning up, and for monitoring and logging purposes.

Overview of the JSF Page Flow

A JSF application is wired to an instance of the FacesContext class. You don't often have to deal with that class explicitly, but it is important to know that each page, once built up, corresponds with a data structure called a *view,* and that this view gets stored in the FacesContext.

When a page gets called the first time, a view gets created that later will contain all the data elements for all the JSF elements defined in the page. This view then gets populated given the JSF elements from the template file (the XHTML file in our case). The view will be directly translated to the data stream sent to the browser.

When a page that already exists gets called as the result of posting a form, the standard JSF lifecycle gets traversed: Restore view ➤ Apply requests values ➤ Process validations ➤ Update model values ➤ Invoke application ➤ Render response. In detail:

1. **Restore View**

    The view gets restored, meaning it will be pulled from the FacesContext given the name of the page.

2. **Apply Request Values**

    The values sent with the form posting will be received, assigned to their corresponding view elements, and saved for future processing. The assignment builds a relationship, but does not yet overwrite old values!

3. **Process Validations**

    The validations associated with the view elements will be processed. Validation get explicitly specified in the template file (XHTML in our case). If all validations on a page succeed, the next phase in the lifecycle gets called. If at least one validation fails, an error message gets generated, the chain gets shortcutted, and the "Render Response" phase will be next instead.

4. **Update Model Values**

    The new values from the "Apply Request Values" as a result of a form post now overwrite the old view values.

5. **Invoke Application**

This is for preparing the navigation to other pages. It includes
calling submit action methods which can perform any suitable
application activities like invoking back-end components.

6. **Render Response**

The data stream to be sent to the browser gets built, and the view
will be stored in the FacesContext

See Figure 4-3.

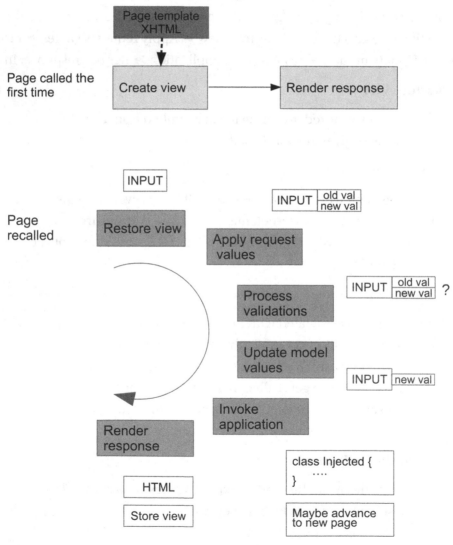

Figure 4-3. *JSF lifecycle and example input field*

This process chain can be altered by adding an XML attribute `immediate="true"` to one or more components. Consider the following example:

```
<h:inputSecret id="password" autocomplete="off"
    value="#{auth.passwd}"
    required="true"
    requiredMessage="Password is Required" />

<p:commandLink action="#{auth.forgotPassword}"
    immediate="true">
  <h:outputText value="#{bundle.link_forgotpasswd']}" />
</p:commandLink>
```

Here the `immediate="true"` for the "forgot password" link leads to the validation of the password field's getting skipped. Which makes sense, since for cases when this link gets pressed the password entry no longer is needed. More precisely, what `immediate` does is the following: if added to input components like input fields (subclasses of `UIInput`), their validation gets brought forward to the "Apply Request Values" phase. This means that if their validation fails, components not marked with `immediate="true"` will just be ignored as far as concerns the "Process Validations" phase, so they won't get validated. If a command field (button or link, subclass of `UICommand`) gets marked with `immediate="true,"` invoking it leads to the skipping of the three phases "Apply Request Values," "Process Validations," and "Update Model Values" for all fields *except for those also marked with* `immediate="true."`

If during the "Process Validations" phase a component validation fails, the `FacesContext` gets an error message added for this component and the chain fast-forwards to the "Render Response" phase, skipping "Update Model Values" and "Invoke application."

If at any stage a programmatic `renderResponse()` gets called on `FacesContext`, the current phase gets completed but immediately afterward the "Render Response" phase will be called, skipping the other phases which have not been invoked yet. By calling `responseComplete()` even the "Render Response" phase can be skipped - you'd use this if you want to leave JSF processing and establish non-JSF means to generate a HTTP response data stream.

For any phase except the "Restore View" phase, event listeners can be registered, which you can use for additional processing steps. This is also the place where you can call `renderResponse()` to fast-forward to the "Render Response" phase, or `responseComplete()` to quit JSF processing altogether.

Exercise 8

Add a phase listener tag to your page, and let it output diagnostic info. Hint: Use `event.getPhaseId().getName()` for the diagnostic output. Hint: In the listener class, let method `getPhaseId()` return `PhaseId.ANY_PHASE`. Load and reload any page to see the listener in action.

CHAPTER 5

Building Single-Page Web Applications with REST and JSON

In Chapter 4 we talked about creating multi-page web applications via Java server faces (JSF). The central paradigm of JSF is the communication between the user (browser) and the server via forms, although using the `<f:ajax>` tag makes a more fine-grained communication possible because only the form part needs to be transmitted to the server.

A totally different paradigm operates under the name *single-page application* or SPA. Here, only one page gets loaded for the whole application, the user interaction or front-end logic gets handled by JavaScript, and the communication between the page on the browser and the server happens via AJAX using data snippets formatted as JSON.

To this aim, different JavaScript frameworks exist that help to streamline the front-end logic. There, you will also find ways to handle menus for structuring the application, as well as techniques to handle user interaction in an elegant if not beautiful manner. In this chapter, we will talk about SPAs, but we will keep the front-end logic at a minimum and leave the discussion about JavaScript frameworks for a follow-up book. For our purposes, it is enough to include the jQuery library, which is not a full-fledged SPA framework but helps a lot for demonstrating SPA techniques.

A RESTful Server Inside Jakarta EE

A Jakarta EE 8 server by default comes with all that we need for a single-page application. Consider a very simple application that just provides a REST interface for reading the current date and time. Let us call it "rest-date." To create it, in the Project Explorer pane

© Peter Späth 2019
P. Späth, *Beginning Jakarta EE*, https://doi.org/10.1007/978-1-4842-5079-2_5

on the left side of the Eclipse window, right-click and select New ➤ Project... and select Maven ➤ Maven Project. Choose "maven-archetype-quickstart" from the archetypes catalog, and then enter the following project data:

```
Group-Id:    book.jakarta8
Artifact-Id: restdate
Version:     0.0.1-SNAPSHOT
```

Rename the package to "book.jakarta8.restdate."

Next, we add the Jakarta EE API library to the project. To do so, open the pom.xml file and, in the dependencies section, add the following:

```
<dependency>
    <groupId>javax</groupId>
    <artifactId>javaee-api</artifactId>
    <version>8.0</version>
</dependency>
```

In the same file, change the packaging to <packaging>war</packaging>.

Make sure the Java JDK gets used in version 8. To check that, right-click on the project in the Project Explorer, then go to Properties. Navigate to "Java Build Path" ➤ "Libraries" tab. Make sure the correct JRE system library is shown.

To also make sure the build tool Maven uses the correct Java version, open pom.xml. Check that it contains or add the following:

```
<project ...>
    ...
    <build>
      <plugins>
        <plugin>
          <artifactId>maven-compiler-plugin</artifactId>
          <configuration>
            <source>1.8</source>
            <target>1.8</target>
          </configuration>
        </plugin>
      </plugins>
    </build>
  </project>
```

If you changed something in the pom.xml file, right-click on the project, and then invoke Maven ➤ Update Project....

Next, we convert the project to a *faceted* project. To do so, right-click on the project in the Project Explorer, then select Configure ➤ Convert to Faceted Form.... If this menu entry does not exist, the project is already faceted. In the Facets dialog, which you see after you click "Convert to Faceted Form..." or via right-clicking on the project name ➤ Properties ➤ Project Facets, check and enter the following:

```
Dynamic Web Module 4.0
Java 1.8
JavaScript 1.0
JAX-RS 2.1
```

If it is not possible to change a version, remove the check, click "Apply and Close," and open the dialog again. Then you can recheck and select the desired version.

Make sure the following folder exists: "src/main/webapp/WEB-INF"—if the folder doesn't exist, create it.

If it does not yet exist, create the file src/main/webapp/WEB-INF/glassfish-web.xml. Let its contents read as follows:

```
<?xml version="1.0" encoding="UTF-8"?>
<!DOCTYPE glassfish-web-app PUBLIC
    "-//GlassFish.org//DTD GlassFish Application Server
    3.1 Servlet 3.0//EN"
    "http://glassfish.org/dtds/glassfish-web-app_3_0-1.dtd">
<glassfish-web-app error-url="">
    <class-loader delegate="true"/>
</glassfish-web-app>
```

(the DOCTYPE element in one line, one space after PUBLIC, just one space in front of 3.1, and one space before the http...).

Create an empty file, src/main/webapp/WEB-INF/beans.xml. If the file exists, make sure it is empty, but do not delete the file.

If it does not exist yet, create the file src/main/webapp/WEB-INF/web.xml. It must contain the following lines:

```
<?xml version="1.0" encoding="UTF-8"?>
<web-app xmlns:xsi=
        "http://www.w3.org/2001/XMLSchema-instance"
  xmlns="http://xmlns.jcp.org/xml/ns/javaee"
  xsi:schemaLocation="http://xmlns.jcp.org/xml/ns/javaee
        http://xmlns.jcp.org/xml/ns/javaee/web-app_4_0.xsd"
  id="WebApp_ID" version="4.0">

  <display-name>julian</display-name>
  <servlet>
    <servlet-name>
      javax.ws.rs.core.Application
    </servlet-name>
  </servlet>
  <servlet-mapping>

    <servlet-name>
      javax.ws.rs.core.Application
    </servlet-name>
    <url-pattern>/webapi/*</url-pattern>
  </servlet-mapping>
</web-app>
```

This file is responsible for mapping URL requests starting with /webapi/ to a REST processing engine.

Create a class, book.jakarta8.restdate.RestDate, and let it read as follows:

```
package book.jakarta8.restdate;

import java.time.ZonedDateTime;
import javax.ws.rs.GET;
import javax.ws.rs.Path;
import javax.ws.rs.Produces;
```

```
/**
 * REST Web Service
 */
@Path("/d")
public class RestDate {
  @GET
  @Produces("text/plain")
  public String stdDate() {
    return ZonedDateTime.now().toString();
  }
}
```

Make sure you have the CURL application installed on your system. You can use any other RESTful client software as well, but for the rest of this chapter we will use CURL because it is both straightforward and powerful. Start the server, install the rest-date application on it (for example, via the menu Run As ➤ Run on Server), and inside a terminal enter the following:

```
curl -X GET http://localhost:8080/restdate/webapi/d
```

The output should be something like 2019-03-31T16:13:25.083+02:00[Europe/Berlin].

Even with this small class and just a few lines in the file web.xml, and by adding a couple of annotations, we already have a fully functional RESTful server running.

Single-Page Web Applications

In a single-page web application we have two kinds of data: static content comprising HTML pages, style sheets, images, and script files, and dynamic content for the dynamic data in JSON format. It is important to know that for a real SPA everything gets handled over a REST interface, even the static content. If you enter a URL in your browser, a command GET/some/url/path gets sent to the server, and the same GET command with different paths gets sent for the style sheets, scripts, and images the page wants to load. If you submit a form, a POST/some/url/path gets sent with the posted data as a message body. In a JSF environment, all those GETs and POSTs and the page navigation can be handled by JSF, but for a REST interface we go one step back and explicitly take care of GETs and POSTs, and we circumvent the page navigation by loading just one static HTML page. The dynamic content of the page then gets handled by JavaScript.

This is what we begin with for our first steps in the SPA world: static content. To elaborate more features for the date output application we started at the beginning of the chapter and to serve as a blueprint for your own SPAs, we create a folder called "src/main/webapp/static." First, we put a `main.html` file there, as follows:

```
<!DOCTYPE html>
<html>
<head>
<meta charset="UTF-8">
<title>RESTful Dates</title>
</head>

<body>
Content of the document......
</body>

</html>
```

Next, we write a controller whose sole purpose is to serve static content. This is a Java class, `book.jakarta8.restdate.StaticContent`:

```
package book.jakarta8.restdate;

import java.io.InputStream;

import javax.ejb.Stateless;
import javax.inject.Inject;
import javax.servlet.ServletContext;
import javax.ws.rs.GET;
import javax.ws.rs.Path;
import javax.ws.rs.PathParam;
import javax.ws.rs.core.Response;

@Path("")
@Stateless
public class StaticContent {
  @Inject ServletContext context;
```

```
@GET
@Path("{path: ^static\\/.*}")
public Response staticResources(
        @PathParam("path") final String path) {
  final InputStream resource = context.
        getResourceAsStream(
        String.format("/static/%s", path));

  return null == resource
    ? Response.status(Response.Status.NOT_FOUND).build()
    : Response.ok().entity(resource).build();
  }
}
```

The @Path annotation makes this a class that responds to REST requests, and it tells which URLs are necessary in order for clients to use the REST interface. The @Inject uses CDI (context and dependency injection, which we already used in the JSF chapter) to get hold of the servlet context. We need the context in order to address application files deployed as resources. The @GET tells which REST verb is needed in order for a method to be responsible for the REST service method; the name of the method is arbitrary.

Do you see that we have two places where we use the @Path annotation? The class-level @Path in front of the class serves as a basis URL path, but the methods declare their own path parts using their own @Path annotations. The effective path used for matching an incoming URL path is the concatenation of the class-level @Path and each method's @Path. In the example, we use an empty string for the class-level @Path, meaning that the methods describe the full path pattern.

We can now load our first static HTML page. Deploy the application by pressing CTRL+ALT+P on the server in the "Servers" view, then in a browser window enter the following:

```
http://localhost:8080/restdate/static/main.html
```

Note   We don't pay particular attention to things like caching and expiry for static content. For production-level applications, such things should be taken into account.

About REST

REST is an acronym for *representational state transfer*. It is an architectural style for web-related operations. Clients use a predefined set of operations or HTTP methods on data—GET, POST, PUT, DELETE (and a few more)—to communicate with servers, and as concerns the communication no state is involved. This means the client communicates using one of the verbs GET, DELETE, POST, PUT, and so on, and immediately after the server has performed the operation and/or returned data, the server forgets about the communication step. The name "representational state transfer" stems from the fact that, from the client's point of view, the representation of data queried from the server changes between communication steps (or might change).

The communication verbs have been part of the HTTP specification from the early infancy of the web. In more detail, we have the following:

– **GET**

Used to retrieve a resource. Resources are identified by URIs, so the communication might be described by something like GET http://some.server.com/myclub/member/37. A GET operation is *not allowed* to change any data (except for access statistics and the like), and it must be idempotent. That means a second GET using the same URI with no intermediate operations between those two GETs must return *exactly* the same data. Note that GET operations were commonly widely abused for any kind of operations, including changing data. With REST we return to the roots, and data must not be changed.

– **DELETE**

Used to delete a datum. Again, the resource in question gets addressed by an URI, so you write DELETE http://some.server. com/myclub/member/37. A DELETE must be idempotent, which means deleting again using the same URI must not change the data. In this case, the second DELETE is of course superfluous— deleting what was already deleted is not supposed to do anything. As a characteristic of REST, concerning a second DELETE, the server must not return an error message, but should just ignore the request instead.

- **POST**

    Used to post a new datum. POSTs commonly happen if the
    user submits a form. POSTs are *not* idempotent—a second POST
    using the same data will lead to a second data set on the server
    side. A POST might be described by POST http://some.server.
    com/myclub/member/37 [data], where [data] stands for the
    transmitted data, usually in the form of XML or JSON, passed over
    in the transmitted message body.

- **PUT**

    Used to store data. If the resource described by the data already
    exists, the resource will be altered according to the data. If it
    does not exist yet, the server might decide to act as if a POST were
    specified. A PUT is idempotent—PUTting again using the same
    input data will not change the data on the server.

The other verbs less frequently get used in real-world applications. HEAD is for
retrieving metadata about a resource (information about it, but not the resource itself).
Using a TRACE, you can see what happens to the data on the way to the server. This is
more a technical operation and does not pay particular attention to the data payload.
A PATCH is like a PUT with partial data. Usually a PUT with the complete datum gets used
instead of a PATCH. The OPTIONS verb is a facility to request the server's capability for a
dedicated resource (like telling what can be done with the resource). CONNECT gets used
for establishing transparent tunnels on the server side. Again, this is more a technical
facility and does not tell about the transmitted data.

Note   The part of Jakarta EE that handles REST is called JAX-RS. You will find
more information online, including the official specification, if you enter "jax-rs" in
your favorite search engine.

About JSON

REST does not make an explicit assumption as to what format data are sent in to the server or received in from it. For the page to be rendered by the browser, we take HTML, and for the static page assets like style sheets, script files, images, and so on the format gets dictated by the assets themselves—REST just passes them over to the client. For dynamic data you are free to choose whatever you like, but as a simple lightweight format, JSON, which is an acronym for *JavaScript object notation*, is a very good candidate that often gets used nowadays. The syntax is simple, as seen here:

- For objects, which are data holders and contain key–value pairs, you use { [object property1], [object property2], ... }.

- An object property writes "propertyName" : [property value], where a property value might be a string like "Hello," a number like 7 or -3.4, a Boolean like true or false, null for the NULL value, or any other object or array.

- For arrays, which are just collections of elements (any type, including changing types inside one array), you write [item1, item2, ...], where array members can have the same value types as object property values.

An example showing all possible JSON constructs is as follows:

```
{
  "ID" : 5616,
  "name" : "John Doe"
  "children" : [
      { "name": "Sue Ann Doe" },
      { "name": "Patt Doe" }
  ],
  "weight": 145.5,
  "spouse": true,
  "cars": null,
  "record": [ 12734, "QBA", true ]
}
```

Exercise 1

Provide a JSON representation of the following object:

```
class MusicRecord {
    static class Composer {
        String firstName;
        String lastName;
        Composer(String firstName, String lastName) {
            ...
        }
    }
    String title;
    Composer[] composers;
    String performer;
    int makeYear;

    MusicRecord(String title, Composer[] composers,
            String performer, int makeYear) {
        ...
    }
}

MusicRecord rec = new MusicRecord(
    "Somewhere over the Rainbow",
    new MusicRecord.Composer[] {
        new MusicRecord.Composer("Harold", "Arlen"),
        new MusicRecord.Composer("E. Y.", "Harburg")
    },
    "Judy Garland",
    1939
);
```

Including Page Assets

HTML pages need to load style sheets for design and layout, JavaScript files from JavaScript libraries, or custom script files, images, and other resources. Those files are static by nature, and we use `GET` operations to retrieve them and load them from the same "static/" folder where the main HTML file was loaded from.

For the date output application, we define a simple CSS file that just changes the font color. You can freely extend it and adapt it for your other single-page applications. Create a folder "src/main/webapp/static/css" and put the following `styles.css` file there:

```
body { color: #000044; }
div.clearfloat { clear: both; }
.err { color: red; };
```

Inside the `main.html` file, we add a link to refer to this style file, as follows:

```
...
<head>
  <meta charset="UTF-8">
  <title>RESTful Dates</title>
  <link rel="stylesheet" type="text/css"
        href="css/styles.css" />
</head>
...
```

Next, we include the jQuery library. Download it from the jQuery home page and save it inside a folder "src/main/webapp/static/js." Inside the `main.html` file, add a link to this jQuery file as follows:

```
...
<head>
  <meta charset="UTF-8">
  <title>RESTful Dates</title>
  <link rel="stylesheet" type="text/css"
        href="css/styles.css" />
  <script src="js/jquery-3.3.1.min.js"></script>
</head>
...
```

(or whatever version you downloaded).

Input, Output, and Action Components

For input, you can use any HTML input field you like. This is one of the strengths of single-page applications—with the power of JavaScript, the source for user input is totally up to you. As an example, we will continue with the date output application and allow the user to specify the date output format in a text-input field. To this aim, we add an input and an output field into the body of the HTML page, together with a button to submit the request, as follows:

```
...
<body>
Date format: <input id="dateFormat" type="text" />
<div class="clearfloat"></div>
<button id="submitButton">Get date!</button>
<div class="clearfloat"></div>
<div id="errOutput" class="err"></div>
<div class="clearfloat"></div>
<div id="dateOutput"></div>
</body>
...
```

Note   We are not going to use form-based communication with the server—that is why we don't need to have the `<input>` elements enclosed inside a `<form>` tag.

Adding Input to the REST Controller

Until now our date output application has not had any functionality. It is fully laid out though—we don't have to add more output and input fields. This is another strength of single-page applications: you can produce the HTML file without any logic or communication functionality going to the server or the outside world, and nevertheless hand it over to the designers to graphically beautify the application and improve usability.

Before we add the front-end logic we must first improve the REST controller. Remember that it is able to output the date, but the format cannot be passed over as an input parameter. Open the Java class RestDate and change it to the following:

```
package book.jakarta8.restdate;

import java.time.ZonedDateTime;
import java.time.format.DateTimeFormatter;

import javax.ws.rs.DefaultValue;
import javax.ws.rs.GET;
import javax.ws.rs.Path;
import javax.ws.rs.Produces;
import javax.ws.rs.QueryParam;
import javax.ws.rs.core.Response;

/**
 * REST Web Service
 */
@Path("/")
public class RestDate {
  @GET
  @Path("date")
  @Produces("application/json")
  public Response date(
      @QueryParam("dateFormat") @DefaultValue("")
      String dateFormat) {
    ZonedDateTime zdt = ZonedDateTime.now();
    String outStr = "";
    String errMsg = "";
    try {
      outStr = ("".equals(dateFormat) ?
          zdt.toString() :
          zdt.format(DateTimeFormatter.
                    ofPattern(dateFormat)));
      errMsg = "";
    } catch(Exception e) {
```

```
    errMsg = e.getMessage();
  }
  return Response.ok().entity(
    "{" +
      "\"date\":\"" + outStr + "\"," +
      "\"errMsg\":\"" + errMsg + "\"" +
    "}"
  ).build();
  }
}
```

Observe the following changes:

- The date calculation response type was changed from `String` to `javax.ws.rs.core.Response`. The latter allows for more options with which to tailor the method invocation result.

- Another `@Path` annotation was added to the method—this makes for two path definitions, from the method added. The final URL to address the method thus will read `http://localhost:8080/restdate/webapi/date`.

- The `@Produces` was changed to `application/json` as a resulting content type. Using JSON simplifies the processing for the browser, and we can hand over more complex data.

- The JAX-RS method returns a JSON object `{"date": "[RETURNED_DATE]", "errMsg": "[SOME_ERR]"}`

- Because of the `@QueryParam` the JAX-RS method is able to receive and handle a query parameter `dateFormat`. Because of the `@DefaultValue` the empty string will be used if the query parameter is not part of the request.

Once you deploy this you can test the new functionality by entering the following in a terminal (one line and no spaces in front of the `dateFormat=`):

```
curl -X GET http://localhost:8080/restdate/webapi/date? dateFormat=yyyy-
MM-dd%20HH:mm:ss
```

147

Its output should be similar to the following:

```
{"date":"2019-04-02 09:49:38","errMsg":""}
```

Note   We used GET to retrieve time and date. You maybe remember that earlier we stated that a second GET must return exactly the same data. So is this a violation of REST rules? Not really. It exactly returns the current date and time, although what "current" means obviously changes between subsequent retrievals.

Adding Front-end Logic

For the front-end logic, we create a JavaScript file src/main/webapp/static/js/script.js. As its contents write the following:

```
$(function() {
  $('#dateFormat').val("yyyy-MM-dd HH:mm:ss.SSSXXX");

  $('#submitButton').click(function(){
    var fmt = $('#dateFormat').val();
    var url = "../webapi/date";

    $.ajax({
      method: "GET",
      url: url,
      data: { dateFormat: fmt }
    })
    .done(function(msg) {
      $('#errOutput').html(msg.errMsg);
      $('#dateOutput').html("Current date/time: " +
          msg.date);
    })
    .fail(function(jqXHR, textStatus, errorThrown) {
      $('#errOutput').html("AJAX error: " +
```

```
    errorThrown);
  });
 });
})
```

The characteristics of this JavaScript code are as follows:

1. Any $(something) addresses a jQuery object.

2. The surrounding #(function(){ ... }) makes sure the code gets
   executed only *after* the page is fully loaded.

3. The $('#dateFormat') addresses the field with ID dateFormat.
   The .val(...) enters data into the text-input field.

4. The $.ajax(...) performs an asynchronous AJAX call. The
   function inside done() gets called when the AJAX call returns
   successfully. The function inside fail() gets called on errors.

5. Because the REST call returns a JSON code, the msg inside done()
   contains a JavaScript object that directly corresponds to the JSON
   data. So, we can access the date and a possible error message via
   property accessors .date and .errMsg, respectively.

What finally needs to be done is to load this JavaScript code from inside main.html.
To this aim, write the following in main.html:

```
...
<head>
  <meta charset="UTF-8">
  <title>RESTful Dates</title>
  <link rel="stylesheet" type="text/css"
        href="css/styles.css" />
  <script src="js/jquery-3.3.1.min.js"></script>
  <script src="js/script.js"></script>
</head>
...
```

The date application is now fully functional at `http://localhost:8080/restdate/static/main.html` (see Figure 5-1). Try different formats (see the `DateTimeFormatter` API documentation for patterns), and also check out what happens if you enter an invalid format.

Date format: yyyy-MM-dd HH:mm:ss.SSSXXX

Get date!

Current date/time: 2019-04-02 16:05:14.117+02:00

Figure 5-1. *The date single-page application at work*

Data-centric Operations with SPAs

From a data communication point of view, the date/time example application we have developed so far is very simple. It used a `GET` operation to query the current date and time. That is it.

If we have a data-centric application or part of an application, the story gets a little bit more complex. We want to be able to retrieve records and lists of records, register or update records, and delete records. Fortunately, we can still use REST operations for all we might think of—we can create, query, alter, and delete entities using `POST`, `GET`, `PUT`, and `DELETE` operations.

As an example, we pretend that we own a club named "Calypso" and need a web application to administer club members. Start a new REST application exactly as you did for the date/time–retrieval application from earlier in this chapter (including the configuration files under `WEB-INF`), but use Maven coordinates as follows:

```
Group-Id:    book.jakarta8
Artifact-Id: calypso
Version:     0.0.1-SNAPSHOT
```

As a package name, use "book.jakarta8.calypso."

As a `main.html` file inside "src/main/webapp/static," use the following:

```
<!DOCTYPE html>
<html>
<head>
  <meta charset="UTF-8">
  <title>Calypso</title>
```

```
<link rel="stylesheet" type="text/css"
  href="css/styles.css" />
<script src="js/jquery-3.3.1.min.js"></script>
<script src="js/script.js"></script>
</head>

<body>
  <div id="memberEntry">
  </div>
  <div id="errMsg">
  </div>
  <div id="memberList">
  </div>
</body>
</html>
```

You can see that it is very simplistic and contains only container divs. The rendering of the contents and the user interactions will be handled by JavaScript functions we are going to add later.

Next, copy the static content controller StaticContent from earlier in this chapter into the package "book.jakarta8.calypso." Also, provide a copy of the jQuery JavaScript library in the folder "src/main/webapp/static/js." Make sure the file name matches the file name specified in the corresponding <script> tag in main.html.

Create a stylesheet file src/main/webapp/static/css/styles.css and let it read as follows:

```
.clearfloat {
    clear: both;
}
#errMsg {
    width: 85%;
    margin-left: 7.5%;
    color: red;
}
#memberEntry {
    display:block;
    width: 85%;
```

```
        margin-left: 7.5%;
        background-color: #DDDDFF;
}
#memberList {
        display:block;
        width: 85%;
        margin-left: 7.5%;
        margin-top: 1em;
        background-color: #FFFFDD;
        height: 10em;
        overflow: scroll;

#idView {
        float:right;
        margin-right: 2em;
        margin-top:0.3em;
        color:#888888;
}
#submitButton {
        float: right;
}
.listTable td {
        padding-right: 1em;
}
```

These styles add some margins to make the output appear more pleasant, apply a red foreground (text) color to the error message area, and otherwise color the different parts (entry area, members list). The `height` and `overflow` declarations inside the member list part make sure the list will get a vertical scroll bar if it becomes too big.

Now, let us continue with the JavaScript front-end logic. It goes into the `src/main/webapp/static/js/script.js` file, and we start with the following functions to handle the "form" area inside `<div id="memberEntry">` (we don't need a `<form>` tag, because the communication with the server gets handled solely by AJAX):

```
function showEntry(entity) {
  $('#lastName').val(entity.lastName);
  $('#firstName').val(entity.firstName);
```

```
  $('#birthday').val(entity.birthday);
  $('#idView').html((entity.id && entity.id !="")?
    'ID: ' + entity.id : ");
}

function clearEntry() {
  $('#lastName').val("");
  $('#firstName').val("");
  $('#birthday').val("");
  $('#idView').html("");
}

function makeForm() {
  function formLine(label, id) {
    return '<tr>' +
        '<td>' + label + ':</td><td><input id="' + id
            + '" type="text"/></td>' +
      '</tr>';
  }

  $('#membcrEntry').html(
    '<table><tbody> \
    ' + formLine("Last name", "lastName") + '\
    ' + formLine("First name", "firstName") + '\
    ' + formLine("Birthday", "birthday") + '\
    </tbody></table>'
  )
  .append(
    '<span>' +
    '<button id="clearButton"' +
        ' onclick="clearEntry()">Clear</button>' +
    '<button id="submitButton"' +
        ' onclick="submit()">Submit</button> \
    </span>'
  )
```

```
  .append(
    '<span id="idView"></span> \
    <div class="clearfloat"></div>'
  );
}
```

The function makeForm() needs to be called just once to build the form contents without the values. The function showEntry() reads in the object passed as a parameter and fills the form from it, and the function clearEntry() clears the form. For all these functions, and also the functions we describe in the following paragraphs, we heavily use jQuery functionalities and techniques.

Note   The "\" at the end of the line disregards the following line break, so we can distribute longer string literals over several lines. Just make sure in your JavaScript files there are no spaces behind the backslashes.

The printing of error messages gets handled by two functions, showErr(msg) and clearErr(), which just enter data into the error message area or clear it, as follows:

```
function showErr(msg) {
  $('#errMsg').html(msg);
}

function clearErr() {
  $('#errMsg').html("");
}
```

Another set of functions is responsible for the members list area, as follows:

```
function clearList() {
  $('#memberList').html("");
}

function makeList(data) {
  clearList();
```

```
function tableRow(lastName, firstName, birthday, id) {
  return '<tr id="tab-'+id+'"> \
          <td>'+lastName+'</td> \
          <td>'+firstName+'</td> \
          <td>'+birthday+'</td> \
          <td><button onclick="edit('+id+')">
              EDIT</button></td> \
          <td><button onclick="del('+id+')">
              DEL</button></td> \
      </tr>';
}

var tab = $('<table class="listTable"></table>');
tab.html('<tbody>');
$.each(data, function(ind,val) {
    tab.append(tableRow(val.lastName, val.firstName,
        val.birthday, val.id));
});
tab.append('</tbody>');
$('#memberList').append(tab);
}

function removeEntry(id) {
  $('#tab-' + id).remove();
}
```

The clearList() function clears the list area. The function makeList() enters the given data into the list area. The data passed to this function must be an array of objects, with each object having the following properties: lastName, firstName, birthdayName, and id. The function removeEntry() removes a row from the rendered list.

The remaining function handles all the AJAX calls we need to get, post, delete, and update entities, as follows:

```
function submit() {
  var id = $('#idView').html();
  if(id.length > 4) id = id.substring(4);
```

```
    var lastName = $('#lastName').val();
    var firstName = $('#firstName').val();
    var birthday = $('#birthday').val();

    var url = (id == "") ?
        "../webapi/member" : "../webapi/member/" + id;
    var meth = (id == "") ?
        "POST" : "PUT";

    $.ajax({
      method: meth,
      url: url,
      data: { lastName:lastName,
              firstName:firstName,
              birthday:birthday }
    })
    .done(function(msg) {
      clearErr();
      loadList();
    })
    .fail(function(jqXHR, textStatus, errorThrown) {
      showErr("AJAX: " + errorThrown);
    });
  }

  function loadList() {
    var url = "../webapi/member";
    $.ajax({
      method: "GET",
      url: url
    })
    .done(function(msg) {
      clearErr();
      makeList(msg);
    })
```

```
  .fail(function(jqXHR, textStatus, errorThrown) {
    showErr("AJAX: " + errorThrown);
  });
}
function edit(id) {
  var url = "../webapi/member/" + id;
  $.ajax({
    method: "GET",
    url: url
  })
  .done(function(msg) {
    clearErr();
    showEntry(msg);
  })
  .fail(function(jqXHR, textStatus, errorThrown) {
    showErr("AJAX: " + errorThrown);
  });
}

function del(id) {
  clearEntry();
  var url = "../webapi/member/" + id;
  $.ajax({
    method: "DELETE",
    url: url
  })
  .done(function(msg) {
    clearErr();
    removeEntry(id);
  })
  .fail(function(jqXHR, textStatus, errorThrown) {
    showErr("AJAX: " + errorThrown);
  });
}
```

The submit() function collects the user entries from the form (and an ID, if it exists) and issues a POST call if the entries belong to a new member, or a PUT if a member gets updated. On a successful AJAX call, the whole list gets reloaded. The corresponding API call reads POST/webapi/member/[data] or PUT/webapi/member/{ID} [data], where [data] gets passed to the message body before the message is sent to the server. The function loadList() loads the complete list using GET/webapi/member and then renders it. The function edit() loads a single member from the REST API (GET/webapi/member/{ID}) and fills the form with the data retrieved. Function del() deletes a member and then reloads and rebuilds the members list.

The final JavaScript parts wait until the HTML page is fully loaded (the surrounding $(function(){ ... }, you remember), makes (prepares) the form, and then loads the list as follows:

```
$(function() {
  makeForm();
  loadList();
})
```

For the REST interface, create a class book.jakarta8.calypso.Calypso and let it read as follows:

```
package book.jakarta8.calypso;

import java.util.ArrayList;
import java.util.List;
import java.util.Optional;
import java.util.stream.Collectors;

import javax.ws.rs.*;
import javax.ws.rs.core.Response;

/**
 * REST Web Service
 */
@Path("/member")
public class Calypso {
```

We provide an inner `Member` class for members. Since the API communicates using JSON (by virtue of the `@Produces( "application/json" )`) and not a direct representation of the class, this member class can be declared private, as follows.

```
... (inside the Calypso class!)
private static class Member
        implements Comparable<Member>{
  public String firstName;
  public String lastName;
  public String birthday;
  public int id;
  public static Member UNKNOWN =
          new Member("","","",0);
  public Member(String firstName,
        String lastName, String birthday, int id) {
    this.firstName = firstName;
    this.lastName = lastName;
    this.birthday = birthday;
    this.id = id;
  }
  @Override
  public int compareTo(Member o) {
    if(o.birthday.compareTo(birthday) != 0)
      return o.birthday.compareTo(birthday);
    if(o.lastName.compareTo(lastName) != 0)
      return -o.lastName.compareTo(lastName);
    return -o.firstName.compareTo(firstName);
  }
}
...
```

The member listing itself is maintained as a static class field, as follows; for production-level applications this should go into a database layer!

```
...
private static List<Member> members =
    new ArrayList<>();
static {
    members.add(new Member("John","Smith",
        "2001-03-24", 1));
    members.add(new Member("Linda","Green",
        "1997-04-01", 2));
    members.add(new Member("Alice","Cloud",
        "1997-04-01", 3));
}
...
```

Here, we also populated the list with a few members for demonstration purposes. The following are the REST interface methods:

```
...
@GET
@Path("/")
@Produces("application/json")
public Response list() {
    StringBuilder outStr = new StringBuilder();
    outStr.append("[");
    outStr.append(
        members.stream().sorted().
        map(itm ->
            "{\"firstName\":\"" + itm.firstName + "\"," +
            "\"lastName\":\"" + itm.lastName + "\"," +
            "\"birthday\":\"" + itm.birthday + "\"," +
            "\"id\":" + itm.id + "}"
        ).collect(Collectors.joining(","))
    );
    outStr.append("]");
    return Response.ok().entity(
        outStr.toString()
    ).build();
}
```

```java
@GET
@Path("/{id}")
@Produces("application/json")
public Response entity(@PathParam("id") int id) {
  Member m = members.stream().
      filter(itm -> itm.id == id).
      findFirst().orElse(Member.UNKNOWN);

  return Response.ok().entity(
    "{\"lastName\":\"" + m.lastName + "\", " +
    "\"firstName\":\"" + m.firstName + "\", " +
    "\"birthday\":\"" + m.birthday + "\", " +
    "\"id\":" + m.id + "}"
  ).build();
}

@POST
@Path("/")
@Produces("application/json")
public Response post(
      @FormParam("lastName") String lastName,
      @FormParam("firstName") String firstName,
      @FormParam("birthday") String birthday) {
  int maxId = members.stream().mapToInt(m -> m.id).
      max().orElse(0);
  int newId = maxId + 1;
  Member m = new Member(firstName, lastName,
      birthday, newId);
  members.add(m);

  return Response.ok().entity("{\"id\":"+ newId +"}").
      build();
}

@PUT
@Path("/{id}")
@Produces("application/json")
```

```java
    public Response put(
            @FormParam("lastName") String lastName,
            @FormParam("firstName") String firstName,
            @FormParam("birthday") String birthday,
            @PathParam("id") int id) {
        Optional<Member> m = members.stream().
                filter( itm -> itm.id == id).findFirst();
        if(m.isPresent()) {
          members.remove(m.get());
          Member m2 = new Member(firstName, lastName,
                  birthday, id);
          members.add(m2);
        }
        return Response.ok().entity("{}").build();
    }

    @DELETE
    @Path("/{id}")
    @Produces("application/json")
    public Response del(@PathParam("id") int id) {
      Member m = members.stream().
              filter(itm -> itm.id == id).
              findFirst().orElse(Member.UNKNOWN);
      members.remove(m);
      return Response.ok().entity("{}").build();
    }
  }
```

The method list() returns the complete members list and reacts to GET/webapi/
member/ (remember the /webapi comes from a configuration entry in the web.xml file).
The method retrieves the members list data, sorts it, and converts it to JSON before
returning it. The method entity() returns a single member as a JSON object. It listens to
GET/webapi/member/{ID}. The method post() reacts to POST /webapi/member/ [data]
and registers new members. The method put() is similar, but it listens to PUT/webapi/
member/{ID} and updates a member. The last method, del(), reacts to DELETE/webapi/
member/{ID} and deletes an entry.

Observe that we used {id} as a placeholder to fetch dynamic URL path parts. This is a common resource-coordinate definition pattern for RESTful applications. The JAX-RS API takes such dynamic path parts and passes them over to appropriately annotated method parameters (see the @PathParam annotation).

The application is now fully functional. Deploy it on the server, and in the browser navigate to

```
http://localhost:8080/calypso/static/main.html
```

to see it working. The output will look like that shown in Figure 5-2.

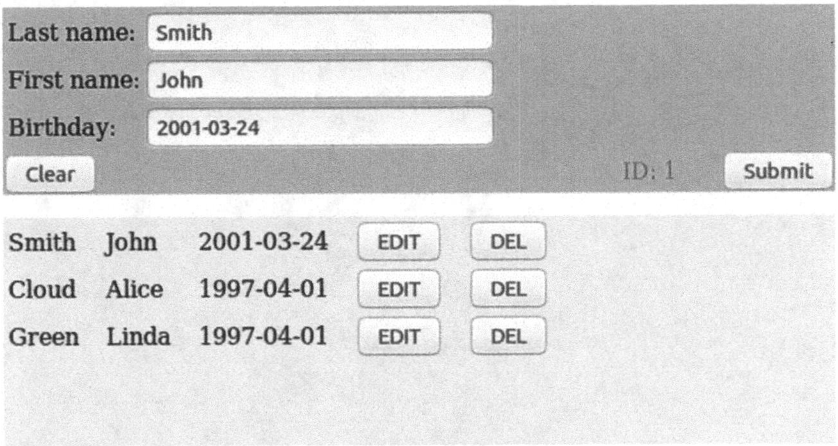

Figure 5-2. *Calypso member registration application*

Exercise 2

From the internet, fetch appropriate icons of your choice for editing and deleting, put them into an "images" folder, and replace the text buttons inside the list with buttons that use the new images.

CHAPTER 6

Adding a Database with JPA

JPA (Java Persistence API) is the dedicated technology for accessing relational databases from inside Jakarta EE. Its aim is to provide a bridge between SQL tables and Java objects. This is a task that is far from simple for other than the most basic data schemes. The reason for this is that in relational database schemes there are associations between different tables: one row from one table may refer to one or many rows from another table or the other way around, and there could be references spanning three or more tables. And think of column-type conversions—a database may have different ideas about numbers, Boolean indicators, dates, and times compared to Java, and also null values in database tables require increased attention if used in table references and while converting to Java values.

In this chapter, we will talk about basic issues when using JPA, and we will extend the Calypso bar example application we started in Chapter 5. For a complete and deep overview of JPA that covers more-complex issues than we will in this chapter, please consult the online documentation and specifications you can find about JPA on the web.

Abstracting Away Database Access with JPA

One of the primary purposes of JPA is to abstract away database access and map database objects to Java classes. In the end, we want to be able to query the database and get Java objects, or to put Java objects into the database. JPA helps to hide away the details of how this is done, including connection properties like username and password, and also including handling connection lifecycles.

The central class with which JPA performs these tasks is the `EntityManager` class, which uses a single configuration file, `persistence.xml`, and some settings inside the

© Peter Späth 2019
P. Späth, *Beginning Jakarta EE*, https://doi.org/10.1007/978-1-4842-5079-2_6

Jakarta EE application server. On the Java side, the classes that correspond to table rows get called *entity* classes. See Figure 6-1 for an overview of JPA.

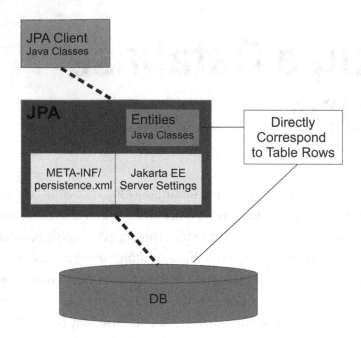

Figure 6-1. *JPA inside Jakarta EE at work*

Setting Up a SQL Database

The Jakarta EE 8 Glassfish server includes a Derby (or JavaDB) database we can use for development purposes. To start it, open a terminal, then enter the following:

```
cd [GLASSFISH_INST]
cd bin
./asadmin start-database
```

(or just `asadmin start-database` for Windows) where `[GLASSFISH_INST]` is the installation folder of your Glassfish server.

Note   The Derby database runs independently of the application server. You can start it even if the Glassfish application server is not running, and stopping the application server will *not* stop the database.

Since we want to extend the Calypso bar example application we started in Chapter 5, we must create a new database for Calypso and appropriately name it "calypso." To do so, in the same terminal we used to start the database, enter the following:

```
cd [GLASSFISH_INST]
cd javadb/bin
# start the DB client
./ij
```

(or ij for windows). We are now inside the ij database client, which you can see since the ij> prompt appears in the terminal. Enter the following:

```
ij> connect 'jdbc:derby://localhost:1527/calypso;
    create=true;user=user0';
```

(enter this in one line without spaces in front of "create="). The database now is created with an owner named "user0," but we must also add a password for the user, as follows:

```
ij> call SYSCS_UTIL.SYSCS_CREATE_USER('user0','pw715');
```

Note   JavaDB by default does not enable authentication for new databases. This normally does not cause problems if using the database just for development, because network access is restricted to local users only. Many Java applications and database tools, however, behave strangely if trying to access the database without authentication, so we add a password.

Next, restart the database for the authentication to start working, as follows:

```
cd [GLASSFISH_INST]
cd bin
./asadmin stop-database
./asadmin start-database
```

This needs to be done only once. Quit and reopen the connection inside the `ij` tool (or quit `ij` altogether by pressing CTRL+D, then restart `ij` and connect again), as follows:

```
ij> disconnect;
ij> connect 'jdbc:derby://localhost:1527/calypso;
    user=user0;password=pw715';
```

(enter the last `ij` command in one line). You can check the authentication mechanism: if you omit user or password or both, you'll get an appropriate error message.

For a transparent and simple connection to the database, we create two resources in the Glassfish server configuration, as follows:

```
cd [GLASSFISH_INST]
cd bin
./asadmin create-jdbc-connection-pool \
    --datasourceclassname \
      org.apache.derby.jdbc.ClientDataSource \
    --restype javax.sql.DataSource \
    --property \
      portNumber=1527:password=pw715:user=user0:
      serverName=localhost:databaseName=calypso:
      securityMechanism=3 \
    Calypso

./asadmin create-jdbc-resource \
   --connectionpoolid Calypso jdbc/Calypso
```

(no line break and no spaces after `user=user0:` and `databaseName = calypso`). This creates a connection pool and a JDBC resource connecting to it. We will later use the `jdbc/Calypso` identifier to let JPA connect to the database.

For the rest of the chapter, we will assume you know how to enter database commands. Either use the `ij` tool (don't forget to connect once you start it) or use any other database client, like the open source tool Squirrel.

For the Calypso application, the SQL commands to create the table and a sequence generator for the unique ID generation read as follows:

```
CREATE TABLE MEMBER (
    ID          INT             NOT NULL,
    LAST_NAME   VARCHAR(128)    NOT NULL,
    FIRST_NAME  VARCHAR(128)    NOT NULL,
    BIRTHDAY    CHAR(10)        NOT NULL,
  PRIMARY KEY (ID));

INSERT INTO MEMBER (ID, LAST_NAME, FIRST_NAME, BIRTHDAY)
    VALUES (-3, 'Smith', 'John', '1997-11-05'),
           (-2, 'Tender', 'Linda', '1997-11-05'),
           (-1, 'Quast', 'Pat', '2003-04-13');

CREATE SEQUENCE MEMBER_SEQ start with 1 increment by 50;
```

where we also added a couple of example entries.

Adding EclipseLink as ORM

For JPA to work, we need to add an *object relational mapping* (ORM) library to the project. You have several options here, but we choose EclipseLink as the ORM library, since EclipseLink is the reference implementation of JPA 2.2.

To add EclipseLink to the project, download the EclipseLink installer ZIP (for example, version 2.7.4) and extract the archive somewhere on your computer.

Next, create a new project, "calypso-jpa," with all the characteristics of the non-JPA Calypso from Chapter 5. The only thing to change apart from the project name is the Maven coordinate set, as follows:

```
Group-Id:    book.jakarta8
Artifact-Id: calypso-jpa
Version:     0.0.1-SNAPSHOT
```

Also rename the package to be used to "book.jakarta8.calypsojpa." Copy all the files from the original Calypso project to the new project, and then check that it runs on the server just as well as the original Calypso application did. The URL to check the browser access reads: http://localhost:8080/calypsojpa/static/main.html.

Next, create a folder, "src/main/webapp/WEB-INF/lib," and copy the library files as follows:

```
eclipselink.jar
jakarta.persistence_x.y.z.jar
org.eclipse.persistence.jpa.modelgen_*.jar
org.eclipse.persistence.jpars_*.jar
```

from the EclipseLink distribution into the "WEB-INF/lib" folder. Add those JARs to the "Libraries" tab of the project properties (section: "Java Build Path").

Create a file, src/main/resources/META-INF/persistence.xml, and let it read as follows:

```
<persistence
    xmlns=
        "http://java.sun.com/xml/ns/persistence"
    xmlns:xsi=
        "http://www.w3.org/2001/XMLSchema-instance"
    xsi:schemaLocation=
        "http://java.sun.com/xml/ns/persistence
         persistence_1_0.xsd"
    version="1.0">
<persistence-unit name="default"
      transaction-type="JTA">
    <jta-data-source>jdbc/Calypso</jta-data-source>
    <exclude-unlisted-classes>
      false
    </exclude-unlisted-classes>
    <properties />
</persistence-unit>
</persistence>
```

This is the central configuration file for JPA. Here, we tell how the database gets connected to from the application. You can see we refer to resources we created earlier in this chapter.

> **Note**   The Eclipse IDE has a few helper wizards for JPA-related development, and
> also has a JPA facet you can add to projects. I decided against using these for this
> introductory-level book so as to avoid vendor lock-in and show the basics needed
> to follow the JPA specification. You are free to later also try the JPA facet of Eclipse
> (you will have to remove the EclipseLink JARs from the "WEB-INF/lib" folder).

Adding Data Access Objects

A data access object or DAO is a Java class that encapsulates database operations like
CRUD (create, read, update, delete). A client of the DAO then doesn't have to know *how*
the DAO does its work and only needs to take care of the business functionality. For this
reason, we first change the REST controller class Calypso to the following:

```
package book.jakarta8.calypsojpa;

import java.util.List;
import java.util.stream.Collectors;

import javax.ejb.EJB;
import javax.ws.rs.*;
import javax.ws.rs.core.Response;

import book.jakarta8.calypsojpa.ejb.MemberDAO;
import book.jakarta8.calypsojpa.jpa.Member;

/**
 * REST Web Service
 * http://localhost:8080/calypso-jpa/static/main.html
 */
@Path("/member")
public class Calypso {
    @EJB private MemberDAO members;

    @GET
    @Path("/")
    @Produces("application/json")
    public Response list() {
```

```
    List<Member> memberList = members.allMembers();
    StringBuilder outStr = new StringBuilder();
    outStr.append("[");
    outStr.append(
      memberList.stream().sorted().
      map((Member itm) ->
        "{\"firstName\":\"" +
            itm.getFirstName() + "\"," +
        "\"lastName\":\"" +
            itm.getLastName() + "\"," +
        "\"birthday\":\"" +
            itm.getBirthday() + "\"," +
        "\"id\":" + itm.getId() + "}"
      ).collect(Collectors.joining(","))
    );
    outStr.append("]");
    return Response.ok().entity(
      outStr.toString()
    ).build();
  }

  @GET
  @Path("/{id}")
  @Produces("application/json")
  public Response entity(@PathParam("id") int id) {
    Member m = members.getMember(id);
    return Response.ok().entity(
      "{\"lastName\":\"" +
          m.getLastName() + "\", " +
      "\"firstName\":\"" +
          m.getFirstName() + "\", " +
      "\"birthday\":\"" +
          m.getBirthday() + "\", " +
      "\"id\":" + m.getId() + "}"
    ).build();
  }
```

```
@POST
@Path("/")
@Produces("application/json")
public Response post(
        @FormParam("lastName") String lastName,
        @FormParam("firstName") String firstName,
        @FormParam("birthday") String birthday) {
    int newId = members.newMember(lastName, firstName,
        birthday);
    return Response.ok().entity("{\"id\":"+ newId +"}").
        build();
}

@PUT
@Path("/{id}")
@Produces("application/json")
public Response put(
        @FormParam("lastName") String lastName,
        @FormParam("firstName") String firstName,
        @FormParam("birthday") String birthday,
        @PathParam("id") int id) {
    members.updateMember(lastName, firstName, birthday,
        id);
    return Response.ok().entity("{}").build();
}

@DELETE
@Path("/{id}")
@Produces("application/json")
public Response del(@PathParam("id") int id) {
    members.deleteMember(id);
    return Response.ok().entity("{}").build();
}
}
```

Concerning the REST interface, that is the way the class gets addressed from outside; nothing changed. The most noticeable changes of how the code works are as follows:

- A DAO class MemberDAO gets injected via the @EJB annotation. We will talk about EJBs in a later chapter; for now it is enough to know that EJBs are objects that get controlled by the server. This includes when and the way instances get created, how many of them will be created, how long they live, access restrictions, and more. We will implement the DAO class (or DAO EJB) later.

- We introduce a so-called *entity* class Member. As far as class Calypso is concerned, this just represents a member with properties of last name, first name, birthday, and ID. It is something JPA returns if we look for a particular record from the database, or that gets sent to the database for insert or update operations. We will implement the entity class in a later section.

The DAO class MemberDAO itself goes to the package book.jakarta8.calypsojpa.ejb. Create the package and the class, and as the class code write the following:

```
package book.jakarta8.calypsojpa.ejb;

import java.util.List;

import javax.ejb.Singleton;
import javax.persistence.EntityManager;
import javax.persistence.PersistenceContext;
import javax.persistence.TypedQuery;

import book.jakarta8.calypsojpa.jpa.Member;

@Singleton
public class MemberDAO {
    @PersistenceContext
    private EntityManager em;

    public List<Member> allMembers() {
      TypedQuery<Member> q = em.createQuery(
          "SELECT m FROM Member m", Member.class);
      List<Member> l = q.getResultList();
```

```
    return 1;
  }

  public Member getMember(int id) {
    return em.find(Member.class, id);
  }

  public int newMember(String lastName,
        String firstName, String birthday) {
    Member m = new Member();
    m.setFirstName(firstName);
    m.setLastName(lastName);
    m.setBirthday(birthday) ;
    em.persist(m);
    em.flush(); // needed to get the ID
    return m.getId();
  }

  public void updateMember(String lastName,
        String firstName, String birthday, int id) {
    Member m = cm.find(Member.class, id);
    m.setLastName(lastName);
    m.setFirstName(firstName);
    m.setBirthday(birthday);
    em.persist(m);
  }

  public void deleteMember(int id) {
    Member m = em.find(Member.class, id);
    em.remove(m);
  }
}
```

You can see that database operations exclusively get handled by an EntityManager that gets injected by the @PersistenceContext annotation. By the configuration file persistence. xml JPA knows which database needs to be accessed by the entity manager. For most operations we can use the methods from class EntityManager—the only exception is the complete list, for which we use a JPA query language expression SELECT m FROM Member m.

The application knows that this DAO is an EJB by the @Singleton class annotation. Thus, the container (the part of the server that handles EJB objects) knows that for all threads we only ever need one single instance of this class. This can be done because instances of this class don't have a state, and for simplicity we don't pay particular attention to concurrency.

Note   For production-level applications, concurrency needs to be taken into account on both the Java language level and the database level (transactionality).

Exercise 1

Which of the following are true?

1. DAOs are needed to connect to databases via JPA.

2. DAOs are needed to provide database user and password.

3. In DAOs, database column names have to be specified.

4. DAOs are used to avoid using database table details in JPA client classes.

5. To use DAOs, they must be injected as EJBs.

Adding Entities

An entity is a representation of a table row as an object. If we think of the MEMBER table from the Calypso application, an entity is something that has a single first name, a single last name, a single birthday, and a single ID. Obviously, this corresponds to a Java class with fields firstName, lastName, birthday, and id. So, we create such a class and put it into the package book.jakarta8.calypsojpa.jpa, as follows:

```
public class Member {
  private int id; // + getter/setter
  private String lastName; // + getter/setter
  private String firstName; // + getter/setter
  private String birthday; // + getter/setter
}
```

To complete the interfacing to the database, we need to add meta-information: the information that this is an entity class, the table name, column names, a dedicated ID column name, a unique ID generator specification, and database field-value constraints. As is usually the case for Java, we use annotations for such meta-information. Our class with all those amendments reads as follows:

```
package book.jakarta8.calypsojpa.jpa;

import javax.persistence.*;
import javax.validation.constraints.*;

@Entity
@Table(name="MEMBER")
@SequenceGenerator(name="MEMBER_SEQ",
                   initialValue=1, allocationSize = 50)
public class Member implements Comparable<Member> {
    @Id
    @GeneratedValue(strategy = GenerationType.SEQUENCE,
                   generator="MEMBER_SEQ")
    @Column(name = "ID")
    private int id;

    @NotNull
    @Column(name = "LAST_NAME")
    private String lastName;

    @NotNull
    @Column(name = "FIRST_NAME")
    private String firstName;

    @NotNull
    @Column(name = "BIRTHDAY", length = 10)
    @Pattern(regexp = "\\d{4}-\\d{2}-\\d{2}",
            message="Birthday format: yyyy-MM-dd.")
    private String birthday;

    @Override
    public int compareTo(Member o) {
      if(o.birthday.compareTo(birthday) != 0)
```

```
        return o.birthday.compareTo(birthday);
    if(o.lastName.compareTo(lastName) != 0)
        return -o.lastName.compareTo(lastName);
    return -o.firstName.compareTo(firstName);
    }

    // + getters and setters for all properties
}
```

where I also added the `Comparator` interface; this has nothing to do with JPA, but helps to construct a sorted list of members. In detail, the annotations added are as follows:

- **@Entity**

  Marks this as an entity so JPA knows this is an entity class.

- **@Table**

  Used to specify the table name. If omitted, the class name (without package) will be used as a table name.

- **@SequenceGenerator**

  Used to specify a sequence generator for unique IDs.

- **@Id**

  Relays that the corresponding field refers to the unique ID of the entity.

- **@GeneratedValue**

  Relays that new entities will auto-generate values for this field.

- **@Column**

  Used to specify the column name corresponding to this field. If unspecified, the field name will be used as a column name instead.

- **@NotNull**

  A constraint relaying that neither the field nor the database field can be `null`.

- **@Pattern**

  Another constraint for text fields, relaying that the field must match the pattern specified.

Given the entity classes, JPA now knows how to map database entry fields to Java classes. With the REST interface adapted and the DAO and entity classes added, the application has a fully functional JPA support engaged, and you can deploy and try it at `http://localhost:8080/calypso-jpa/static/main.html`. Also try restarting the server and check that the entries were persisted and survive a server restart. You can also directly check the database using a database client tool and investigate the table rows that were added there.

Exercise 2

Which of the following are true?

1. One entity class corresponds to one database table.

2. An entity class must have the same name as the database table.

3. Properties (fields) of entity classes must have the same names as the columns in the database table.

4. Properties of entity classes can have restrictions added.

In the following section, we will learn how to map table relations to several interconnected entities.

Adding Relations

Relational data is about relations, like one table entry referring to entries from other tables. JPA provides a solution to such relations, again by special annotations you can add to entity classes.

Consider the following example: in our Calypso application we add another table, STATUS, which contains membership status entries like "Gold," "Platinum," "Senior," or whatever you might think of. Each member may have zero to N status entries added, so we talk about a "one-to-many" relationship between members and status entries.

To achieve this, we first create the STATUS table and a sequence STATUS_SEQ for it, as follows:

```
CREATE TABLE STATUS (
    ID          INT             NOT NULL,
    MEMBER_ID   INT             NOT NULL,
    NAME        VARCHAR(128)    NOT NULL,
  PRIMARY KEY (ID));

CREATE SEQUENCE STATUS_SEQ start with 1 increment by 50;
```

Next, we create a new entity class, Status, inside the package book.jakarta8. calypsojpa.jpa and let it read as follows:

```
package book.jakarta8.calypsojpa.jpa;

import javax.persistence.*;
import javax.validation.constraints.*;

@Entity
@Table(name="STATUS")
@SequenceGenerator(name="STATUS_SEQ",
                    initialValue=1, allocationSize = 50)
public class Status implements Comparable<Status> {
    @Id
    @GeneratedValue(strategy = GenerationType.SEQUENCE,
                    generator="STATUS_SEQ")

    @Column(name = "ID")
    private int id;

    @NotNull
    @Column(name = "MEMBER_ID")
    private int memberId;

    @NotNull
    @Column(name = "NAME")
    private String name;
```

```
public Status() {
}

public Status(String name) {
  this.name = name;
}

@Override
public int compareTo(Status o) {
  return -o.name.compareTo(name);
}

// + getters and setters
}
```

We added a constructor for easy construction using the name. It is important to know that the JPA specification requires that there is a public no-argument constructor, so in this case we have to add it as well.

Inside the entity class `Member`, we add a field that corresponds to the actual relationship between member and status, as follows:

```
...
@JoinColumn(name = "MEMBER_ID")
@OneToMany(cascade = CascadeType.ALL, orphanRemoval=true)
private Set<Status> status; // + getter / setters
...
```

Everything else stays untouched. The `@JoinColumn` refers to a member in the *associated* class or table, so we don't have to update the member table for this new field.

Because of the two entity classes and their relationship announced via `@OneToMany`, any entity-manager operations will automatically take care of correctly cascading database operations to related entities. For example, to create a new member inside the Calypso application, you can write the following:

```
...
Member m = new Member();
m.setFirstName(firstName);
m.setLastName(lastName);
m.setBirthday(birthday);
```

```
Set<Status> status = new HashSet<>();
status.add(new Status("Platinum"));
status.add(new Status("Priority"));
m.setStatus(status);

em.persist(m);
...
```

Thus, you don't have to explicitly tell the entity manager to persist the related Status entity.

In the front-end code, you can add a text field with a comma-separated list of status values, or a select listbox or select menu to reflect the relationship. The same holds for update and delete operations—because of the cascade = CascadeType.ALL inside the @OneToMany annotation, JPA will even delete related Status entries from the STATUS table if members get deleted.

Exercise 3

Update the Calypso front-end code and add the status to members. For simplicity, use a text field where a comma-separated list of status values can be entered.

There are other association types in a relational data model. The list of possible association types you can declare for entities in JPA is as follows:

- **@OneToMany**

  For entities of entity class A zero-to-many related entries of entity class B exist. Inside class A you define a field of type Set with annotation OneToMany. Inside entity B's table you then have a foreign key ID_A (or whatever name you like), and inside the entity class B a field aId (or whatever name you like) pointing to A IDs. To tell A how it is related to B you then add another annotation @JoinColumn as in

  ```
  @OneToMany
  @JoinColumn(name="ID_A")   // In table B!
  private Set<B> b;
  ```

or add an attribute to @OneToMany as in

```
@OneToMany(mappedBy = "aId") // Field in class B!
private Set<B> b;
```

- **@ManyToOne**

  For zero or many entities of entity class A one related entry of
  entity class B exists. Inside class A you add a field of type B with
  annotations @ManyToOne and @JoinColumn, where for the latter
  you provide a column name (inside A's table) for the join, as
  follows:

  ```
  @ManyToOne
  @JoinColumn(name="ID_B") // In table A
  private B b;
  ```

- **@OneToOne**

  For one entity of entity class A one related entry of entity class B
  exists. Inside class A you add a field of type B with annotations @
  OneToOne and @JoinColumn, where for the latter you provide a
  column name (inside A's table) for the join, as follows:

  ```
  @OneToOne
  @JoinColumn(name="ID_B") // In table A
  private B b;
  ```

- **@ManyToMany**

  For zero or many entities of entity class A zero or many related
  entries of entity class B exist. Here, we need a third table serving
  as an intermediate join table; for example, MTM_A_B, with columns
  ID_A and ID_B. The annotations in entity class A (with ID column
  "ID") then read as follows:

  ```
  @ManyToMany
  @JoinTable(
    name = "MTM_A_B",
  ```

```
        joinColumns = @JoinColumn(
          name = "ID_A",
          referencedColumnName="ID"),
        inverseJoinColumns = @JoinColumn(
          name = "ID_B",
          referencedColumnName="ID"))
    private Set<B> b;
```

## CHAPTER 7

Modularization with EJBs

Enterprise Java Beans (EJBs) are classes that encapsulate business functionality, each of a certain kind. Thus far this is the same characterization as we have for normal Java classes. EJBs, however, run in a *container* environment, which means the server adds system-level services to them, which includes lifecycle management (instantiate and destroy when and how), transactionality (building logical, atomic, rollback-enabled units of work), and security (which user can invoke which methods).

The EJB technology comprises *session* beans and *message-driven beans*. However, the latter will get handled in their own chapter, so here we will talk about *session* EJBs.

Types of Session EJBs

Session EJBs can be accessed locally (the same application), remotely (over the network, method invocation), or via a web-service interface (distributed applications across heterogeneous networks; HTML, XML, or JSON data formats).

Concerning the instance creation and destruction of session EJBs, there exist the following three types:

- **Singleton**

  For a singleton session EJB the container instantiates only one instance, and all clients share this single instance. You can do this if the EJB does not have a state that discriminates between clients, and if concurrent access does not impose problems.

- **Stateless**

  EJBs of the "stateless" kind do not maintain a state, so a particular client can for subsequent EJB invocations have different instances assigned to it (the container handles this; the client doesn't know about this assignment).

© Peter Späth 2019
P. Späth, *Beginning Jakarta EE*, https://doi.org/10.1007/978-1-4842-5079-2_7

– **Stateful**

  Stateful EJBs maintain a state, and a client can be sure it will for
  subsequent usage of the same EJB receive the same session EJB
  instance from the container. You will often hear that stateful
  EJB clients maintain a *conversational* state concerning their use
  of stateful EJBs. Stateful session EJBs cannot implement web
  services, because web services are not allowed to have state, and
  no session information gets communicated.

Defining EJBs

To define a singleton EJB, a stateless EJB, or a stateful EJB, you add one of the
annotations @Singleton, @Stateless, or @Stateful, respectively, to the EJB
implementation.

  Consider three examples: an EJB Configuration for encapsulated access to
application-wide configuration settings, another EJB Invoice that handles invoice
registration and inquiries given some invoice ID, and a third EJB TicTacToe for a simple
tic-tac-toe game implementation. Obviously, for the configuration EJB we can use a
singleton EJB, since neither local state nor concurrency matter. Similarly, for the invoice
EJB we can use a stateless EJB, since the state is mediated by the ID, which does not access
an EJB state but rather a database state. The last one, the tic-tac-toe EJB, needs to maintain
the game board per client, and we thus use a stateful EJB for it. See the following:

```
import javax.ejb.Singleton;
import javax.ejb.Stateless;
import javax.ejb.Stateful;
...
@Singleton
public class Configuration {
    ... configuration access methods
}

@Stateless
public class Invoice {
    ... invoice access methods
}
```

```
@Stateful
public class TicTacToe {
    ... tic-tac-toe methods
}
```

Of course, all those classes must go into different files. We put them together for illustration purposes only.

Concerning their accessibility from client code, session EJBs can use one or a combination of three methods (all annotations shown are from package javax.ejb), as follows:

- **No-interface**

  You use this method if you don't want to describe the EJB access via an interface. This is only possible for local clients running inside the same application. While the separation into interfaces (describing *what* gets done in interfaces) and implementation (the how, implemented in non-abstract classes) is generally a good idea for clean code, a no-interface view can make sense for simple EJBs. For no-interface EJBs you just declare the implementation, as in the following:

  ```
  @Stateless public class Invoice {
      ... implementation
  }
  ```

  The EJB clients can then only access the implementation class directly, without mediating interfaces.

- **Local**

  If you want to define local access to session EJBs (EJBs and EJB clients running in the same application) and use an interface view for that, you can either mark the interface with @Local and let the EJB implementation class implement the interface, as follows:

  ```
  @Local public interface InvoiceInterface {
      ... abstract interface methods
  }
  ```

```
@Stateless public class Invoice
        implements InvoiceInterface {
    ... implementation
}
```

Or you can use the @Local annotation in the implementation class, as follows:

```
public interface InvoiceInterface {
    ... abstract interface methods
}

@Stateless
@Local(InvoiceInterface.class)
public class Invoice implements InvoiceInterface {
    ... implementation
}
```

You can even omit the implementation as in the following:

```
public interface InvoiceInterface {
    ... abstract interface methods
}

@Stateless
@Local(InvoiceInterface.class)
public class Invoice {
    ... implementation
}
```

to further reduce the coupling of the interface, although this is, in general, not recommended.

– **@Remote**

Use the @Remote annotation to make a session EJB accessible from outside the application. You can just replace @Local with @Remote, and everything that was just said for the local access and concerning the interfaces can be transcribed unaltered for remote access. So, you would write, for example:

```
public interface InvoiceInterface {
    ... abstract interface methods
}

@Stateless
@Remote(InvoiceInterface.class)
public Invoice
        implements InvoiceInterface {
    ... implementation
}
```

EJBs can have a local *and* a remote interface—just use both annotations together, as follows:

```
public interface InvoiceLocal {
    ... abstract interface methods
}
public interface InvoiceRemote {
    ... abstract interface methods
}

@Stateless
@Local(InvoiceLocal.class)
@Remote(InvoiceRemote.class)
public Invoice
        implements InvoiceLocal,
                   InvoiceRemote {
    ... implementation
}
```

Also, nobody will stop us from using the same interface for both local and remote access, as follows:

```
public interface InvoiceInterface {
    ... abstract interface methods
}

@Stateless
@Local(InvoiceInterface.class)
```

```
@Remote(InvoiceInterface.class)
public Invoice implements InvoiceInterface {
    ... implementation
}
```

Caution   Remote access means parameters in method calls get passed by value, not by reference! Passing by value means that if you change the parameters, changes won't be reflected on the caller side. So, although local and remote interfaces get declared connatural to each other, concerning method parameters you must be careful under all under some circumstances.

Accessing EJBs

Accessing local EJBs from a client is easy: you just use the @EJB injection to let CDI (context and dependency injection) assign an instance access to an EJB, as follows:

```
public class SomeCdiManagedClass {
    ...
    @EJB
    private SomeEjbInterface theEjb;

    // or, for no-interface EJBs
    @EJB
    private SomeEjbClass theEjb;
    ...
}
```

The SomeCdiManagedClass is just any class eligible for CDI management. This could be a class annotated with @Named, as is often the case for classes used with JSF or other EJBs.

Addressing remote EJBs is considerably more complicated than local access to EJBs. What you have to do is set up a JNDI context and then use it to do a lookup of a remote instance, as follows:

```
...
String remoteServerHost = "localhost";
// or "192.168.1.111" or something
String remoteServerPort = "3700";
// Port 3700 is part of the Glassfish conf
```

```
Properties props = new Properties();
props.setProperty("java.naming.factory.initial",
  "com.sun.enterprise.naming."+
  "SerialInitContextFactory");
props.setProperty("java.naming.factory.url.pkgs",
  "com.sun.enterprise.naming");
props.setProperty("java.naming.factory.state",
  "com.sun.corba.ee.impl.presentation.rmi."+
  "JNDIStateFactoryImpl");
props.setProperty("org.omg.CORBA.ORBInitialHost",
  remoteServerHost);
props.setProperty("org.omg.CORBA.ORBInitialPort",
  remoteServerPort);

try {
  InitialContext ic = new InitialContext(props);

  // Use this to see what EJBs are available
  // and how to name them
  //NamingEnumeration<NameClassPair> list =
  //      ic.list("");
  //while (list.hasMore()) {
  //  System.out.println(list.next().getName());
  //}

  // Looking up a remote EJB
  SomeEjbRemote testEJB = (SomeEjbRemote)
      ic.lookup(
      "book.jakarta8.testEjbServer.SomeEjbRemote");

  // Invoking some EJB method
  System.out.println(testEJB.tellMe());
}catch(Exception e) {
  e.printStackTrace(System.err);
}
```

This example assumes that on the remote server side you created a session EJB with a remote interface, as follows:

```
package book.jakarta8.testEjbServer;

public interface SomeEjbRemote {
  String tellMe();
}
```

And an implementation like the following:

```
package book.jakarta8.testEjbServer;

import javax.ejb.Remote;
import javax.ejb.Stateless;

@Stateless()
@Remote(SomeEjbRemote.class)
public class SomeEjb implements SomeEjbRemote {
  @Override
  public String tellMe() {
    return "Hello World";
  }
}
```

Obviously, for this to work the client must have access to the compiled remote interfaces. That means you must have somehow included a step in the EJB server build to extract the interfaces from the generated classes.

Note   For testing and a proof of concept it is enough to build a JAR in the "remote" EJB project by, for example, running Run As ➤ Maven build... with goal "package." You can then extract the JAR you find in the "target" folder (it is just a ZIP file), remove everything but the remote interfaces, repackage it, and put the result into the WEB-INF/lib of the client project.

If the remote EJB server is a Glassfish server, you can also use its `asadmin` command to see which EJBs are eligible for remote access and how they are named, as follows:

```
cd [GLASSFISH_INST]
cd bin
./asadmin list-jndi-entries

# output for example:
# UserTransaction: com.sun.enterprise.transaction...
#    startup.TransactionLifecycleService$2
# ejb: com.sun.enterprise.naming.impl.TransientContext
# book.jakarta8.testEjbServer.SomeEjbRemote__3_x_
#    Internal_RemoteBusinessHome__: javax.naming.Reference
# java:global: com.sun.enterprise.naming.impl.
#    TransientContext
# book.jakarta8.testEjbServer.SomeEjbRemote:
#    javax.naming.Reference
# book.jakarta8.testEjbServer.SomeEjbRemote#book.
#    jakarta8.testEjbServer.SomeEjbRemote:
#    javax.naming.Reference
# jdbc: com.sun.enterprise.naming.impl.TransientContext
# concurrent: com.sun.enterprise.naming.impl.
#    TransientContext
# com.sun.enterprise.container.common.spi.util.
#    InjectionManager:
# com.sun.enterprise.container.common.impl.util.
#    InjectionManagerImpl
# jms: com.sun.enterprise.naming.impl.TransientContext
```

The fifth entry from the example output shows the remote EJB JNDI name "book. jakarta8.testEjbServer.SomeEjbRemote" used in the EJB client lookup code just listed.

Other Java Enterprise Edition (JEE or Jakarta EE) application servers probably apply other naming schemes for remotely accessible EJBs. You must consult their documentation and/or get the remotely visible JNDI entry listing. For the latter, you can try a programmatic access (commented out in the preceding listing) or use some administration features implemented for the remote EJB server.

Exercise 1

Which of the following is/are true?

1. EJBs must have a local *and* a remote interface.

2. Not providing interfaces means EJBs automatically get assigned to local and remote interfaces by the EJB container (the part of the Jakarta EE server that handles EJBs).

3. A remote EJB means the EJB can be accessed from other applications on the same server. Access from other Jakarta EE servers is not possible.

4. EJBs cannot have a state.

5. If a client accesses an EJB, a new instance of the EJB gets created on the server side.

6. To access any EJB from a client, you must do a lookup in a JNDI context.

7. To use an EJB from a client, the EJB's interfaces and its implementation must be imported into the client project.

EJB Projects

Jakarta EE projects don't have to be web projects—they can also just expose services to clients accessing their remote EJB interfaces. Web interfaces like REST or web-service interfaces are your first choice for interoperability with web browsers and non–Jakarta EE servers, but for faster communication among Jakarta EE participants in a larger system comprising different network nodes, using component-to-EJB communication might be a better choice.

Web projects also can expose remote EJBs to appropriate clients. In case you want to have a streamlined project without web capabilities, the procedure to do that inside Eclipse gets described in the following paragraphs.

Start a new Maven project, similar to the web projects we have created so far, but change the packaging declaration inside pom.xml to `<packaging> ejb </packaging>`. For example:

```
<groupId>book.jakarta8</groupId>
<artifactId>testEjbServer</artifactId>
<version>0.0.1-SNAPSHOT</version>
<packaging>ejb</packaging>
```

For the project facets, uncheck all facets other than "EJB Module," "Java," and "JavaScript." Change the EJB Module version to 3.2.

Note   Eclipse version 2018-12 (and maybe later versions) under certain circumstances disallows unchecking the "Dynamic Web Module" facet. If this is the case for you, quit Eclipse, go to the ".settings/" folder, open file `org.eclipse.wst. common.project.facet.core.xml`, and remove the unwanted facets there.

From there, create the EJBs and their remote interfaces as described previously, with the following additional constraint: move the EJB interfaces to their own package. For example:

```
book.jakarta8.ejbproj.ejb              <- Implementation
book.jakarta8.ejbproj.ejb.interfaces   <- Interfaces
```

We know that for an EJB client we only need the EJB interfaces, not the EJB implementations. Maven can help us here: go inside the `pom.xml` file and add the following within the `<build><plugins>` section:

```
<plugin>
  <groupId>org.apache.maven.plugins</groupId>
  <artifactId>maven-ejb-plugin</artifactId>
  <version>3.0.1</version>
  <configuration>
    <generateClient>true</generateClient>
    <ejbVersion>3.2</ejbVersion>
    <clientExcludes>
      <clientExclude>
        book/jakarta8/ejbproj/ejb/*
      </clientExclude>
    </clientExcludes>
  </configuration>
</plugin>
```

The `<clientExclude>` tag will make sure only the interfaces will be exported to a client-specific JAR archive.

If you now invoke Run As ➤ Maven build... ➤ goals="package" you'll find a client JAR with the compiled EJB interface in the "target" folder. Maybe you have to press F5 first on that folder to update the view. Look for the JAR with ending "-client.jar." Any client wishing to communicate with the EJBs must include this client JAR as a dependency. Of course, the EJB project itself must be deployed on the server for the EJBs to work.

EJBs with Dependencies

Until now we have developed only very simple EJBs without the need to use library JARs. Once you need to add libraries to an EJB, you'll run into trouble. This is because there is no standard way to add dependencies to isolated EJB modules. If you need to add library JARs, there are basically two ways to achieve this: either you add the libraries globally to your Jakarta EE server, or you pack the EJB module into an enterprise archive (EAR). We will talk about both possibilities.

Adding Dependencies to the Server

You can add dependencies in the form of library JARs globally to your server. While this is a quick and easy solution in many cases, there are three big disadvantages with this approach, as follows:

- You cannot deploy and undeploy such dependencies while the server is running. So you would have to stop the server, add the library JARs to some special folder, start the server again, and then deploy your EJB.

- Such solutions are global to the complete server. If one application needs a version x.y.z of the library and another application needs version p.q.r, a conflict appears that cannot be solved.

- Such solutions are not portable. One Jakarta EE 8 server product requires that such a global library JAR be put into some folder "BASE-DIR/libs/ext," while another server needs it inside "BASE-DIR/server/domain1/lib" and so on.

If you still think this is the solution for your EJBs, the procedure for Glassfish 5.1 is as follows:

1. Stop the server.

2. Put the library JARs into folder "[INST-DIR]/glassfish/modules" *or* put it into "[INST-DIR]/glassfish/domains/domain1/lib/ext." In the former case, the library applies to really all applications, while in the latter case the library is restricted to a *domain*. We don't talk about different domains in this beginner's book, so for our purposes there is practically no difference between those two options.

3. Start the server.

4. Deploy the EJBs.

Creating EARs

EARs are archives that bundle EJBs, web applications (WARs), and library JARs. Dealing with EARs instead of isolated EJBs somewhat increases the complexity of administration activities. But adding library JARs to EARs is a standard way of including dependencies with applications and is thus preferable over the global approach we just described.

To add EAR functionality to an application inside Eclipse, you basically have to do the following:

1. Build a new EAR project: Go to New ➤ Project... ➤ JavaEE ➤ Enterprise Application Project.

2. Choose any name you like and add the EJB module project as a dependency (you are being asked for dependencies in a dialog).

3. Create a folder "EarContent/lib."

4. Copy the library JARs into "EarContent/lib."

5. Stop deploying the isolated EJB module projects on the server. Instead, deploy the EAR project onto the server by clicking Run As ➤ Run on Server on the EAR project.

If you change the EJB's source code, just redeploy the EAR project—Eclipse will correctly take care of updating the EAR's EJB modules.

Exercise 2

Create the following four projects:

- A JRE project (no Jakarta EE capabilities) with a single class MyDateTime and a method date(String format) that returns the LocalDateTime according to the format string specified as a parameter. Make it a Maven project with "jar" packaging. Hint: Enter Run As ➤ Maven build... ➤ Goals "package install" to create a JAR file that can be used by other projects, as well as to install the JAR in the local Maven repository. You'll find the JAR in the "target" folder (press F5 to update the folder view in Eclipse after the generation).

- An EJB project with a single EJB, MyDateTimeEjb, and local and remote interfaces. Let it use the JAR file generated from the preceding JRE project. Hint: Even without using a remote repository, the JAR from the preceding project can be referred to like any other Maven artifact.

- An EAR project that contains the EJB project and adds the JAR dependency needed.

- A simple no-Jakarta-EE EJB client project that tests the remote interface from the MyDateTimeEjb EJB. Hint: Include the gf-client. jar file from Glassfish's "lib" folder as a library dependency.

Asynchronous EJB Invocation

EJB methods can be called asynchronously by an EJB client. This means the client invokes an EJB method that was marked eligible for asynchronous invocation, immediately regains control of the program execution, and handles the result from the EJB invocation later when it is available.

To mark an EJB method for asynchronous invocation, you add the annotation @Asynchronous from package javax.ejb to the method, as follows:

```
import java.util.concurrent.Future;
import javax.ejb.AsyncResult;
import javax.ejb.Asynchronous;
import javax.ejb.Singleton;
```

```
@Singleton // Example only, all EJB types work!
public class SomeEjb {
  @Asynchronous
  public Future<String> tellMeLater() {

    // Simulate some long-running calculation
    try {
      Thread.sleep(2000);
    } catch (InterruptedException e) {
    }

    return new AsyncResult<String>(
        "Hi from tellMeLater()");
  }
}
```

This example EJB uses the no-interface method, but asynchronous invocation works for local and remote interfaces as well. The AsyncResult is a convenience class that allows for the easy creation of a Future object. This Future object will not really be exposed to the client; its main purpose is to obey the method signature. The Future returned to the client will instead be transparently created by the EJB container.

On the EJB client side you invoke the EJB as usual and handle the Future you received from the EJB invocation as you are used to from the JRE concurrency API, as follows:

```
...
@EJB
private SomeEjb someEjb;
...
Future<String> f = someEjb.tellMeLater();
try {
    // Example only: block until the result
    // is available:
    String s = f.get();
    System.err.println(s);
} catch (Exception e) {
    e.printStackTrace(System.err);
}
```

Timer EJBs

EJBs can be equipped with timer facilities, like delayed execution of some task or reoccurring automatic method invocations. You have two options: automatic timers and programmatic timers.

For automatic timers, you add a @Schedule or @Schedules annotation (from the javax.ejb package) to any void method (the visibility doesn't matter) without parameters, or with a javax.ejb.Timer parameter. The parameters of the @Schedule annotation describe the frequency, as in the following:

```
@Stateless
public class SomeEjb {
  @Schedule(minute="*", hour="0", persistent=false)
  // every minute during the hour between 00:00 and 01:00
  public void timeout1() {
    System.err.println("Timeout-1 from " + getClass());
  }
}
```

A delayed execution like "Do something once 10 seconds after the server has started" is not possible for automatic timers.

The following is a listing of some example schedules you can use inside automatic timers:

```
@Schedule(second="10", minute="0", hour="0")
  // <- at 00:00:10 every day

@Schedule(minute="30", hour="0",
      dayOfWeek="Tue")
  // <- at 00:30:00 on Tuesdays (second defaults to 00)

@Schedule(minute="11", hour="15",
      dayOfWeek="Mon,Tue,Fri")
  // <- at 15:11:00 on Mondays, Tuesdays and Fridays

@Schedule(minute="*/10", hour="*")
  // <- every 10 minutes, every hour

@Schedule(minute="25/10", hour="1")
  // <- 01:25, 01:35, 01:45 and 01:55
```

```
@Schedule(hour="*", dayOfMonth="1,2,3")
  // <- every hour at 1st, 2nd, and 3rd each month
  // (minute defaults to 00)

@Schedule(hour="*/10")
  // <- every 10 hours

@Schedule(month="Feb,Aug")
  // <- 00:00:00 each February and August
  // (hour defaults to 00)

@Schedule(dayOfMonth="1", year="2020")
  // <- 00:00:00 each 1st each month during 2020

@Schedule(dayOfMonth="1-10")
  // <- 00:00:00 each 1st to 10th each month
```

The @Schedules annotation can be used to apply several @Schedule specifications to a timer callback, as follows:

```
@Schedules({
  @Schedule(hour="*"),
  @Schedule(hour="0", minute="30")
})
private void someMethod(Timer tm) {
    ...
}
```

which means: every x:00:00 (x = 00 through 23), but also at 00:30:00.

Unless you also give a persistent=false to the @Schedule annotation, a timer survives an application and a server restart.

Timers can also be defined programmatically. Here it is also possible to define a one-time shot, like, for example, in the following:

```
@Singleton
@Startup
public class Timer1 {
  @Resource
  private SessionContext context;
```

201

```
@PostConstruct
public void go() {
  context.getTimerService().
        createSingleActionTimer(5000, new TimerConfig());
}

@Timeout
public void timeout(Timer timer) {
  System.err.println("Hello from " + getClass());
}
}
```

Here, the method annotated with @Timeout gets called every time the timer fires. For this example, this will be 5,000 milliseconds after EJB creation because of the createSingleActionTimer() invocation. The timer service you get with context. getTimerService() allows for various scheduling options; please see the API documentation for details.

CHAPTER 8

Dealing with XML Data

One important part of enterprise applications is the capability to produce, emit, receive, and investigate XML data. This is similar to the JSON data format we talked about in Chapter 5, but XML allows for a higher complexity compared to JSON. The advantages and disadvantages of XML over JSON are as follows:

- **Advantages**

  XML documents introduce schema declarations for structure validation and element validation. This means it can be precisely described how an XML document must be structured and which values elements and attributes are allowed to have.

- **Disadvantages**

  What can be an advantage can also be a disadvantage. So, while important for the stability of enterprise applications, schema validation and element and attribute value constraints may lead to a performance degradation if processing XML data, and the comprehensiveness of documents may prominently suffer from this increased complexity.

If document structure and values validation are an issue or if you have to deal with legacy systems with components talking to the outside world via XML, Jakarta EE 8 allows for both communication via XML and XML processing.

SOAP Web Services

The dedicated Jakarta EE 8 technology to let components talk via XML messages and to translate between XML data and Java objects gets called JAX-WS. The data protocol used for that is SOAP (simple object access protocol). Services producing and consuming SOAP messages also sometimes get called *web services* in the traditional sense.

© Peter Späth 2019
P. Späth, *Beginning Jakarta EE*, https://doi.org/10.1007/978-1-4842-5079-2_8

Note   To draw a distinction between REST services using JSON as a message format and SOAP web services using XML messages, we will keep using "REST services" for the former and "SOAP web services" for the latter.

The idea behind JAX-WS is the following:

1. On the server side, we declare one or more Java classes and methods, therein encapsulating functionalities we want to be able to address via SOAP.

2. JAX-WS takes these classes and methods and produces a web service endpoint addressable from inside and outside the application via SOAP.

3. JAX-WS also allows us to generate the web service artifacts needed in order for SOAP web service clients to communicate with the web service endpoint. This happens only during development.

4. Import the client artifacts generated by JAX-WS into client projects. Implement the JAX-WS client and deploy it.

5. As an alternative to Java clients' importing JAX-WS artifacts, any SOAP client using any platform can be used to communicate with the JAX-WS server.

6. As another alternative to the former, you can read and process the raw XML data outside JAX-WS. This is a more low-level approach for SOAP clients. Expect more work compared to using JAX-WS.

SOAP documents get described by WSDL documents (web service description language), which tell about their structure. JAX-WS and the Jakarta EE 8 server provide an HTTP endpoint where clients can directly retrieve the WSDL documents describing a SOAP web service endpoint. In fact, the WSDL information is all a client needs in order to learn how to talk with the SOAP web service.

As an example, let us reimplement the REST data and time retriever from Chapter 5, this time using a SOAP web service instead of a REST controller. To start the example, create a new Maven project with coordinates, as follows:

```
Group-Id:    book.jakarta8
Artifact-Id: wsdate
Version:     0.0.1-SNAPSHOT
```

As usual, make sure the project uses and compiles for Java 8. As project facets use the following:

```
Dynamic Web Module 4.0
Java 1.8
JavaScript 1.0
```

As the Maven build file pom.xml, use the following as its content:

```xml
<project xmlns="http://maven.apache.org/POM/4.0.0"
  xmlns:xsi="http://www.w3.org/2001/XMLSchema-instance"
  xsi:schemaLocation="http://maven.apache.org/POM/4.0.0
      http://maven.apache.org/xsd/maven-4.0.0.xsd">
  <modelVersion>4.0.0</modelVersion>

  <groupId>book.jakarta8</groupId>
  <artifactId>wsdate</artifactId>
  <version>0.0.1-SNAPSHOT</version>
  <packaging>war</packaging>

  <name>wsdate</name>
  <url>http://maven.apache.org</url>

  <properties>
    <project.build.sourceEncoding>
      UTF-8
    </project.build.sourceEncoding>
    <failOnMissingWebXml>false</failOnMissingWebXml>
  </properties>
```

```xml
  <dependencies>
    <dependency>
      <groupId>javax</groupId>
      <artifactId>javaee-api</artifactId>
      <version>8.0</version>
    </dependency>
    <dependency>
      <groupId>junit</groupId>
      <artifactId>junit</artifactId>
      <version>3.8.1</version>
      <scope>test</scope>
    </dependency>
  </dependencies>
  <build>
    <plugins>
      <plugin>
        <artifactId>maven-compiler-plugin</artifactId>
        <configuration>
          <source>1.8</source>
          <target>1.8</target>
        </configuration>
      </plugin>
    </plugins>
  </build>
</project>
```

Compared to the build files we've used up to now, this one has an additional `<failOnMissingWebXml> false </failOnMissingWebXml>`. Without this entry, Eclipse would complain about a missing `web.xml` file.

Note   Although with project facet Dynamic Web Module configured and producing a WAR deployable, the project does not need a `WEB-INF/web.xml` file. JAX-WS takes care of correctly exposing the SOAP web service endpoint without a `web.xml`.

Create a Java class representing the SOAP web service endpoint for the date and time retrieval, as follows:

```java
package book.jakarta8.wsdate;

import java.time.ZonedDateTime;
import java.time.format.DateTimeFormatter;

import javax.jws.WebMethod;
import javax.jws.WebService;

@WebService
public class WsDate {
  @WebMethod
  public String date(String dateFormat) {
    ZonedDateTime zdt = ZonedDateTime.now();
    String outStr = "";
    String errMsg = "";
    try {
      outStr = ("".equals(dateFormat) ?
        zdt.toString() :
        zdt.format(
            DateTimeFormatter.ofPattern(dateFormat)));
      errMsg = "";
    } catch(Exception e) {
      errMsg = e.getMessage();
    }
    // errMsg currently ignored
    return outStr;
  }
}
```

Because of the @WebService annotation, JAX-WS knows that this class describes a SOAP web service. The @WebMethod annotation in front of a method further describes a sub-activity that a web service client is allowed to invoke. Obviously, there can be more such methods, and the class may have non-annotated methods not exposed to the SOAP web service.

Once deployed and running, the Glassfish web administration page lists the new SOAP web service and tells us about its capabilities. With the browser, go to the admin page at `http://localhost:4848`.

By default, the user name is "admin" and there is no password. If you navigate to Applications ➤ wsdate, there is a "View Endpoint" link you can use to navigate to a page that lets you see the WSDL information and even provides an online testing tool for the web service. See Figures 8-1 and 8-2.

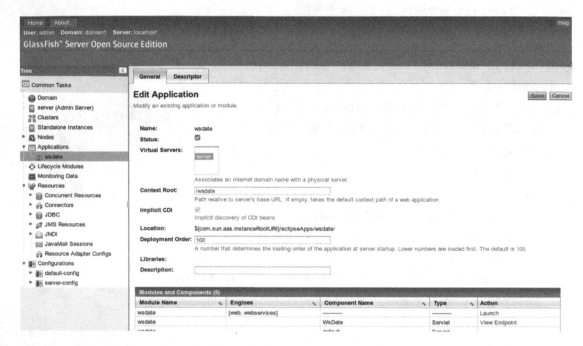

Figure 8-1. *Web services in the admin page*

Web Service Endpoint Information

View details about a web service endpoint.

Application Name:	wsdate
Tester:	/wsdate/WsDateService?Tester
WSDL:	/wsdate/WsDateService?wsdl
Endpoint Name:	WsDate
Service Name:	WsDateService
Port Name:	WsDatePort
Deployment Type:	109
Implementation Type:	SERVLET
Implementation Class Name:	book.jakarta8.wsdate.WsDate
Endpoint Address URI:	/wsdate/WsDateService
Namespace:	http://wsdate.jakarta8.book/

Figure 8-2. *Information about a web service*

You can also directly download the WSDL data and the associated XSD file (for the validation) using your browser: just navigate to one of the following:

```
http://localhost:8080/wsdate/WsDateService?wsdl
http://localhost:8080/wsdate/WsDateService?xsd=1
```

The SOAP web service tester that the Glassfish web administrator provides is quite nice. If you use it, it will tell you both the SOAP request message and the response. For the wsdate sample and some date/time format input as "yyyy," the messages read as follows:

```
Request:
<?xml version="1.0" encoding="UTF-8"?>
<S:Envelope xmlns:S=
     "http://schemas.xmlsoap.org/soap/envelope/"
          xmlns:SOAP-ENV=
     "http://schemas.xmlsoap.org/soap/envelope/">
   <SOAP-ENV:Header/>
   <S:Body xmlns:ns2="http://wsdate.jakarta8.book/">
```

```
        <ns2:date>
            <arg0>yyyy</arg0>
        </ns2:date>
    </S:Body>
</S:Envelope>
```

Response:
```
<?xml version="1.0" encoding="UTF-8"?>
<S:Envelope xmlns:S=
    "http://schemas.xmlsoap.org/soap/envelope/"
        xmlns:SOAP-ENV=
    "http://schemas.xmlsoap.org/soap/envelope/">
    <SOAP-ENV:Header/>
    <S:Body xmlns:ns2="http://wsdate.jakarta8.book/">
        <ns2:dateResponse>
            <return>2019</return>
        </ns2:dateResponse>
    </S:Body>
</S:Envelope>
```

This is a lot of stuff for such a simple method call! Remember the same application using REST and JSON instead, as follows:

Request:
```
    GET http://localhost:8080/restdate/webapi/date?
        dateFormat=yyyy
```

Response:
```
    {"date":"2019","errMsg":""}
```

Exercise 1

Add a new method, date2(), to the SOAP web service class that consumes the same parameter and returns a string array [outStr, errMsg].

Let's get back to the SOAP web service. With the SOAP web service running, we develop a client application to access this service. This could be a JSF application, a single-page application, or any other Jakarta EE application. As an example, we will build a simple application that directly implements an HTTP servlet. To start the client coding, create a new Maven project with the following coordinates:

```
<groupId>book.jakarta8</groupId>
<artifactId>wsdate-client</artifactId>
<version>0.0.1-SNAPSHOT</version>
<packaging>war</packaging>
```

As project facets, use the following:

```
Dynamic Web Module 4.0
Java 1.8
JavaScript 1.0
```

As usual, make sure the project correctly uses Java 8.

To generate the artifacts that a Java client needs to communicate with the SOAP web service, we add a build configuration to the pom.xml build file. Inside the `<build><plugins>` tag add the following:

```
<plugin>
  <groupId>org.codehaus.mojo</groupId>
  <artifactId>jaxws-maven-plugin</artifactId>
  <version>1.12</version>
  <executions>
    <execution>
      <id>wsimport-from-jdk</id>
      <goals>
        <goal>wsimport</goal>
      </goals>
    </execution>
  </executions>
  <configuration>
    <!-- using wsdl from an url -->
    <wsdlUrls>
      <wsdlUrl>
        http://localhost:8080/wsdate/WsDateService?wsdl
      </wsdlUrl>
    </wsdlUrls>
```

```
<!-- or reading wsdls from file directory -->
<!-- <wsdlDirectory>src/wsdl</wsdlDirectory> -->
<!-- wsdl files -->
<!-- <wsdlFiles> -->
<!-- <wsdlFile>theWSDL.wsdl</wsdlFile> -->
<!--</wsdlFiles> -->
<!-- Keep generated files -->
<keep>true</keep>
<!-- Package name -->
<packageName>book.jakarta8.wsdate.generated</packageName>
<!-- generated source files destination -->
<sourceDestDir>src/main/java</sourceDestDir>
    </configuration>
</plugin>
```

Now run Run As... ➤ Maven build... ➤ goals "jaxws:wsimport." This generates the Java files needed to talk to the web service. In Eclipse, update the sources by pressing F5 on the Sources directory. This generation needs to be done only once during development, unless you change the SOAP web service, which requires another client artifacts generation.

Next, we create the servlet. It is a single Java class that reads as follows:

```
package book.jakarta8.wsdate_client;

import java.io.IOException;
import java.io.PrintWriter;

import javax.servlet.ServletException;
import javax.servlet.annotation.WebServlet;
import javax.servlet.http.HttpServlet;
import javax.servlet.http.HttpServletRequest;
import javax.servlet.http.HttpServletResponse;
import javax.xml.ws.WebServiceRef;

import book.jakarta8.wsdate.generated.WsDate;
import book.jakarta8.wsdate.generated.WsDateService;
```

```java
@WebServlet(name = "WsDateServlet",
        urlPatterns = { "/WsDateServlet" })
public class WsDateServlet extends HttpServlet {
    private static final long serialVersionUID =
        -1651237748783635642L;

    @WebServiceRef(wsdlLocation =
        "http://localhost:8080/wsdate/WsDateService?wsdl")
    private WsDateService service;

    private
    void processRequest(HttpServletRequest request,
            HttpServletResponse response)
            throws ServletException, IOException {
        response.setContentType("text/html;charset=UTF-8");
        try (PrintWriter out = response.getWriter()) {
            out.println("<html lang=\"en\">");
            out.println("<head>");
            out.println("<title>Servlet WsDateServlet</title>");
            out.println("</head>");
            out.println("<body>");
            out.println("<h1>Servlet WsDateServlet at " +
                request.getContextPath() + "</h1>");
            out.println("<p>" + date("yyyy-MM-dd HH:mm:ss") +
                "</p>");
            out.println("</body>");
            out.println("</html>");
        }
    }

    @Override
    protected void doGet(HttpServletRequest request,
        HttpServletResponse response)
            throws ServletException, IOException {
        processRequest(request, response);
    }
```

```
    private String date(String dateFormat) {
      WsDate port = service.getWsDatePort();
      return port.date(dateFormat);
    }
}
```

You can see it refers to the WSDL URL and to the Java classes we just generated. You may also notice that you don't have to deal with XML directly—JAX-WS does all the SOAP XML creating, parsing, and converting tasks for us. Deploy this on the server, and in a browser of your choice navigate to the following URL:

```
    http://localhost:8080/wsdate-client/WsDateServlet
```

This will call the SOAP web service and print the result on the browser page generated.

Exercise 2

Let the client call the `date2()` web method (results from the previous exercise) instead and output any error messages on the page.

Application Startup Activities

Up until now, any activities performed by our Jakarta EE 8 server applications have been triggered from outside, like from a browser, from some client application also started in Jakarta EE, or from some client tool like CURL. In the following sections, we are going to talk about XML handling algorithms, and it would be nice if we had something similar to the JRE construct `public static void main(String[] args) { ... }` to run any code unconditionally.

You will find a lot of ideas on the internet about how this can be done. However, most of the described ideas are more or less ugly hacks, which stems from the fact that in older versions of Java enterprise servers there was nothing like a genuine startup hook method. With EJB version 3.1 and up we are fortunately in a better situation. We know there is a `@Singleton` annotation for EJBs for which we need only a single instance, and, more important at this point, there is also a `@Startup` class-level annotation that unconditionally creates the EJB upon application startup. This in turn triggers a method annotated with `@PostConstruct`.

So, the Jakarta EE 8 equivalent of a `public static void main(String[] args) {`
`... }` reads as follows:

```
import javax.annotation.PostConstruct;
import javax.ejb.Singleton;
import javax.ejb.Startup;

@Singleton
@Startup
public class App {
  @PostConstruct
  public void postConstruct() {
    System.err.println("!!!!!!!!!!!!!!!!!!!!!!!!!!!!!!!!!!!");
    System.err.println("!!!!!!!!!!!!!!!!!!!!!!!!!!!!!!!!!!!");
    System.err.println("!!!!!!!!!!!!!!!!!!!!!!!!!!!!!!!!!!!");

    ... any startup code ...
  }
}
```

You can put this anywhere. Also, you can rename the class and its single method
to anything you like—names don't matter here, because only the annotations are
important.

This code will be executed at server startup *and* every time the application gets
redeployed, which for an application containing nothing but this startup procedure
won't take longer than maybe two seconds.

Note   To deploy or redeploy an application you can press CTRL+ALT+P on the
server in Eclipse's "Servers" view.

XML Processing

If, for whatever reason, you need to process XML data directly, outside JAX-WS, Jakarta EE 8 also includes several technologies to create and parse XML data:

- **JAXP 1.6**

    Java API for XML Processing

- **StAX 1.0**

    Streaming API for XML. Included within JAXP.

- **JAXB 2.2**

    Java XML Binding

The following paragraphs will describe JAXP, more precisely its parts DOM, SAX, and StaX, from a use case–centric view. JAXB will require a follow-up book. For detailed instructions and a more complete API survey, please see the specification manuals you can find on the internet.

In all examples and unless otherwise noted, we use the following input document:

```
<?xml version="1.0" encoding="UTF-8"?>
<recordings>
  <recording genre="classic">
    <composer>Haydn</composer>
    <composerFirst>Joseph</composerFirst>
    <title>The Creation</title>
    <make>1797</make>
  </recording>
  <recording genre="classic">
    <composer>Haydn</composer>
    <composerFirst>Joseph</composerFirst>
    <title>The Seasons</title>
    <make>1801</make>
  </recording>
  <recording genre="rock">
    <composer>U2</composer>
    <lyrics>Bono</lyrics>
```

```
        <performer>U2</performer>
        <title>A Sort of Homecoming</title>
        <make>1984</make>
    </recording>
</recordings>
```

DOM: In-Memory Representation of a Complete XML Document

If an XML document is not too big you can let JAXP read in the complete document and produce an in-memory tree representation from that. Such a representation gets called a *document object model* or DOM.

Inside the DOM methodology, any leaf or sub-tree root gets called a *node*. A node is an instance of the interface org.w3c.dom.Node. The children of a DOM tree node are of type org.w3c.dom.NodeList. To build a Java 8 stream from that we use a helper class, as follows:

```
class DOMIterator {
  private int i = 0;
  private Node n;
  public DOMIterator(Node n) { this.n = n; }
  public Stream<Node> stream() {
    NodeList nl = n.getChildNodes();
    int len = nl.getLength();
    return len == 0 ?
      Stream.empty()
      : Stream.iterate(nl.item(0), n2 -> {
        i++; return nl.item(i); }).limit(len);
  }
  public static Stream<Node> stream(Node n) {
    return new DOMIterator(n).stream();
  }
}
```

To read in a document and build an in-memory DOM representation, you write the
following:

```
import java.util.stream.Stream;
import javax.xml.parsers.DocumentBuilder;
import javax.xml.parsers.DocumentBuilderFactory;
import org.w3c.dom.Document;
import org.w3c.dom.Node;
import org.w3c.dom.NodeList;
import org.xml.sax.InputSource;
...

  String xml = ...;
  DocumentBuilderFactory dbf =
      DocumentBuilderFactory.newInstance();
  DocumentBuilder db = dbf.newDocumentBuilder();
  InputSource is = new InputSource(
      new ByteArrayInputStream(xml.getBytes()));
  Document doc = db.parse(is);
```

From there we can navigate through the tree, investigate nodes, retrieve node
attributes and node text content, and add nodes and attributes, as follows:

```
Node root = doc.getDocumentElement();

// Getting a node name
System.err.println("Name = " + root.getNodeName());
// -> recordings

// Iterate through child elements
DOMIterator.stream(root).
      filter(n -> n.getNodeType() == Node.ELEMENT_NODE).
      forEach(n -> {
   System.err.println("Child Name = " + n.getNodeName());
   // -> recording, recording, ...
  });
```

```
// Navigating and finding
Node third = DOMIterator.stream(root).
      filter(n -> n.getNodeType() == Node.ELEMENT_NODE).
      skip(2).findFirst().get();
String thrdComposer = DOMIterator.stream(third).
      filter(n -> n.getNodeName().equals("composer")).
      findFirst().get().getTextContent();
String thrdGenre = third.getAttributes().
      getNamedItem("genre").getNodeValue();
System.err.println("3rd Composer = " + thrdComposer);
System.err.println("3rd Genre = " + thrdGenre);

// Changing and adding an attribute
third.getAttributes().getNamedItem("genre").
      setNodeValue("ROCK");
Attr attr = doc.createAttribute("classification");
attr.setNodeValue("kx-7");
third.getAttributes().setNamedItem(attr);

// Adding a node
Node newNode = doc.createElement("country");
newNode.setTextContent("Ireland");
third.appendChild(newNode);
```

To output the complete DOM tree, we first condense it, removing white-space texts, including line breaks, and then use a transformer to output re-indented XML, as follows:

```
TransformerFactory transformerFactory =
      TransformerFactory.newInstance();
Transformer transformer = transformerFactory.
      newTransformer();

// Remove whitespaces outside tags
XPathFactory xfact = XPathFactory.newInstance();
XPath xpath = xfact.newXPath();
NodeList empty = (NodeList) xpath.
      evaluate(
        "//text()[normalize-space(.) = “]",
```

```
        doc, XPathConstants.NODESET);
for (int i = 0; i < empty.getLength(); i++) {
  Node node = empty.item(i);
  node.getParentNode().removeChild(node);
}

// Re-indent
transformer.setOutputProperty(
      OutputKeys.INDENT, "yes");
transformer.setOutputProperty(
      "{http://xml.apache.org/xslt}indent-amount", "2");

DOMSource source = new DOMSource(doc);
StreamResult result = new StreamResult(System.out);
transformer.transform(source, result);
```

StAX: Streaming Pull Parsing

StAX, in contrast to DOM reading, does not read in the complete XML file and save it in memory. Instead, the application maintains an iterator or a cursor for consecutively scanning the whole XML document. So, if you have a really big XML file and need to fetch certain entries from it, StAX might be your best choice for achieving your aim.

StAX is relatively new compared to the other XML-processing technologies. While it is easy to understand, you might sometimes read that it is old-fashioned because in your code you have to add a lot of switch statements to react to cursor or iterator event types—you have to check for start and end elements, characters, namespace, attributes, and more.

The truth is, this is not StAX's fault; it comes from the way you use it. If you use Java 8's streaming capabilities and a helper class to mediate between StAX and streams, you can write really elegant code for StAX processing.

First, we add the protonpack library to the project. It contains Java 8 stream utilities to leverage the power of Java 8 streams even more. In the `pom.xml` build file, add the following inside the `<dependencies>` section:

```
<dependency>
    <groupId>com.codepoetics</groupId>
    <artifactId>protonpack</artifactId>
    <version>1.13</version>
</dependency>
```

Update the project by clicking on Maven ➤ Update Project.... This ensures Eclipse knows about this library, but we still need to make sure the Jakarta EE 8 server knows about it. For simplicity, we add the `protonpack1.13.jar` file (you can find it inside the "[USER]/.m2/repository/com/codepoetics/protonpack/1.13" folder on your PC) to the "[GLASSFISH_INST]/glassfish/domains/domain1/lib/ext" folder.

Restart the Glassfish server now.

Note   A more standard way of adding libraries to EJB projects gets described in the "EJBs with Dependencies" section of Chapter 7.

Next, we create a helper class for mediating between StAX and Java 8 streams, as follows:

```
import java.util.stream.Stream;
import com.codepoetics.protonpack.StreamUtils;

public class StaxIterator {
    private XMLStreamReader parser;
    public StaxIterator(XMLStreamReader parser) {
        this.parser = parser;
    }
    public Stream<XMLStreamReader> stream() {
        return StreamUtils.
            takeWhile(Stream.iterate(parser, pa -> {
          try {
            if(!pa.hasNext())
              return null;
```

```
                pa.next();
            } catch (XMLStreamException e) {
                e.printStackTrace(System.err);
            }
            return pa;
        }), elem -> elem != null);
    }
    public static Stream<XMLStreamReader>
            stream(XMLStreamReader n) {
        return new StaxIterator(n).stream();
    }
    public static String getElementText(
            XMLStreamReader n) {
        try {
            return n.getElementText();
        } catch (XMLStreamException e) {
        return "";
        }
    }
}
```

We again use the XML data presented at the beginning of the "XML Processing" section. Now the code to read in an XML text for StAX parsing reads as follows:

```
ByteArrayInputStream bis =
        new ByteArrayInputStream(xml.getBytes());
XMLInputFactory factory =
        XMLInputFactory.newInstance();
XMLStreamReader parser =
        factory.createXMLStreamReader(bis);
```

Instead of the byte array input stream, you can of course use any other input stream, including reading from a file or even a URL.

From there we can use our stream helper class to create a Java 8 stream, and then use finders, filters, mappers, injectors, collectors, and whatever else streams provide us with. Just a few examples are shown here:

```
// show all elements
StaxIterator.stream(parser).
    filter(elem -> elem.isStartElement()).
    forEach(sr -> {
        System.err.println(sr.getLocalName());
});

// show all composers
bis.reset();
XMLStreamReader parser2 =
      factory.createXMLStreamReader(bis);
System.err.println(
  StaxIterator.stream(parser2).
  filter(elem -> elem.isStartElement()).
  filter(elem -> elem.getLocalName().equals("composer")).
  map(StaxIterator::getElementText).
  distinct().
  collect(Collectors.joining(","))
);

// count records
bis.reset();
XMLStreamReader parser3 =
      factory.createXMLStreamReader(bis);
long recNum = StaxIterator.stream(parser3).
  filter(elem -> elem.isStartElement()).
  filter(elem -> elem.getLocalName().equals("recording")).
  count();
System.err.println(recNum);
```

Note that we have to create a fresh new parser after each stream operation. This is because a parser gets used up and cannot be rewound.

SAX: Event-Based Push Parsing

Reading in an XML document using the SAX technology is different from parsing the complete document to generate an in-memory DOM tree or using StAX streaming. With SAX you tell a parser engine to read in the XML document and call a class you implement as a listener on document parts arriving while the parsing goes on. This sometimes gets called *push* type parsing because the parser engine pushes events to your application.

We first develop a listener class, which for demonstration purposes just outputs diagnostic information. In a real-world application you would use this class to filter and transform values. See the following:

```java
import org.xml.sax.Attributes;
import org.xml.sax.InputSource;
import org.xml.sax.SAXException;
import org.xml.sax.helpers.DefaultHandler;

class UserHandler extends DefaultHandler {
    @Override
    public void startElement(
        String uri, String localName, String qName,
        Attributes attributes)
        throws SAXException {

      String attrs = "[";
      for(int i=0; i < attributes.getLength();i++) {
        attrs += attributes.getLocalName(i) + "=" +
            attributes.getValue(i)+ ",";
      }
      attrs = attrs.length() > 1 ?
          attrs.substring(0, attrs.length()-1) : attrs;
      attrs += "]";

      System.err.println("-> " + localName + " - " +
          uri + " - " + qName + " - " + attrs);
    }
```

```
@Override
public void endElement(String uri,
    String localName, String qName)
    throws SAXException {
  System.err.println("<- " + localName + " - " +
      uri + " - " + qName);
}

@Override
public void characters(char ch[], int start,
      int length) throws SAXException {
  String chars = new String(ch, start, length);
  if(!chars.trim().isEmpty())
    System.err.println("CHARS: " + chars);
}
}
```

For the code to read in the XML data, register the handler you tell a parser engine to read in the (listener), and start the parsing, you need to write the following:

```
ByteArrayInputStream bis =
      new ByteArrayInputStream(xml.getBytes());
InputSource is =
      new InputSource(bis);
SAXParserFactory factory =
      SAXParserFactory.newInstance();
SAXParser saxParser = factory.newSAXParser();
UserHandler userhandler = new UserHandler();
saxParser.parse(is, userhandler);
```

CHAPTER 9

Messaging with JMS

Messaging allows components from one or more applications running on one or more servers in possibly different network nodes to communicate in a loosely coupled way. This means that the senders and receivers don't have to know about each other—there must just be a common understanding about message format and content. In addition, the message processing happens asynchronously, which means senders and receivers don't have to be available at the same time, and the sender is not forced to wait until a message reaches its destination.

In Jakarta EE 8, messaging gets handled by the JMS (Java Messaging Service) technology. In this chapter, we will talk about messaging methodologies, about setting up the infrastructure needed for JMS to work, and about the ways components can send and receive JMS messages.

Messaging Paradigms

We have already pointed out that messaging couples senders and receivers only loosely. This refers to the message format, which must not depend on classes that only the sender or receiver knows about. But it also refers to temporal synchronicity, meaning that a receiver must not necessarily be reachable when the sender transmits a message.

For this to work, messaging requires the collaboration of three types of participants: message senders, message receivers, and a messaging provider, which mediates between the senders and receivers. A Jakarta EE 8 server is not required to include a messaging provider; in a corporate environment you will often have third-party messaging providers at work. It is, of course, not forbidden that a Jakarta EE 8 server provides its own messaging provider, and in fact the Glassfish 5.1 server we are using in this book contains the Oracle Glassfish Server Message Queue or Open Message Queue (OpenMQ) software. Both names refer to the same thing, apart from maybe some legal

© Peter Späth 2019
P. Späth, *Beginning Jakarta EE*, https://doi.org/10.1007/978-1-4842-5079-2_9

issues. We will be using that message provider for our first JMS steps, but you are free to use any other JMS-compliant messaging provider of your choice.

Messaging usually distinguishes between two messaging domains, which further limit the multitude of clients that can participate in messaging connections:

– **Point-to-Point Messaging or Queues**

   Here, the message sender—or several message senders—sends messages to a dedicated message queue, and at most one consumer is eligible to receive the message. The message receiver acknowledges the message, but the message sender is not required to wait until the message is actually consumed by the receiver. There is no temporal dependency—the receiver need not be active at the time the message is sent. It can receive the message later as well. A messaging provider usually allows for an unlimited number of queues to exist.

– **Publish/Subscribe Messaging or Topics**

   Here, one or more message senders send messages to a container-like structure called a *topic*. One or more receivers wishing to read messages that arrive in that topic *subscribe* to it. Usually, messages that arrive in the topic while a potential receiver is not active get lost for that receiver, unless the receiver maintains a *durable* subscription, which leads to topic messages "queuing up" for that receiver. Once such a durable receiver gets active again, it will receive all messages that arrived in the topic while the receiver was inactive. A messaging provider usually allows for an unlimited number of topics to exist.

Setting Up a Messaging Provider

If you start the Glassfish server 5.1, a messaging provider gets started for you automatically. By default, it listens on port 7676, and it is secured by a user–password combination "admin"/"admin."

Note   You can change the JMS user credentials and the port if in the web admin application `http://localhost:4848` you go to Configurations ➤ server-config ➤ Java Message Service ➤ JMS Hosts ➤ default_JMS_host.

In the web admin application `http://localhost:4848` at Resources ➤ JMS Resources ➤ Connection Factories ➤ jms/__defaultConnectionFactory you can find a connection factory that you can use from inside your code to connect to the messaging provider. This one was created by default for you, and we will use it for this book. Important is the value "java:comp/DefaultJMSConnectionFactory" at "Logical JNDI Name" (see Figure 9-1).

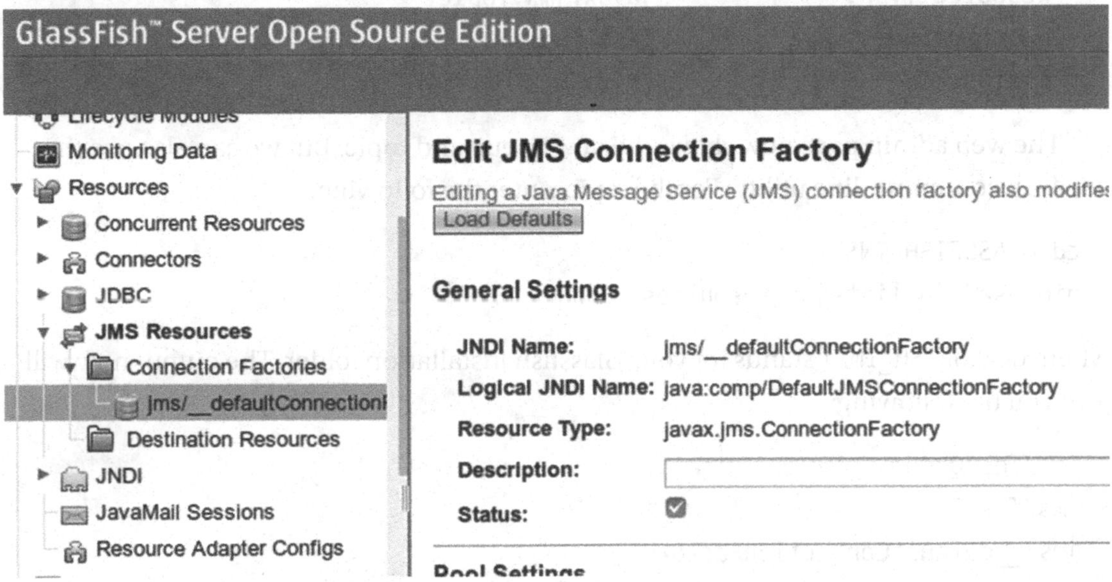

Figure 9-1. *JMS Connection Factory*

Creating Queues and Topics

To create a queue or topic within the Glassfish server's JMS provider, go to Resources ➤ JMS Resources ➤ Destination Resources and click on the "New..." button.

For the examples found in the rest of this chapter, create one queue, "TestQueue," and one topic, "TestTopic." The data for the queue are as follows:

```
JNDI Name:                 jms/TestQueue
Physical Destination Name: TestQueue
Resource Type:             javax.jms.Queue
Description:               Test Queue
Status:                    [x]
```

And for the topic, enter the following:

```
JNDI Name:                 jms/TestTopic
Physical Destination Name: TestTopic
Resource Type:             javax.jms.Topic
Description:               Test Topic
Status:                    [x]
```

The web admin page now shows the new queue and topic. But we can also use the asadmin command-line utility. For the topic, enter the following:

```
cd GLASSFISH_INST
bin/asadmin list-jms-resources
```

where GLASSFISH_INST stands for your Glassfish installation folder. The output now will give you the following:

```
jms/TestQueue
jms/TestTopic
jms/__defaultConnectionFactory
```

Submitting and Receiving Messages

To submit a message to a queue or a topic, you can use an injected JMSContext and JMS resources as follows:

```
@Singleton
@Startup
public class QueueSender {
    @Resource(lookup = "jms/TestQueue")
    private Queue queue;
```

```
  @Inject
  private JMSContext jmsContext;

  @PostConstruct
  public void go() {
    String msg = "My JMS Message";
    jmsContext.createProducer().send(queue, msg);
  }
}
```

You can use this methodology from every class managed by CDI, like an EJB of any type, a SOAP web service, a REST service, and so forth. This example uses a singleton EJB with a startup method (the @Startup and @PostConstruct annotations) to make testing as easy as possible. The lookup parameter in the resource injected must match the queue's JNDI name.

Doing this with a topic as the target instead of a queue looks very similar. We add a delay to the sending process to make sure any topic listener has registered itself before we send messages, as follows:

```
@Singleton
@Startup
public class TopicSender {

  @Resource(lookup = "jms/TestTopic")
  private Topic topic;

  @Inject
  private JMSContext jmsContext;

  @Resource
  private SessionContext context; // needed for the timer

  @PostConstruct
  public void go() {
    // schedule the timer with a 5 secs delay
    context.getTimerService().createSingleActionTimer(
        5000, new TimerConfig());
  }
```

```
@Timeout // called when the timer fires
public void programmaticTimeout(Timer timer) {
  String msg = "My JMS Message";
  jmsContext.createProducer().send(topic, msg);
}
}
```

Similar to the queue example, the `lookup` parameter of the `@Resource` annotation must match the JNDI name of the topic used to handle the message.

For receiving messages there exists a special EJB type we haven't talked about yet: message-driven beans. They allow us to implement message receivers in a very concise way. First, the receiver for the queue is can be written as follows:

```
@MessageDriven(
  activationConfig = {
    @ActivationConfigProperty(
      propertyName = "destinationType",
      propertyValue = "javax.jms.Queue")
  },
  mappedName = "jms/TestQueue")
public class TestQueueReceiverEJB
      implements MessageListener {

  @Resource
  private MessageDrivenContext mdc;

  @Override
  public void onMessage(Message message) {
    try {
      System.err.println("!#!#!#! QUEUE " +
            ((TextMessage)message).getText());
    } catch (JMSException e) {
      e.printStackTrace(System.err);
    }
  }
}
```

The whole magic lies in the @MessageDriven annotation. Here, we tell whether we are listening for messages from a queue or a topic and provide the JNDI name for the queue or topic. The rest gets done by implementing the MessageListener interface.

The receiver for listening for messages handled by a topic looks very similar, as follows:

```java
@MessageDriven(
  activationConfig = {
    @ActivationConfigProperty(
      propertyName = "destinationType",
      propertyValue = "javax.jms.Topic")
  },
  mappedName = "jms/TestTopic")
public class TestTopicReceiverEJB
    implements MessageListener {

  @Resource
  private MessageDrivenContext mdc;

  @Override
  public void onMessage(Message message) {
    try {
      System.err.println("!#!#!#! TOPIC " +
          ((TextMessage)message).getText());
    } catch (JMSException e) {
      e.printStackTrace(System.err);
    }
  }
}
```

Note   Examples you will find on the web often use the older JNDI lookup method for messaging-context retrieval and topic or queue acquisition—you can see we use injection for the same task to write shorter and more elegant code. But, if you like, the old methods are still valid.

Exercise 1

Create an EJB project with a queue and a topic sender and a queue and a topic receiver as described in this section.

Managing the Messaging Provider

Tools for managing the messaging provider are product specific, so there is no standard tool chain we can describe here. But since we are using the OpenMQ messaging provider included within Glassfish, we will take a closer look at the tools this one provides.

With every Glassfish installation, you will find the OpenMQ messaging provider tools in the "GLASSFISH_INST/mq" folder.

If with the Glassfish server running you start the imqadmin tool from this tools folder, you will see a window, as shown in Figure 9-2.

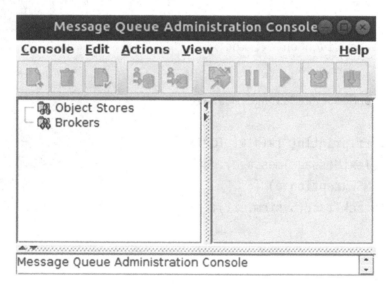

Figure 9-2. *"imqadmin" tool main window*

The JMS provider running inside Glassfish gets called "Broker" in this tool. To see it, we have to register it: click on "Brokers" and then on the "Add" icon (or Actions ➤ Add Broker in the menu). In the dialog that appears, enter the following:

```
Broker Label: Glassfish
Host:         localhost
Primary Port: 7676
Username:     admin
Password:     admin
```

See Figure 9-3.

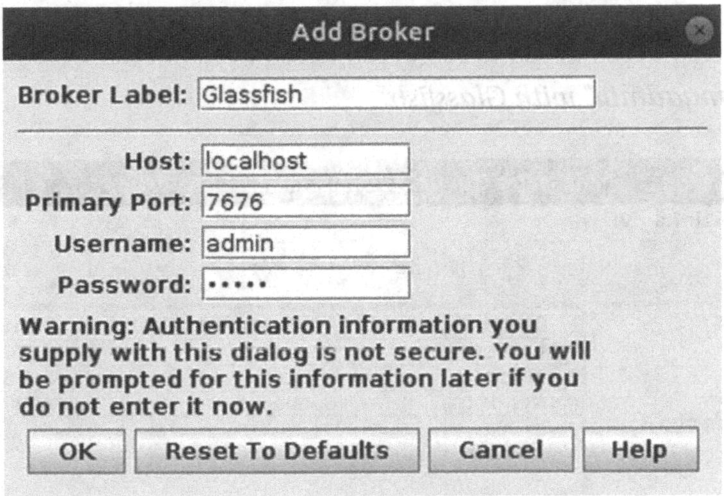

Figure 9-3. "imqadmin" new broker

Click "OK." The new broker gets shown, as in Figure 9-4. Click on "Glassfish" and then go to Actions ➤ Connect to Broker. Click on "Destinations" to see our test queue and test topic. This gets shown in Figure 9-5. To see some information about each of them, right-click on each and in the menu select Actions ➤ Properties....

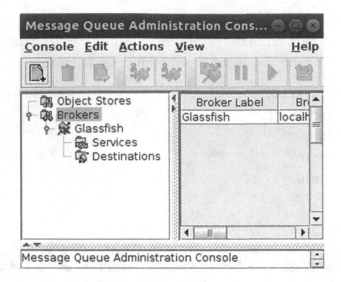

Figure 9-4. *"imqadmin" with Glassfish*

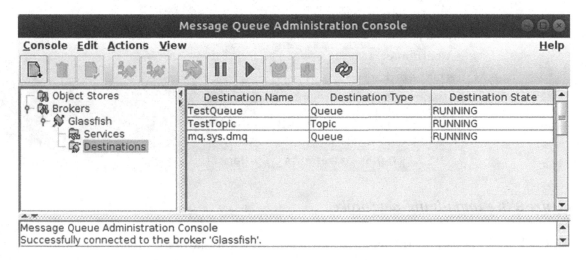

Figure 9-5. *Test queue and topic*

The other tools in the "mq/bin" folder are command-line utilities. All of them have a help facility included—just enter the command and append an "h" to see it. For our purposes, what is particularly interesting is the `imqusermgr` tool. It gets used to administer users for the messaging provider. The following listing shows some use cases for that tool:

```
# ###### List all users ########################
./imqusermgr list
# ->
# User repository for broker instance: imqbroker
# ---------------------------------------
# User Name     Group        Active State
# ---------------------------------------
# admin         admin        true
# guest         anonymous    true

# ###### Change user password #################
./imqusermgr update -u admin -p QW34rtz

# ###### Add new user #########################
./imqusermgr add -u Spongebob -p QW34rt7 -g admin

# ###### Delete user ##########################
./imqusermgr delete -u Spongebob
```

## CHAPTER 10

Maintaining State Consistency with JTA Transactions

Transactions are about units of work, which either succeed in total or produce no result at all. This sounds easy at first, but consider cases where databases are involved, or queues and topics inside an associated messaging provider. Needless to say, in cases where we consider a transaction to have failed, rolling back database changes and messages in a topic or queue can become a complex matter if many tables and queues or topics are involved. The story becomes even more complex if the parties involved run on different network nodes, in which case we are talking about *distributed* transactions.

The Java Transaction API or JTA is a specification that allows parties involved in transactions or distributed transactions, together with a transaction manager, to run in the way desired, with the ability to define units of work that can be committed if they succeed, or rolled back in total in case important business workflow steps fail.

Transaction managers often follow the *two-phase commit protocol*. In the first phase, the transaction manager polls each party of the transaction, and if any of them cannot commit, rolls back the sub-transactions in question. In the second phase, the transaction manager checks whether any party reported a negative result and decides then whether the whole transaction gets committed or rolled back.

© Peter Späth 2019

P. Späth, *Beginning Jakarta EE*, https://doi.org/10.1007/978-1-4842-5079-2_10

Modularization in Time: Transaction Demarcation

Transactions can be considered as modules in the time domain. The responsibility of a transaction is to take exactly one of two possible decisions:

- The transaction can be committed. Once committed, all participants of the transaction are considered to have successfully finished their work. After the commit, the transaction is over and new transactions can be entered.

- The transaction must be rolled back. All participants of the transaction must do their own rollback. After a rollback, the transaction is over and a new transaction (including repeating the failed transaction) can be entered.

Transactions are said to draw a demarcation line between activities that are considered part of the transaction and activities that run outside the transaction. A transaction manager must allow the definition of which activities run inside and which run outside the demarcation line.

Consider, for example, an ATM with four parties: communicating with the accounts database, communicating with the money dispenser, communicating with the receipt printer, and registering performance figures in some database. Surely from a customer's point of view the accounts database, the money dispenser, and the receipt printer are part of the transaction—if any of them fail the whole transaction must be rolled back. A problem with the performance figures database, on the other hand, is not a severe problem, and the customer probably doesn't care about such problems. The performance figure registration thus lies outside the transaction demarcation, and all the other activities described lie inside.

Local and Distributed Transactions

A *local* transaction requires involved parties to run within one process. Local transactions are easier to handle for transaction managers, since no interprocess communication is needed for the transaction handling.

In contrast to that, interprocess communications get handled by XA transactions (eXtended Architecture). Not all database and JMS products are able to handle XA transactions—you would have to consult their feature list to check.

The ACID Paradigm

If databases are involved in transactions, they follow a set of properties in order to guarantee data operation validity. This gets described by the acronym ACID:

- **Atomicity**

    A set of related database operations fulfilling a dedicated business case must be treated as a unit. The statements composing the operation set must either succeed in total or fail completely. This atomicity must be assured in case of software failures, hardware failures, network breakdowns, power failures, and so on.

- **Consistency**

    Database consistency is given if database operations during a transaction cannot possibly leave the database in a corrupted state. This includes constraints, table relations (cascades), and triggers.

- **Isolation**

    During a transaction, different tables and database meta-information undergo consecutive state transitions. The isolation level is a configurable property that defines the visibility of such changes to other database clients. The isolation must be configured in such a way that the database is in a usable state for outside users both during and after the transaction.

- **Durability**

    After the commit, the new state must be able to endure software and hardware problems, including crashes and power shortages.

The transaction management governed by JTA will ensure that all ACID properties are guaranteed for databases participating in transactions.

Transaction Managers

Normally you don't have to care about installing or configuring a transaction manager in a Jakarta EE server—any server compliant with the Jakarta EE specification has a transaction manager included and properly configured.

What you must do is to decide what types of transactions a component or resource supports. First, you have to decide whether you use container-managed transactions or bean-managed transactions. We will talk about this distinction later in this chapter. The other distinction is between XA transactions for distributed components and local transactions. This has to be configured for each resource independently. Do you remember the JDBC connection pool configuration we talked about in Chapter 6? There, we wrote the following to create a pool:

```
./asadmin create-jdbc-connection-pool \
    --datasourceclassname \
      org.apache.derby.jdbc.ClientDataSource \
    --restype javax.sql.DataSource \
    --property \
      portNumber=1527:password=pw715:user=user0:
      serverName=localhost:databaseName=calypso:
      securityMechanism=3 \
    Calypso
```

Actually, because of the `-- restype javax.sql.DataSource` this created a non-XA database resource for local transactions only. If we needed XA transactions, we'd have to use `-- restype javax.sql.XADataSource` instead. Similarly, there are XA and non-XA connection factories for JMS resources. You can see it if you enter the administration web application at `http://localhost:4848`. There at Resources ➤ JMS Resources ➤ Connection Factories ➤ (For example) `jms/__defaultConnectionFactory` you will see a field called "Transaction Support" with possible values "XATransaction," "LocalTransaction," and "NoTransaction." See Figure 10-1, in the bottom input field.

Also, for JPA-enabled projects we had to provide a `persistence.xml` file inside the `META-INF` directory for connecting the JPA project to a data source. An example was the following:

```
<persistence xmlns="http://java.sun.com/xml/ns/persistence"
  xmlns:xsi="http://www.w3.org/2001/XMLSchema-instance"
  xsi:schemaLocation=
      "http://java.sun.com/xml/ns/persistence
      persistence_1_0.xsd"
  version="1.0">
    <persistence-unit name="default"
        transaction-type="JTA">
      <jta-data-source>jdbc/Calypso</jta-data-source>
      <exclude-unlisted-classes>false
      </exclude-unlisted-classes>
      <properties />
    </persistence-unit>
</persistence>
```

Because of the `transaction-type = "JTA"` the JPA project uses JTA transactions. So, don't forget to write the attribute this way if you create JPA projects and need to use transactions.

Edit JMS Connection Factory

Editing a Java Message Service (JMS) connection factory also modifies the a
[Load Defaults]

General Settings

JNDI Name:	jms/__defaultConnectionFactory
Logical JNDI Name:	java:comp/DefaultJMSConnectionFactory
Resource Type:	javax.jms.ConnectionFactory
Description:	
Status:	☑

Pool Settings

Initial and Minimum Pool Size: `1` Connections
Minimum and initial number of connectio

Maximum Pool Size: `250` Connections
Maximum number of connections that ca

Pool Resize Quantity: `2` Connections
Number of connections to be removed w

Idle Timeout: `300` Seconds
Maximum time that connection can rema

Max Wait Time: `60000` Milliseconds
Amount of time caller waits before conne

On Any Failure: ☐ **Close All Connections**
Close all connections and reconnect on f

Transaction Support: `XATransaction ▼`

Figure 10-1. JMS transactionality

Container-Managed Transactions

With container-managed transactions you have the smallest amount of work to be done for enabling transactionality in your processes. As the name says, the transaction demarcation gets handled by the container, more precisely by the EJB container, and as such applies for both session- and message-driven beans.

Consider the example from the JPA chapter, where we talked about the following EJB for handling the members of a club named "Calypso" we own:

```
@Singleton
public class MemberDAO {
    @PersistenceContext
    private EntityManager em;

    public List<Member> allMembers() {
      [ return list of all memebers from the DB ]
    }

    public Member getMember(int id) {
      [ return one member from the DB ]
    }

    public int newMember(String lastName,
            String firstName, String birthday) {
      Member m = new Member();
      [ set member properties ]
      em.persist(m);
      em.flush(); // needed to get the ID
      return m.getId();
    }

    public void updateMember(String lastName,
            String firstName, String birthday, int id) {
      Member m = em.find(Member.class, id);
      [ set member properties ]
      em.persist(m);
    }
```

```
    public void deleteMember(int id) {
      [ delete member from the DB ]
    }
}
```

See Chapter 6 for the details.

Now, all we have to do to add basic container-managed transactionality is to annotate the class as follows:

```
@Singleton
@TransactionManagement(TransactionManagementType.CONTAINER)
public class MemberDAO {
    ...
}
```

In fact, we don't even have to do that, because `TransactionManagementType.CONTAINER` is the default, so without knowing it we already used transactions in Chapter 6! What happened is that if the client—that is, the code that invoked any method of the EJB—runs itself in a transactional context, the EJB method will participate in that transaction. If, however, the client doesn't start a transaction before an EJB method gets called, the container will start a new transaction before the method body gets executed, and it finishes the transaction immediately after the method returns. The transaction is assumed to have succeeded (with a subsequent "commit"), unless the method `setRollbackOnly()` of the session context gets called. We first inject the context into the EJB implementation as follows:

```
@Singleton
@TransactionManagement(TransactionManagementType.CONTAINER)
public class MemberDAO {
    @Resource private SessionContext ejbContext;
    ...
}
```

And then, if a rollback for the transaction is needed, we write the following:

```
    ...
    ejbContext.setRollbackOnly();
    ...
```

So far, this kind of transaction control gets applied to all EJB methods, but it is possible to tune that on a per-method basis. What we must do is add the annotation @TransactionAttribute with one parameter from one of the six constants—REQUIRED, REQUIRES_NEW, MANDATORY, NOT_SUPPORTED, SUPPORTS, or NEVER–from the class TransactionAttributeType. For example:

```
...
import javax.ejb.TransactionAttribute;
import static javax.ejb.TransactionAttributeType.*;

@Singleton
public class MemberDAO {
    ...

    @TransactionAttribute(REQUIRED)
    public List<Member> allMembers() {
      ...
    }

    @TransactionAttribute(NEVER)
    public Member getMember(int id) {
      ...
    }

    ...
}
```

The characteristics of all the possible transaction attribute types are as follows:

- **REQUIRED**

    This is the default; if the EJB uses container-managed transactions and you don't specify an @TransactionAttribute for a method, REQUIRED is assumed for that method. If the client runs itself in a transactional context, the EJB method will participate in that transaction. If the client didn't start a transaction before the EJB method was called, the container will start a new transaction before the method body gets executed, and it finishes the transaction immediately after the method returns.

- **REQUIRES_NEW**

  If the client is not running in a transaction itself, the container will start a new transaction before the method body gets executed, and it finishes the transaction immediately after the method returns. Otherwise, the client's transaction gets temporarily suspended, a new transaction gets created for the method execution, and after the method finishes the client's transaction gets resumed.

- **MANDATORY**

  The client must be running inside its own transaction context, and the EJB method execution participates in that transaction. If the client does not have a transaction, a `TransactionRequiredException` will be thrown.

- **NOT_SUPPORTED**

  If the client runs inside a transaction, it gets temporarily suspended. The EJB method then runs outside any transaction context. After the method returns, the client's transaction gets resumed (if applicable). Use this type if transactionality is not needed and you want improved performance.

- **SUPPORTS**

  Only if the client is running in its own transaction, it will continue to use that one while the method gets executed. Otherwise, no transaction gets used or created.

- **NEVER**

  The client must not run in its own transaction. Otherwise, throw a `RemoteException` exception. The EJB method runs outside any transaction.

Bean-Managed Transactions

If you add a transaction type "bean" to an EJB as follows:

```
@Singleton  // or @Stateful / @Stateless
@TransactionManagement(TransactionManagementType.BEAN)
```

```
public class SomeEjb {
    ...
}
```

the EJB container stops taking care of the transactionality.

Note   Usually container-managed transactions are easier to code compared
to bean-managed transactions. However, with container-managed transactions
EJB methods get associated with exactly one transaction or none at all. If
during a method execution you need several consecutive transactions, you *must*
use bean-managed transactions.

If the EJB container does not help with transaction demarcation, we have to do it
programmatically, and to this aim we need an instance of the UserTransaction interface
(package javax.transaction). We get one via injection, as follows:

```
@Singleton  // or @Stateful / @Stateless
@TransactionManagement(TransactionManagementType.BEAN)
public class SomeEjb {
    @Resource UserTransaction transa;

    ...
}
```

From there, we are able to define the transaction demarcation inside EJB methods,
as follows:

```
    ...
    transa.begin();      // -- start the transaction
    ...
    if(everythingOK) {
      transa.commit();   // -- commit the transaction
    }else{
      transa.rollback(); // -- rollback the transaction
    }
    ...
```

> **Note**   If you use stateful session EJBs, you can leave the transaction open at the
> end of the method execution and postpone a `commit()` or `rollback()` to a later
> point. This is another advantage of bean-managed transactions—they can span
> several method invocations for stateful EJBs.

If you use bean-managed transactions, using the methods getRollbackOnly()
and setRollbackOnly() on the session context is not allowed. Those are for
container-managed transactions only.

Observing Transaction for Stateful EJBs

Only if you use container-managed transactions and only in the case of stateful session
EJBs can you let your EJB implement the SessionSynchronization interface and then
react on transaction boundaries, as follows:

```
...
import javax.ejb.SessionSynchronization;
...
@Stateful
@TransactionManagement(TransactionManagementType.CONTAINER)
public class SomeEjb implements SessionSynchronization {
    @Override
    public void afterBegin() {
        // A transaction has started
        ...
    }

    @Override
    public void beforeCompletion() {
        // A transaction is about to be finished
        ...
    }
```

```
@Override
public void afterCompletion(boolean committed) {
    // A transaction has finished
    ...
}
}
```

Transaction Monitoring

The web administration application has a facility to monitor transactions. To use it, we first have to enable it: go to the web administration console

```
http://localhost:4848
```

Then, navigate to Configurations ➤ server-config ➤ Monitoring, and switch the "Transaction Service" level to "HIGH" (see Figure 10-2).

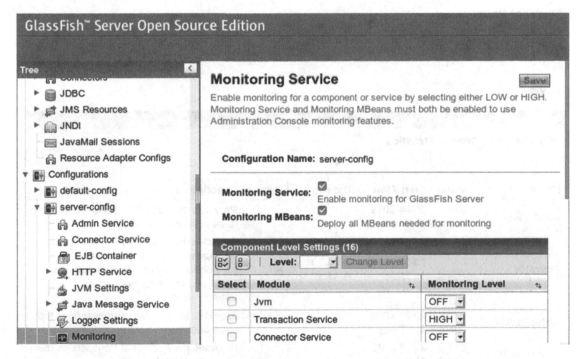

Figure 10-2. Transaction monitoring setting

Click on the "Save" button to register the changed configuration. The transaction figures can then be seen in the admin console at "Monitoring Data." Click on the "Server" link in the column "Monitoring Data" (see Figure 10-3).

Monitoring

View and manage the monitoring information for GlassFish Server instances.

Monitoring (1)			
Instance Name	**Cluster Name**	**Action**	**View Monitoring Data**
server	N/A	Configure Monitoring	Application , Server , Resources

Figure 10-3. *Transaction monitoring link*

This will then show the transaction service statistics (see Figure 10-4).

Server Monitoring   Refresh

Click **Configure Monitoring** and enable monitoring for a component or service by selecting either LOW or HIGH. See the **Online Help** for more information.

Instance Name: server

View : [▾]

Monitor (5 Statistics)					
▽ **Transaction Service Statistics**					
Name	**Value**	**Start Time**	**Last Sample Time**	**Details**	**Description**
CommittedCount	0 count	25.04.2019 11:37:28	--	--	Provides the number of transactions that have been committed.
ActiveIds		25.04.2019 11:37:28	25.04.2019 11:41:37	--	Provides the IDs of the transactions that are currently active a.k.a. in-flight transactions. Every such transaction can be rolled back after freezing the transaction service.
RolledbackCount	0 count	25.04.2019 11:37:28	--	--	Provides the number of transactions that have been rolled back.
ActiveCount	0 count	25.04.2019 11:37:28	--	--	Provides the number of transactions that are currently active.
State	False	25.04.2019 11:37:28	25.04.2019 11:41:37	--	Indicates if the transaction service has been frozen.

Figure 10-4. *Transaction statistics*

The same data can then be viewed via the REST administration interface (only after being configured as described!). Enter the following in a terminal (no line break and no spaces after server/):

```
curl -X GET -H "Accept: application/json" \
http://localhost:4848/monitoring/domain/server/
    transaction-service | jq .
```

Remember the backslash is just for escaping the following line break—remove it if you enter everything in one line. The output should be similar to the following:

```
{
  "message": "",
  "command": "Monitoring Data",
  "exit_code": "SUCCESS",
  "extraProperties": {
    "entity": {
      "activecount": {
        "unit": "count",
        "lastsampletime": 1556189242353,
        "name": "ActiveCount",
        "count": 0,
        "description": "Provides the number of
            transactions that are currently active.",
        "starttime": 1556189216488
      },
      "activeids": {
        "unit": "List",
        "current": "",
        "lastsampletime": 1556190928188,
        "name": "ActiveIds",
        "description": "Provides the IDs of the
            transactions that are currently active a.k.a.
            in-flight transactions. Every such
            transaction can be rolled back after freezing
            the transaction service.",
```

```
      "starttime": 1556189216488
    },
    "committedcount": {
      "unit": "count",
      "lastsampletime": 1556189242353,
      "name": "CommittedCount",
      "count": 7,
      "description": "Provides the number of transactions
          that have been committed.",
      "starttime": 1556189216484
    },
    "rolledbackcount": {
      "unit": "count",
      "lastsampletime": -1,
      "name": "RolledbackCount",
      "count": 0,
      "description": "Provides the number of transactions
          that have been rolled back.",
      "starttime": 1556189216484
    },
    "state": {
      "unit": "String",
      "current": "False",
      "lastsampletime": 1556190928188,
      "name": "State",
      "description": "Indicates if the transaction
          service has been frozen.",
      "starttime": 1556189216488
    }
  },
  "childResources": {}
  }
}
```

As is often the case in Java, times are milliseconds since the epoch 1970-01-01T00:00:00. To make the date readable, write a short Java program as follows:

```
public class Main {
  public static void main(String[] args){
    System.out.println(
      new java.util.Date(1556189216488) );
  }
}
```

Or if you have Groovy installed, enter the following in a terminal:

```
groovy -e "println new java.util.Date(1556189216488)"
```

Note   To freeze or unfreeze the transaction service, enter `./asadmin freeze-transaction-service` or `./asadmin unfreeze-transaction-service` in a terminal inside the "GLASSFISH_INST/bin" folder.

## CHAPTER 11

Securing Jakarta EE Applications

Security plays an important role in Jakarta EE applications. This stems from the fact that communication with the outside world is an integral part of a server application, be it web access for JSF or REST applications, web services, remotely accessible EJBs, an email interface, and so on.

But it is also important to avoid someone's breaking into your system because the administrative interfaces of the Jakarta EE8 server (Glassfish in our case) are not protected, or the database or the JMS provider is not secured. In this chapter, we will talk about both security realms—application protection and securing administrative interfaces.

Securing Administrative Access

There is no set administrative security specification, so each Jakarta EE 8 application server product has its own idea of how to ensure administrative interfaces can't be hacked from outside. You have to consult the server manual to see how this can be done. However, in our case we are using the Glassfish server (version 5.1), and so in the following paragraphs we will spend a few words on administrative security for this particular Jakarta EE 8 server.

Securing the ASADMIN Tool

We learned that with the asadmin command from the Glassfish bin directory we can start and stop the application server and the JavaDB database, change configuration settings, administer resources, and issue commands that control the server's internal

© Peter Späth 2019
P. Späth, *Beginning Jakarta EE*, https://doi.org/10.1007/978-1-4842-5079-2_11

functions. The same tool can be used to change security settings, to deploy and undeploy applications, and to change the monitoring and logging settings. It is even possible to use asadmin to administer Glassfish servers running on remote hosts.

This versatility makes it necessary to secure the server access via asadmin. For a fresh Glassfish installation as described in this book, there is only a single user named "admin" with an empty password. This configuration makes asadmin skip authorization and take that "admin" user by default. So, the first thing we want to do is to give this admin user a decent password. In a terminal, enter the following ("GLASSFISH_INST" is your installation folder):

```
cd GLASSFISH_INST
bin/asadmin change-admin-password
```

You will then be asked for the admin user name. Press Enter to accept the default. Press Enter again when asked for the password (since it is empty). Then, enter the new password twice. To see that the new password got registered, enter the following:

```
bin/asadmin
asadmin> login
```

You will then be asked for the user name and the password. Enter "admin" and the password you have just set. If successfully logged in using the new password, the output of the login command will tell you the following:

```
Command login executed successfully.
```

Eclipse uses administrative access to the Glassfish server for deployment and other purposes, so we have to register the changed administrator password inside Eclipse. Open the "Servers" view, then double-click on the Glassfish server entry. The "Overview" page will appear, as shown in Figure 11-1.

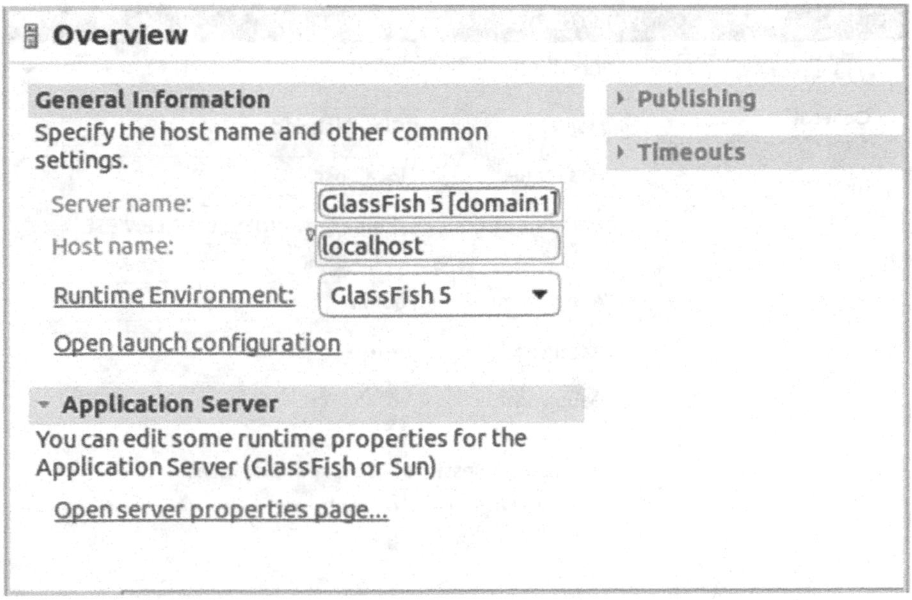

Figure 11-1. *Eclipse server overview*

Click on the link "Open server properties page..." and on the dialog that then appears navigate to the "GlassFish" menu item. On the dialog page enter corresponding entries for "Admin name" and "Admin password." See Figure 11-2. Click the "Apply and Close" button.

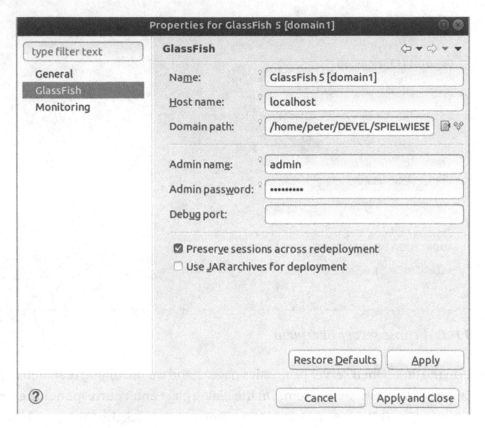

Figure 11-2. *Eclipse server administration*

Securing the Web Administrator Console

Setting the `asadmin` password as described in the preceding paragraphs automatically also sets a password for the web administration console at `http://localhost:4848`. Entering the console in your browser, you will now be asked for the new password. See Figure 11-3. Enter "admin" as the user name, and then enter the password.

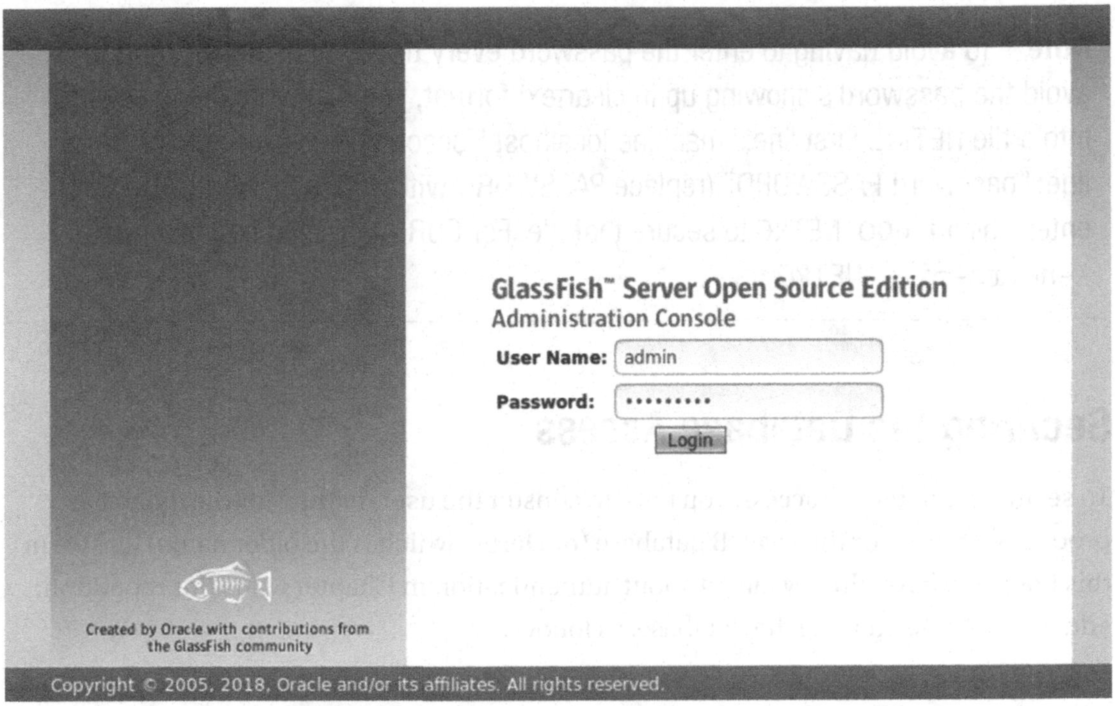

Figure 11-3. *Web administration with password*

Securing the Administrative REST Service

Because the REST interface used for administration uses the same HTTP connector as the web administration console, the same authentication restrictions apply. So, by adding a password to the "admin" user as described for the asadmin tool, the REST interface gets secured as well, and we must supply the same credentials to use it as we do for the asadmin tool and the web administration console.

To use the command-line utility CURL, we have to add user and password as follows:

```
curl -uadmin:PASSWORD [rest of the curl command]
```

The PASSWORD needs to be replaced with the password we assigned to the "admin" user. If you omit :PASSWORD, the curl command will prompt for the password instead.

> **Note**   To avoid having to enter the password every time you use CURL, and to
> avoid the password's showing up in cleartext format, you can write the password
> into a file NETRC. First line: "machine localhost," second line: "user admin," third
> line: "password PASSWORD" (replace PASSWORD with your password). Then,
> enter chmod 600 NETRC to secure that file. For CURL, you then can use curl
> --netrc-file NETRC ....

Securing the Database Access

To secure the database access, you have to consult the user manual for the database
product you use. For the JavaDB database (or Derby, which is the older name) we use in
this book, we have already talked about authentication in Chapter 6. Just for repetition:
add a user while creating the database, as follows:

```
cd [GLASSFISH_INST]
cd javadb/bin
# start the DB client
./ij
ij> connect 'jdbc:derby://localhost:1527/database-name;
    create=true;user=user-name';
```

(Enter the ij command in one line without spaces in front of create=.) Replace
database-name with the name of the database you want to create, and user-name with
the user name of your choice. The database now is created with an owner named "user-
name" (or whatever your choice for the user name was). To add a password for this user,
enter the following (one line):

```
ij> call SYSCS_UTIL.SYSCS_CREATE_USER('user-name', 'pw715');
```

The pw715 is the password of the user; of course, you should use your own password and user. To make sure everything works as expected, restart the database for the authentication to start working, as follows:

```
cd [GLASSFISH_INST]
cd bin
./asadmin stop-database
./asadmin start-database
```

The database credentials, for example, have to be entered in the JDBC connection pools we need for JPA (see Chapter 6).

Securing the JMS Messaging

The JMS messaging provider included within the Jakarta EE 8 Glassfish server comes preconfigured with two users: an administrative user admin with password "admin" and a guest user named guest using password "guest." The admin user belongs to the "admin" group and gets used to configure, administer, and manage message brokers. The guest user belongs to group "anonymous" and is supposed to have limited access rights.

The first thing we do to improve messaging security is to disable the guest user. To do so, in a terminal enter the following (replace GLASSFISH_INST with the installation directory):

```
cd GLASSFISH_INST/mq/bin
./imqusermgr update -u guest -a false
```

You can check the new user database by entering ./imqusermgr list. This should now print something like the following:

```
User repository for broker instance: imqbroker
----------------------------------------
User Name     Group          Active State
----------------------------------------
admin         admin          true
guest         anonymous      false
```

Next, we change the password for the admin user to prohibit unauthorized access to the messaging provider, as follows:

```
./imqusermgr update -u admin -p PW3194
```

Of course, you must choose your own password.

The new admin user password needs to be entered in the "JMS Host" configuration: open the web administration console at http://localhost:4848, navigate to Configurations ➤ server-config ➤ Java Message Service ➤ JMS Hosts ➤ default_JMS_ host. Update the admin password there (see Figure 11-4). Don't forget to click the "Save" button.

Edit JMS Host   Save   Cancel

The Java Message Service (JMS) host specifies the system where the JMS service is running.
Load Defaults

Configuration Name: server-config

Name: default_JMS_host
Host: localhost
                     Name or IP address; if name, must contain only alphanumeric,
                     underscore, dash, or dot characters
Port: ${JMS_PROVIDER_PORT}
                     Listener port for servicing JMS requests
Admin Username: *   admin
                     User name for maintaining the JMS service; can be up to 255
                     characters, must contain only alphanumeric, underscore, dash, or dot
                     characters
Admin Password: *   ••••••
                     Password for JMS administrator
Confirm New Password: * ••••••

***Figure 11-4.** Update JMS host*

Next, we create a dedicated user for JMS operations. In a terminal, enter the following:

```
./imqusermgr add -u user1 -p PW36t3 -g user
```

Instead of PW36t3, choose your own password. This creates a user named "user1" belonging to the "user" group. Update your connection factory to use exactly that user: In the web administration console at http://localhost:4848 navigate to Resources ➤ JMS Resources ➤ Connection Factories ➤ jms/- defaultConnectionFactory (or whatever connection factory you are using from your JMS application) and add the following as "Additional Properties":

```
UserName  =  user1
Password  =  PW36t3
```

(Use your password for that user.) See Figure 11-5. If you like, you can add appropriate descriptions for these fields. Don't forget to click the "Save" button after you enter the properties.

Additional Properties (2)		
Select	Name	Value	Description
☐	Password	PW36t3	
☐	UserName	user1	

Figure 11-5. *New JMS operating user*

Exercise 1

Update the JMS sample application from Chapter 9 to use the "user1" credentials as described in this section.

Securing Web Applications

Caution   Make sure you are using the newest build of JDK 8. Older builds lead to some issues with security providers.

Securing web applications consists of the following measures:

- Switching to using SSL and https:// URLs.

- Restricting access to the complete web application or some parts of it in such a way that only users who have authenticated themselves can access the pages.

265

For SSL, the Jakarta EE 8 Glassfish server out of the box provides an SSL-enabled HTTP connector. If for normal applications the standard URL reads `http://localhost:8080/[path]`, you can just as well use `https://localhost:8181/[path]`. The included server certificate is a self-signed certificate, and your browser will complain about it, but for development purposes it is totally acceptable to use it.

The question is, if we have some web application at `http://localhost:8080/my-web-app` and the user can arbitrarily switch back and forth to and from `https://localhost:8181/my-web-app`, how can we force the user to use the more secure HTTPS protocol? One answer would be to remove the non-SSL HTTP listener or disable the non-SSL network listener from the configuration via the web administration console. However, there is also a more fine-grained way to configure applications to draw this distinction based on URL patterns. We will be talking about it shortly.

First, we have to enable security in a server-wide configuration setting. To achieve this, in the web administration console at `http://localhost:4848` go to Configurations ➤ server-config ➤ Security and enable the "Security Manager" checkbox (see Figure 11-6).

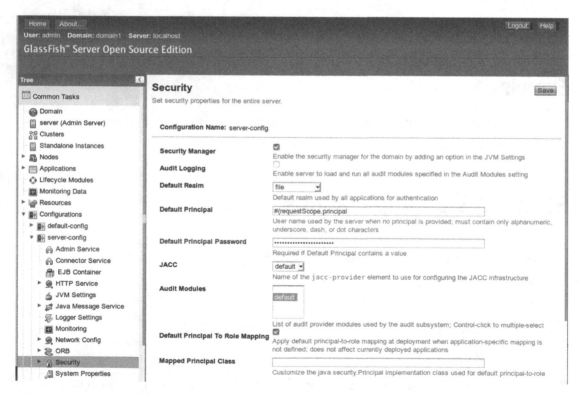

Figure 11-6. *Enable security manager*

Securing web applications by installing URL-based access restrictions is tightly coupled to the concepts of users, groups, roles, authentication, and authorization, which we first want to explain:

- **User**

  A user is an individual person or an application with an identity. For any particular user, an authentication mechanism can be defined, which the user can use to identify himself or herself (no other users!).

- **Group**

  A group is a set of users. A group has an ID (or group name) itself. A particular user can belong to zero or more groups.

- **Authentication**

  An authentication mechanism can be used to prove a user's identity. Unless a security breach happens, a user can only authenticate himself or herself, not other users. A user may have a password to authenticate himself or herself, but authentication by other means like certificates is also possible.

- **Authorization**

  An authorization is a set of activities a user is allowed to perform once authenticated. Authorizations may also be given to groups, which means any user of that group is given that authorization once authenticated.

- **Role**

  A role is an abstract name for a permission. In your application you use roles to specify what can be done or not. A mapping between roles and users or between roles and groups happens declaratively in some server vendor–specific way.

In the rest of this section, we will revisit the Gregorian calendar to Julian day converter we talked about earlier in this book. We have a greetings page that asks for the Gregorian date (our usual calendar system), a "Submit" button for performing the calculation, and another page showing the result of the calculation. We add a third page, which should be accessible only for special administrative users who must authenticate themselves, and we want this admin page to automatically switch to the HTTPS protocol.

We first add a user "AdminUser" to the server's user database. The user has to be assigned to the "ApplAdmin" group. Start the web administration console at `http://localhost:4848`. Navigate to Configurations ➤ serverconfig ➤ Security ➤ Realms ➤ file. Click on "Manage Users" button. On the page that then appears, click on "New...," then enter the following:

```
User ID:     AdminUser
Group List:  ApplAdmin
Password:    pW41834
```

Click "OK." This new user gets stored in a file inside the server's file-tree structure—this is where the name "file" realm comes from.

Contrary to the original `Julian` project, where we had an extra project just for the calculation, this time we put everything into a single project. To this aim, create a new Maven project with the following coordinates:

```
Group-Id:     book.jakarta8
Artifact-Id:  julian-gui-secure
Version:      0.0.1-SNAPSHOT
Packaging:    war
```

And also use `book.jakarta8.julianguisecure` as a Java base package. As usual, make sure the project correctly uses Java 8. The complete `pom.xml` file reads as follows:

```xml
<project xmlns=
    "http://maven.apache.org/POM/4.0.0"
  xmlns:xsi=
    "http://www.w3.org/2001/XMLSchema-instance"
  xsi:schemaLocation=
    "http://maven.apache.org/POM/4.0.0
     http://maven.apache.org/xsd/maven-4.0.0.xsd">
  <modelVersion>4.0.0</modelVersion>

  <groupId>book.jakarta8</groupId>
  <artifactId>julian-gui-secure</artifactId>
  <version>0.0.1-SNAPSHOT</version>
  <packaging>war</packaging>
```

```xml
<name>julian-gui-secure</name>
<url>http://maven.apache.org</url>

<properties>
  <project.build.sourceEncoding>
    UTF-8
  </project.build.sourceEncoding>
 </properties>

<dependencies>
  <dependency>
    <groupId>javax</groupId>
    <artifactId>javaee-api</artifactId>
    <version>8.0</version>
  </dependency>
  <dependency>
    <groupId>junit</groupId>
    <artifactId>junit</artifactId>
    <version>3.8.1</version>
    <scope>test</scope>
  </dependency>
</dependencies>

<build>
  <plugins>
    <plugin>
      <artifactId>maven-compiler-plugin</artifactId>
      <configuration>
        <source>1.8</source>
        <target>1.8</target>
      </configuration>
    </plugin>
  </plugins>
</build>
</project>
```

Convert the project to the faceted form (if it is not already). As facets, add the following:

```
Dynamic Web Module 4.0
Java 1.8
JavaScript 1.0
JavaServer Faces 2.3
```

Add a folder, "src/main/webapp/WEB-INF," and inside add four files: beans.xml, faces-config.xml, glassfish-web.xml, and web.xml. The beans.xml file must stay empty. As the contents of faces-config.xml write the following:

```
<?xml version="1.0" encoding="UTF-8"?>
<faces-config
  xmlns=
    "http://xmlns.jcp.org/xml/ns/javaee"
  xmlns:xsi=
    "http://www.w3.org/2001/XMLSchema-instance"
  xsi:schemaLocation=
    "http://xmlns.jcp.org/xml/ns/javaee
     http://xmlns.jcp.org/xml/ns/javaee/
             web-facesconfig_2_3.xsd"
    version="2.3">

    <application>
      <resource-bundle>
        <base-name>
          julian.web.WebMessages</base-name>
        <var>bundle</var>
      </resource-bundle>
      <locale-config>
        <default-locale>en</default-locale>
        <!--  <supported-locale>es</supported-locale> -->
      </locale-config>
    </application>
</faces-config>
```

(Let there be no line break and no spaces after javaee/). The file glassfish-web.xml for now should read as follows:

```
<?xml version="1.0" encoding="UTF-8"?>
<!DOCTYPE glassfish-web-app PUBLIC
  "-//GlassFish.org//DTD GlassFish Application Server
  3.1 Servlet 3.0//EN"
  "http://glassfish.org/dtds/glassfish-web-app_3_0-1.dtd">
<glassfish-web-app error-url="">
    <class-loader delegate="true"/>
</glassfish-web-app>
```

And for the central web application configuration file web.xml, we write the following:

```
<?xml version="1.0" encoding="UTF-8"?>
<web-app
  xmlns:xsi=
    "http://www.w3.org/2001/XMLSchema-instance"
  xmlns=
    "http://xmlns.jcp.org/xml/ns/javaee"
  xsi:schemaLocation=
    "http://xmlns.jcp.org/xml/ns/javaee
    http://xmlns.jcp.org/xml/ns/javaee/web-app_4_0.xsd"
  id="WebApp_ID"
  version="4.0">

  <welcome-file-list>
    <welcome-file>greeting.xhtml</welcome-file>
  </welcome-file-list>
  <servlet>
    <servlet-name>Faces Servlet</servlet-name>
    <servlet-class>
      javax.faces.webapp.FacesServlet
    </servlet-class>
    <load-on-startup>1</load-on-startup>
  </servlet>
```

```
<servlet-mapping>
  <servlet-name>Faces Servlet</servlet-name>
  <url-pattern>*.xhtml</url-pattern>
</servlet-mapping>
</web-app>
```

Create a file (including directories) called src/main/resources/julian/web/WebMessages.properties, and as its contents write the following:

```
welcome=This is a Gregorian date to Julian day converter.
instructions=Enter a Gregorian UTC date in the form \
    yyyy-mm-dd hh:mm:ss (use 24hr format), then submit.
label_gregorianDate=Gregorian Date:
label_response=The Julian Day Reads:
submit=Submit
back=Back
```

These are the localized texts we use inside the pages. We need a single Java class as a front-end controller to be injected as a JSF bean, as follows:

```
package book.jakarta8.julianguisecure;

import java.io.Serializable;
import java.time.LocalDateTime;
import java.time.ZoneId;
import java.time.format.DateTimeFormatter;
import java.util.Date;
import java.util.function.Function;

import javax.enterprise.context.SessionScoped;
import javax.faces.context.FacesContext;
import javax.inject.Named;
import javax.servlet.http.HttpServletRequest;

@Named
@SessionScoped
public class Julian implements Serializable {
  private static final long serialVersionUID =
    -1110733631543471209L;
```

```java
private Date dateIn; // + getter / setter
private String jd; // + getter / setter

public String convert() {
  jd = convert(getGd());
  return "/response.xhtml";
}

public String getGd() {
  LocalDateTime ldt = LocalDateTime.ofInstant(
      dateIn.toInstant(), ZoneId.of("UTC"));
  return ldt.format(DateTimeFormatter.
      ofPattern("yyyy-MM-dd HH:mm:ss"));
}

private String convert(String inDate) {
  Function<Double, Integer> trunc = (d) -> d.intValue();

  // yyyy-MM-dd-HH-mm-ss
  int inYear = Integer.parseInt(
    inDate.substring(0, 4));
  int inMonth = Integer.parseInt(
    inDate.substring(5, 7));
  int inDay = Integer.parseInt(
    inDate.substring(8, 10));
  int inHour = Integer.parseInt(
    inDate.substring(11, 13));
  int inMinute = Integer.parseInt(
    inDate.substring(14, 16));

  double jd = 367 * inYear -
      trunc.apply(7.0 * (inYear +
          trunc.apply((inMonth + 9.0) / 12)) / 4)
    + trunc.apply(275.0 * inMonth / 9)
      + inDay + 1721013.5 + 1.0 *
          (inHour + inMinute / 60.0) / 24
```

```
        - 0.5 * Math.signum(100 * inYear
            + inMonth - 190002.5) + 0.5;

    return "" + jd;
  }
}
```

The greetings page greeting.xhtml and the response page response.xhtml go into the "src/main/webapp" folder. Let the first one read as follows:

```
<!DOCTYPE html>
<html xmlns:h="http://xmlns.jcp.org/jsf/html"
      xmlns:f="http://xmlns.jcp.org/jsf/core"
      xmlns:pt="http://xmlns.jcp.org/jsf/passthrough">
<h:head><title>Julian Converter</title></h:head>
<h:body>
  <h:messages globalOnly="true"/>
  <h:form id="form">
    <h2>
        <h:outputText value="#{bundle.welcome}"/>
    </h2>
    <h:outputText value="#{bundle.instructions}"/>
    <p/>
    <h:outputText
        value="#{bundle.label_gregorianDate} "/>
    <h:inputText id="getdate"
        value="#{julian.dateIn}">
      <f:convertDateTime
            pattern="yyyy-MM-dd HH:mm:ss" />
    </h:inputText>
    <h:message for="getdate" style="color:red" />
    <p/>
    <h:commandButton value="#{bundle.submit}"
                        action="#{julian.convert}"/>
    <h:outputLink value="admin/admin.xhtml">
      <f:param name="backref" value="#{view.viewId}"/>
      <h:outputText value="#{bundle.adminlink} "/>
```

```
    </h:outputLink>
  </h:form>
</h:body>
</html>
```

This page looks like the original Julian day converter from earlier in this book, but it contains an additional link to the admin page, as follows:

```
<h:outputLink value="admin/admin.xhtml">
  <f:param name="backref" value="#{view.viewId}"/>
  <h:outputText value="#{bundle.adminlink} "/>
</h:outputLink>
```

We add a "backref" parameter to the link so we can navigate back from the admin page via a button placed there.

The response page response.xhtml gets navigated to when the user clicks the "Submit" button. Its contents are the same as from earlier in this book, as follows:

```
<!DOCTYPE html>
<html xmlns:h="http://xmlns.jcp.org/jsf/html"
      xmlns:f="http://xmlns.jcp.org/jsf/core"
      xmlns:pt="http://xmlns.jcp.org/jsf/passthrough">
  <h:head>
    <title>Julian Response Page</title>
  </h:head>
  <h:body>
    <h:form>
      <h:outputText value="#{bundle.label_response}"/>
      <p/>
      <h:outputText value="#{julian.gd} -> "/>
      <h:outputText value="#{julian.jd}"/>
      <p/>
      <h:commandButton id="back"
        value="#{bundle.back}"
        action="greeting"/>
    </h:form>
  </h:body>
</html>
```

The new admin page `admin.xhtml` goes into the "src/main/webapp/admin" folder. We use a new folder here so we can later apply a path pattern to secure the access to exactly this page. Let it read as follows:

```
<!DOCTYPE html>
<html xmlns:h="http://xmlns.jcp.org/jsf/html"
      xmlns:f="http://xmlns.jcp.org/jsf/core"
      xmlns:pt="http://xmlns.jcp.org/jsf/passthrough">
<h:head><title>Julian Converter</title></h:head>
<h:body>
  <h:messages globalOnly="true"/>
  Admin Page ...<p/>
  <h:outputLink
      value="#{request.contextPath}#{param['backref']}">
    <h:outputText value="#{bundle.back}"/>
  </h:outputLink>
</h:body>
</html>
```

We did not yet add any security features to the web application, but it should be fully functional now, and you can deploy and try it. See Figure 11-7.

Figure 11-7. *The Julian day converter*

We now add the security features to the web application. This mainly happens inside the src/main/webapp/WEB-INF/web.xml file. Inside this file, directly underneath the `<servlet-mapping> ... </servlet-mapping>` element, add the following:

```
...
</servlet-mapping>

<security-constraint>
  <display-name>Admin Constraint</display-name>
  <web-resource-collection>
    <web-resource-name>members</web-resource-name>
    <description />
    <url-pattern>/admin/*</url-pattern>
  </web-resource-collection>
  <auth-constraint>
    <description />
    <role-name>admin</role-name>
  </auth-constraint>
  <user-data-constraint>
    <transport-guarantee>
      CONFIDENTIAL
    </transport-guarantee>
  </user-data-constraint>
</security-constraint>
```

The `<url-pattern>` element with text value "/admin/*" specifies that the security constraint applies to all URLs starting with "/admin." The `<authconstraint>` element specifies that users wishing to use admin pages need to have the role "admin." The `<transport-guarantee>` with contents "CONFIDENTIAL" will force the application to switch to HTTPS before the admin pages get shown.

The mapping from roles ("admin" in this case) to users or user groups lies outside the Jakarta EE 8 specification. It is the Glassfish server's business to provide this mapping. How Glassfish does this works as follows: inside the `src/main/webapp/WEB-INF/glassfish-web.xml` file we exactly specify the following mapping:

```
<?xml version="1.0" encoding="UTF-8"?>
<!DOCTYPE glassfish-web-app PUBLIC
  "-//GlassFish.org//DTD GlassFish Application Server 3.1
   Servlet 3.0//EN"
  "http://glassfish.org/dtds/glassfish-web-app_3_0-1.dtd">
<glassfish-web-app error-url="">

    <!-- <security-role-mapping>
         <role-name>SomeRole</role-name>
         <principal-name>SomeUser</principal-name>
     </security-role-mapping>  -->

    <security-role-mapping>
         <role-name>admin</role-name>
         <group-name>ApplAdmin</group-name>
    </security-role-mapping>

    <class-loader delegate="true"/>

</glassfish-web-app>
```

Here, we can see that the role "admin" gets mapped to the user group "ApplAdmin." The commented out part in this file is just for illustration purposes—there, a mapping from a role to a particular user gets shown.

Those changes in `web.xml` and `glassfish-web.xml` already add all that is needed to secure the admin pages. Deploy and try it in your browser. If you click on the "Admin" link the browser will first complain that you are trying to use a self-signed certificate. Allow it by adding an exception. Then, a login dialog gets shown, where you have to enter "AdminUser" as a user name and the password you chose for that user earlier in this section (see Figure 11-8).

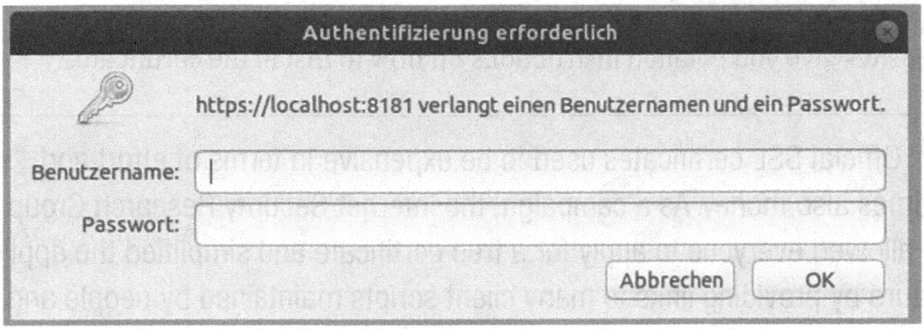

Figure 11-8. *The Julian day converter login*

Only if you enter the password correctly will you be allowed to see the admin page, and it will have automatically switched to HTTPS.

Rendering Dependent on Security Conditions

Once in a while, inside JSF template pages, you need a switch controlling whether some page element gets rendered or not, based on some security condition. This is easy to achieve, since there is a method isUserInRole() inside the request object that gets injected by default. You can use this inside a "rendered" attribute of any HTML element, as follows:

```
<h:commandButton value="Delete"
      action="#{bean.delete}"
      rendered="#{request.isUserInRole('admin')}" />
```

Here, the request object refers to the HttpServletRequest instance injected by default into any JSF page. The preceding code will lead to the button's only being rendered if the user has the "admin" role. Similar checks can be performed for any other tags supporting the "rendered" attribute.

Importing SSL Certificates for Web Applications

The Glassfish Jakarta EE 8 server (Glassfish 5.1) comes with a pre-installed SSL certificate. It is not an official certificate, because official certificates get issued on a per-domain basis. Instead, the pre-installed SSL certificate is a self-signed certificate, which means you can use it for development and maybe intranet purposes, but the browser will complain about it, and you have to tell the browser to accept it as an exception case.

You apply for an official certificate at a *certificate authority* (CA), and in many cases their websites give you detailed instructions on how to install the certificate.

Note   Official SSL certificates used to be expensive in terms of effort and sometimes also money. As a campaign, the Internet Security Research Group (ISRG) allowed everyone to apply for a free certificate and simplified the application procedure by providing links to many client scripts maintained by people and organizations on the internet. The website `https://letsencrypt.org/` gives you more information about it.

Without going into too much into detail, for the Glassfish server there are three central places you need to know about if you install an official certificate you receive from a CA. First, there are two central files where your private key and the CA certificate get stored. They are called `keystore.jks` and `cacerts.jks`, and you will find them in the "GLASSFISH_INST/glassfish/domains/domain1/config/" folder.

The third place is the Glassfish configuration, where we assign the certificate to the SSL HTTP listener.

Once you receive a certificate from a CA, you can import it into the `keystore.jks` and `cacerts.jks` Java keystore files. Usually you will receive instructions from the CA on how to do that. Showing all possibilities goes beyond the scope of this book—only if you acquired the certificate from `letsencrypt.org` does the story go as follows: you received the following files:

```
cert.pem
chain.pem
fullchain.pem
privkey.pem
```

This is the actual server certificate without the certificate chain (`cert.pem`), the intermediates from the certificate chain (`chain.pem`), the combination of these two (`fullchain.pem`), and the private key (`privkey.pem`). From here, we can generate the files `keystore.jks` and `cacerts.jks` from scratch using the following BASH script:

```
#!/bin/bash

#Alias of the certificate
NAME=my_alias
```

```
#The domain registered in letsencrypt
DOMAIN=www.server.com

#The keystore password, default is <changeit>
KEYSTOREPW=changeit

#The full absolute path of the folder where you have put
#the files received from letsencrypt
LIVE=/some/path/on/your/pc/$DOMAIN

mkdir temp-ssh-123
cd temp-ssh-123

# ### start building keystore.jks keystore ##############

# Create cert_and_key.p12 from private key and a
# certificate from the CA confirming that the private
# key belongs to the domain you were using while applying
# for the certificate. PKCS12 is a standardized archive
# format for cryptographic objects
openssl pkcs12 -export -in $LIVE/fullchain.pem \
   -inkey $LIVE/privkey.pem \
   -out cert_and_key.p12 \
   -name $NAME \
   -CAfile $LIVE/chain.pem -caname root \
   -password pass:$KEYSTOREPW

# Create a new keystore file keystore.jks from
# cert_and_key.p12
keytool -importkeystore \
   -destkeystore keystore.jks \
   -srckeystore cert_and_key.p12 -srcstoretype PKCS12 \
   -alias $NAME \
   -srcstorepass $KEYSTOREPW \
   -deststorepass $KEYSTOREPW \
   -destkeypass $KEYSTOREPW
```

```
# Add the certificate chain to keystore.jks
keytool -import -noprompt \
  -trustcacerts \
  -alias root \
  -file $LIVE/chain.pem -keystore keystore.jks \
  -srcstorepass $KEYSTOREPW \
  -deststorepass $KEYSTOREPW \
  -destkeypass $KEYSTOREPW

# Create file pkcs.p12 containing the private key again,
# this time use name "glassfish-instance." This is one
# of the keys Glassfish uses for its normal functioning.
openssl pkcs12 -export \
  -in $LIVE/fullchain.pem -inkey $LIVE/privkey.pem \
  -out pkcs.p12 \
  -name glassfish-instance \
  -password pass:$KEYSTOREPW

# ... Import exactly this key into keystore.jks
keytool -importkeystore -destkeystore keystore.jks \
  -srckeystore pkcs.p12 -srcstoretype PKCS12 \
  -alias glassfish-instance \
  -srcstorepass $KEYSTOREPW \
  -deststorepass $KEYSTOREPW \
  -destkeypass $KEYSTOREPW

# And one more key Glassfish needs as a default key. This
# time the name is "s1as."
openssl pkcs12 -export -in $LIVE/fullchain.pem \
  -inkey $LIVE/privkey.pem -out pkcs.p12 -name s1as \
  -password pass:$KEYSTOREPW

# ... Also import this one into keystore.jks
keytool -importkeystore \
  -destkeystore keystore.jks \
  -srckeystore pkcs.p12 -srcstoretype PKCS12 \
```

```
    -alias s1as \
    -srcstorepass $KEYSTOREPW \
    -deststorepass $KEYSTOREPW \
    -destkeypass $KEYSTOREPW

# ### start building cacerts.jks keystore ###############

# Create a new keystore file cacerts.jks from
# cert_and_key.p12
keytool -importkeystore \
    -destkeystore cacerts.jks \
    -srckeystore cert_and_key.p12 -srcstoretype PKCS12 \
    -alias $NAME \
    -srcstorepass $KEYSTOREPW \
    -deststorepass $KEYSTOREPW \
    -destkeypass $KEYSTOREPW

# Imports the chain.pem file into cacerts.jks
keytool -import -noprompt -trustcacerts \
    -alias root -file $LIVE/chain.pem \
    -keystore cacerts.jks \
    -srcstorepass $KEYSTOREPW \
    -deststorepass $KEYSTOREPW \
    -destkeypass $KEYSTOREPW

# Imports fullchain.pem into cacerts.jks,
# use name glassfish-instance
openssl pkcs12 -export -in $LIVE/fullchain.pem \
    -inkey $LIVE/privkey.pem -out pkcs.p12 \
    -name glassfish-instance -password pass:$KEYSTOREPW
keytool -importkeystore -destkeystore cacerts.jks \
    -srckeystore pkcs.p12 -srcstoretype PKCS12 \
    -alias glassfish-instance \
    -srcstorepass $KEYSTOREPW \
    -deststorepass $KEYSTOREPW \
    -destkeypass $KEYSTOREPW
```

```
# Imports privkey.pem into cacerts.jks, use name s1as
openssl pkcs12 -export -in $LIVE/fullchain.pem \
  -inkey $LIVE/privkey.pem -out pkcs.p12 -name s1as \
  -password pass:$KEYSTOREPW
keytool -importkeystore -destkeystore cacerts.jks \
  -srckeystore pkcs.p12 -srcstoretype PKCS12 \
  -alias s1as \
  -srcstorepass $KEYSTOREPW \
  -deststorepass $KEYSTOREPW \
  -destkeypass $KEYSTOREPW

# ===========================================================
# Download latest list of cacert and import it into the
# cacerts.jks

wget https://curl.haxx.se/ca/cacert.pem \
  --no-check-certificate -O cacert.pem
# number of certificates in the PEM file
CERTS=$(grep 'END CERTIFICATE' cacert.pem | wc -l)

# Extract all certificates from the PEM file and insert \
# them into cacerts.jks
for N in $(seq 0 $(($CERTS - 1))); do
  PEM_FILE=cacert.pem
  ALIAS="${PEM_FILE%.*}-$N"
  echo $ALIAS
  cat cacert.pem |
    awk "n==$N { print }; /END CERTIFICATE/ { n++ }" |
    keytool -noprompt -import -trustcacerts \
            -alias $ALIAS -keystore cacerts.jks \
            -storepass $KEYSTOREPW
done
```

You can now use the files keystore.jks and cacerts.jks and overwrite the files from "GLASSFISH_INST/glassfish/domains/domain1/config/." Just make a backup of the old files first. Restart Glassfish after you replace these two keystores.

> **Note**   You could also selectively update the existing entries from the files
> `keystore.jks` and `cacerts.jks` using a similar script.

The SSL certificate is now ready to use for Glassfish. Which certificate gets used for HTTPS can be specified in the web administration console at `http://localhost:4848`. Navigate to Configurations ➤ server-config ➤ Network Config ➤ Network Listeners ➤ http-listener-2 ➤ Tab "SSL." Because we updated the preconfigured "s1as" certificate in the script we just used, you change the settings in the admin console only if you want to use a different certificate you created in addition to what we did in the script.

Preparing EJB Security

Securing components does not stop at web applications. We can also secure EJB access. But before we can examine that for our Julian day converter, we first need to add EJBs to it. Create an EJB project `julian-secure-ejb` and add the following EJB class to it:

```
package book.jakarta8.juliansecureejb.ejb;

import javax.ejb.Local;
import javax.ejb.Remote;
import javax.ejb.Singleton;

import book.jakarta8.juliansecureejb.ejb.interfaces.
    NameEjbLocal;
import book.jakarta8.juliansecureejb.ejb.interfaces.
    NameEjbRemote;

@Singleton
@Local(NameEjbLocal.class)
@Remote(NameEjbRemote.class)
public class NameEjb
        implements NameEjbLocal, NameEjbRemote {
    public String hello(String name) {
        return "Hello " + name + " (admin)";
    }
}
```

Exercise 2

Implement the EJB project `julian-secure-ejb`.

Next, we will create an *Enterprise Application Project* that gathers the two projects, `julian-gui-secure` and `julian-secure-ejb`.

Note   This way we don't have to export EJB client artifacts in order for the GUI project to be able to use the EJB interfaces. Using an Enterprise Application Project also helps to include libraries. We already talked about Enterprise Application Projects in Chapter 7.

To do so, inside Eclipse select New ➤ Project.... Select Java EE ➤ Enterprise Application Project. See Figure 11-9.

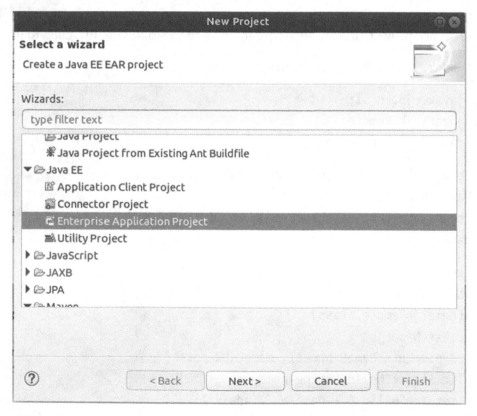

Figure 11-9. *New Enterprise Application Project*

Click on the "Next" button, and in the dialog that appears enter "julian-secure-ear" as the project name (see Figure 11-10).

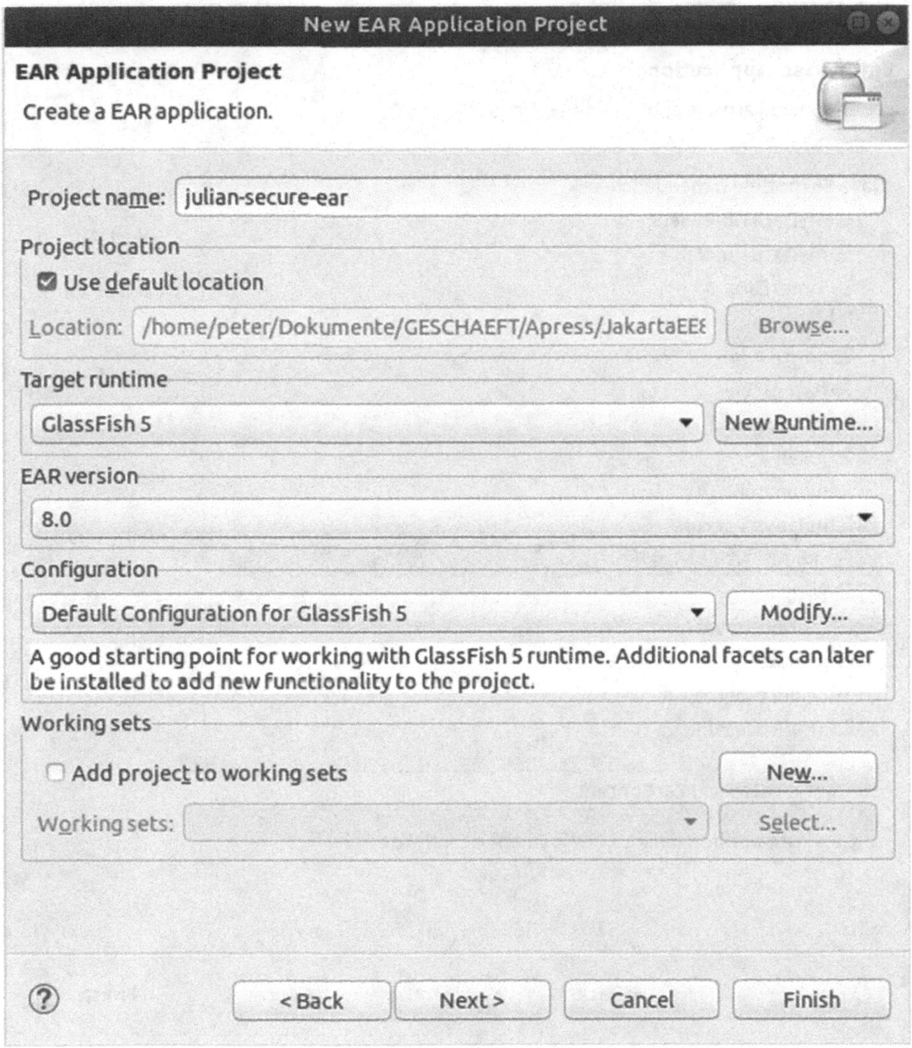

Figure 11-10. Enterprise Application Project name

In the following dialog, add the `julian-gui-secure` and `julian-secure-ejb` projects to the member list of the Enterprise Application Project (see Figure 11-11).

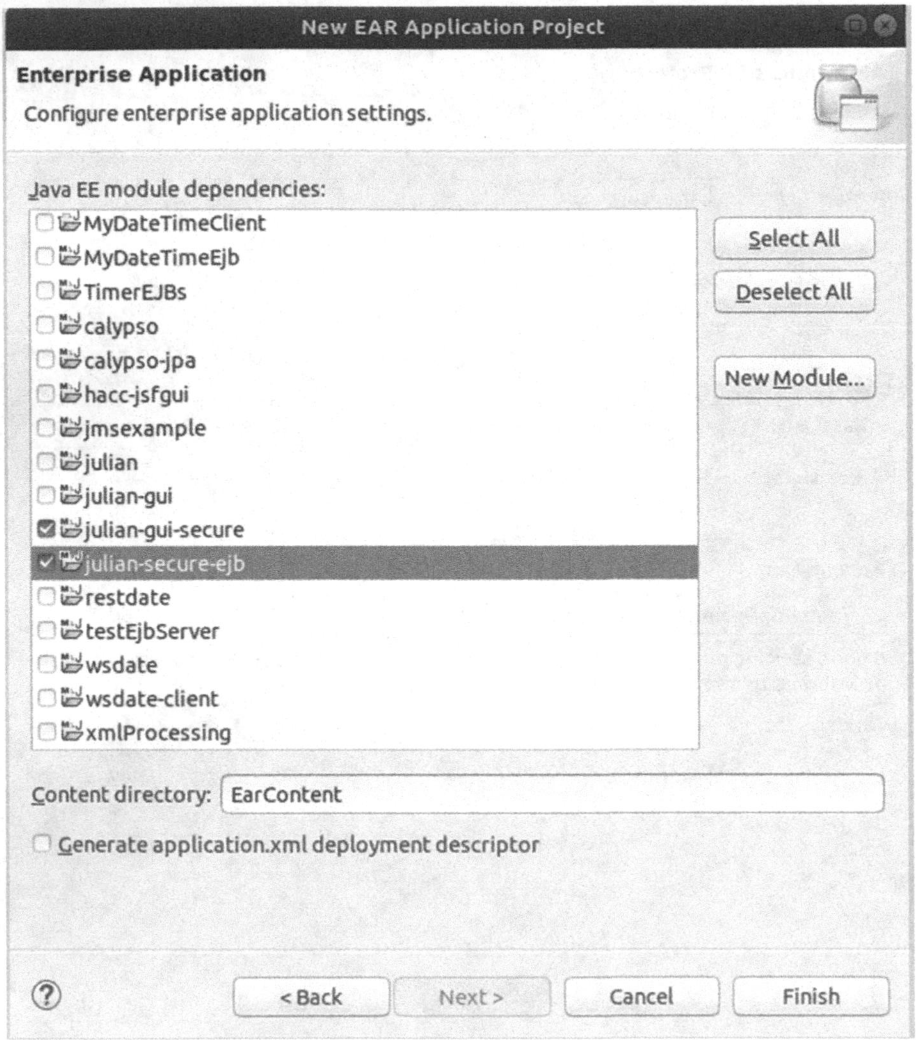

Figure 11-11. *Enterprise Application Project members*

Click on the "Finish" button. The new Enterprise Application Project will now appear in the Project Explorer view of Eclipse's main window. One thing is left to do before we can deploy `julian-secure-ear`: because from a project view the `julian-gui-secure` project does not yet know about the EJB classes it will be using, we must add the `julian-secure-ejb` project to the dependencies of the `julian-gui-secure` project. To do so, in the "Properties" view of `julian-gui-secure`, navigate to Java Build Path, "Projects" tab, and add the `julian-secure-ejb` project (see Figure 11-12). Click "Apply and Close" to finish the wizard.

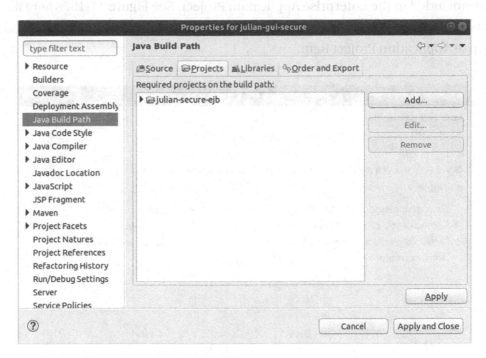

Figure 11-12. *Secure Julian cross-reference*

To let the GUI project use the EJB, we add a text-output field to the admin page. Inside `admin.xhtml`, write the following anywhere inside the `<h:body>` tag:

```
<h:outputText value="#{julian.greetingTxt}"/>
<p/>
```

Also add the following inside the `Julian` class:

```
@EJB
private NameEjbLocal nameEjb;
...

public String getGreetingTxt() {
    return nameEjb.hello("User");
}
```

The EJB access is not secured yet; we will catch up on that soon. But it is now possible to deploy and run the application. Invoke Run As ➤ Run on Server on the `julian-secure-ear` project and remove the orphaned `julian-guisecure` project since it is now included in the Enterprise Application Project. See Figure 11-13, where the projects `julian-gui-secure` and `julian-secure-ejb` are only shown if you expand the Enterprise Application Project item.

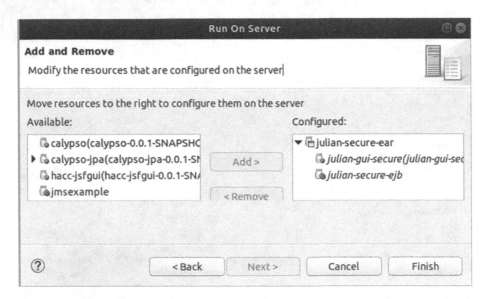

Figure 11-13. *Running the Enterprise Application Project*

Declarative EJB Security

To secure the EJB access, you can add a couple of annotations to the EJB class. Similar to web applications, EJBs use roles to restrict access to EJB classes and methods. The first annotation we can use is @DeclareRoles (from package `javax.annotation.security`), as follows:

```
@DeclareRoles("role1")
... more annotations ...
public class SomeEjb {
}
```

Or, if you have more than one, use the following:

```
@DeclareRoles({"role1","role2", ...})
... more annotations ...
public class SomeEjb implements ... {
}
```

This `@DeclareRoles` gets used to list all roles that are of any interest for the EJB. This annotation by itself does not restrict access to the EJB; it is a mere listing of role names that play a role in the EJB's security. The information available about `@DeclareRoles` elsewhere is a little bit confusing—sometimes it seems that you could omit it altogether, while sometimes it seems obligatory to add all roles referred to in the EJB. To be on the safe side, it is better to always list all roles used from inside the EJB in the `@DeclareRoles` annotation.

For the Julian day converter EJB from the preceding section, we want to restrict the EJB access to admin users, so we write the following:

```
import javax.annotation.security.*;
...

@Singleton
@Local(NameEjbLocal.class)
@Remote(NameEjbRemote.class)
@DeclareRoles({"admin"})
public class NameEjb
        implements NameEjbLocal, NameEjbRemote {
    public String hello(String name) {
        return "Hello " + name + " (admin)";
    }
}
```

As pointed out earlier, this does not yet restrict access to the EJB. To actually install a restriction you use the `@RolesAllowed` annotation, either at the class level or via methods, as follows:

```
import javax.annotation.security.*;
...

@DeclareRoles({"rx1", "rx2", "ry1", "ry2", ...})
// restricting access to the whole EJB:
@RolesAllowed({"rx1", "rx2", ...})
```

```
... more annotations ...
public class SomeEjb implements ... {
    // restricting access to some method
    @RolesAllowed({"ry1", "ry2", ...})
    public void someMethod() {
        ...
    }
    ...
}
```

If there is just one role, you can also write @RolesAllowed ("role1"). Back to our Julian day converter, we only have one role, "admin." To apply it at the method level, we write the following:

```
import javax.annotation.security.*;
...

@Singleton
@Local(NameEjbLocal.class)
@Remote(NameEjbRemote.class)
@DeclareRoles({"admin"})
public class NameEjb
        implements NameEjbLocal, NameEjbRemote {
    @RolesAllowed({"admin"})
    public String hello(String name) {
        return "Hello " + name + " (admin)";
    }
}
```

With these additions to the EJB, only clients (code accessing the EJB) that have acquired the "admin" role are allowed to use this method of the EJB. If you redeploy the Enterprise Application Project, the new security roles apply.

Exercise 3

Implement the access restrictions to the Julian day converter Enterprise Application Project. If you change the "admin" role declarations inside the Julian day converter EJB to "adminX," what do you expect to happen?

Programmatic EJB Security

In case the granularity declarative EJB security offers does not fit your needs, it is also possible to perform security checks from inside the EJB code. You need to inject an instance of SessionContext (from package javax.ejb). From this object, you can check a role membership via the isCallerInRole() method, as follows:

```
import javax.ejb.SessionContext;
...
public class SomeEjb implements ... {
    @Resource private SessionContext ctx;
    ...

    public void someMethod() {
        if(ctx.isCallerInRole("SomeRole")) {
            ...
        } else {
            throw new SecurityException(...);
        }
    }
    ...
}
```

Role Mimic: Propagating Roles

EJBs can be called from other EJBs. If there needs to be a mapping between role names from the calling EJB to the called EJB, the @RunAs annotation comes in handy. Consider, for example, the following:

```
public class SomeEjb implements ... {
    @EJB private SomeOtherEjb ejb2;
    ...
```

```
@RunAs("member")
public void someMethod() {
    ejb2.doSomething();
}
...
}
```

Here, when the someMethod() method gets entered, the current execution thread gets assigned the role "member" when calling the other EJB.

Because the Glassfish server by default assumes unlimited trust between different containers, the called EJB assumes the "member" role got authenticated correctly, even if no authentication actually happens. You must be careful when you use @RunAs to not open security holes.

## CHAPTER 12

Deployment Artifacts

So far, we have developed Jakarta EE 8 applications using the Eclipse IDE. Eclipse knows what to do with Java classes, configuration files, and resources like images, scripts, and language text files by virtue of a special plugin that knows how to talk to a Jakarta EE 8 server like Glassfish. We installed that plugin for Glassfish at the beginning of the book.

This deployment process, including server handling like starting, stopping, and restarting the server, only partially gets covered by a Jakarta EE 8 specification. In fact, for the deployment processes inside Eclipse there exist server plugins for all major Jakarta EE 8 servers and their predecessors. We already used the Glassfish server plugin in this book. The deployment processes and server-handling procedures for all possible servers are out of scope, but we will talk in more detail about how all this is implemented for the Glassfish 5.1 server. Later in this chapter, we will talk about the more standardized aspects of application deployment, exemplified also for the Glassfish server.

The Eclipse Plugin's Deployment Process

If from the Eclipse IDE you deploy a Jakarta EE 8 application, the plugin performs as follows:

1. If the Glassfish server is not yet running, the plugin starts the server.

2. Given the project files—this is all compiled Java classes, all configuration files, and all resources—the plugin reorganizes them according to a standard format required by the Glassfish server for the "Directory"-style deployment.

3. The plugin moves the deployment directory to the "GLASSFISH_INST/glassfish/domains/domain1/eclipseApps" folder.

© Peter Späth 2019
P. Späth, *Beginning Jakarta EE*, https://doi.org/10.1007/978-1-4842-5079-2_12

4. Similar to what the `asadmin` command-line utility does, the plugin
    sends an HTTP request `POST command/deploy` with appropriate
    POST body data to the administration port (normally 4848) of
    Glassfish.

5. If the deployment succeeds, the deployed application now is
    available on the server and ready to do its work.

Note   How do we know about the HTTP request used to start a deployment? It
is easy. From the corresponding `asadmin` sub-command `deploy` we take the
"deploy" and build the following URL from it:

`http://localhost:4848/command/deploy`

Enter this URL in a browser, and you will get an information page telling you
about all deployment options. Actually, the returned data format is JSON, but your
browser will appropriately render it. In fact, you can use a REST client and bypass
the `asadmin` tool for all kinds of administrative work in addition to the dedicated
administrative REST interface we already talked about.

Deploying Jakarta EE 8 applications in the form of directories that contain the
application's files in a special format is a good method for development purposes.
It is fast, and you can easily look at the files using a file explorer. The more portable
way of handling enterprise applications, however, consists of using ZIP archives in a
standardized format.

In the following paragraphs we will talk about such archives and only later will we
talk about the details of directory deployment. It is easier to understand if we describe
the various alternatives of deployment processes this way because the directory
structure used for the "directory"-style deployment closely follows the structure of the
archives used for the "archive" style.

Using Deployment Archives

Packaging Jakarta EE 8 applications in ZIP archives according to some standardized format specification shows a couple of advantages:

- Handling applications in the form of single archive files simplifies the deployment process. Give the server a single file, tell it to deploy this file, and ready you are.

- You can hand around Jakarta EE 8 applications more easily if they are just single archive files. Using single files, for example, allows for uploading an application using a web front end.

- If given as archive files, applications show improved coherence. Adhering to standards for formatting such archives lowers the probability of later corrupting the application by accidentally changing or removing archive members.

For Jakarta EE 8 there exist basically four types of deployable application artifacts:

- **Web Applications**

  Web applications are Jakarta EE applications serving a web GUI. But also, applications providing a REST interface, a web service, or any other interface using HTTP or HTTPS as a protocol are considered to be web applications. A web application archive is a ZIP archive using the file ending .war. We will talk about the structure of WARs shortly.

- **Resource Adapters (Connectors)**

  Resource adapters are Jakarta EE application components that implement the Jakarta EE connector architecture. Resource adapters frequently get used to connect to other, possibly non-Java enterprise systems commonly referred to as EISs (enterprise information systems). We do not handle resource adapters in this book, although, strictly speaking, adapters for accessing databases or messaging via JMS may be considered resource adapters as well. If given as deployable archives, resource adapters are ZIP files with the suffix .rar

- **Application Clients**

  Application clients are Java components with access to server
  components like EJBs. While normal clients access the server
  through web interfaces, application clients can directly connect to
  the business tier. And they run as server components themselves.
  Application clients usually provide a GUI using the Swing
  technology, but a CLI (command-line interface) is also possible.

- **Enterprise Applications**

  Enterprise applications in a narrow sense are applications that
  combine web applications, EJBs, and resource adapters. If given
  as an archive, it will be a ZIP archive with the ending `.ear`. We will
  talk about the structure of EARs shortly.

Web Application Archives

Web application archives are ZIP archives with the ending `.war` (instead of `.zip`). They
contain all files that are necessary for a web application to do its work. This includes
non-GUI applications with an HTTP or HTTPS interface like web services and RESTful
applications. The standard structure of such a WAR archive is as follows:

```
WEB-INF/
    classes/
        [Java classes]
    lib/
        [Libraries / JARs]
    web.xml
    [more configuration]
[web resources]
```

For example, if we have a JSF web application, the template file `index.xhtml` as a
landing page, and furthermore put all JavaScript files into a "js" folder, all CSS files into
"css," and all images into "images," the structure would read as follows:

```
WEB-INF/
    classes/
        [Java classes]
```

```
lib/
    [Libraries / JARs]
beans.xml
faces-config.xml
web.xml
glassfish-web.xml
[More configuration]
index.xhtml
js/
    [JavaScript files]
css/
    [Style sheets]
images/
    [Images]
[more pages]
[more resources]
```

Sometimes you will also see a top-level "META-INF" folder that contains some manifest files, but this is optional and depends on the tools you use and whether you actually need it.

However, the structure of the web resources is totally up to you. For example, you could decide to put all JavaScript files and CSS files into the root of the structure, or you could use "script" and "style" as folder names for the JavaScript and style sheet files, and so on.

Note   The precise specification of the structure of WAR files is part of the servlet specification to be found, for example, at https://jcp.org.

To deploy a WAR file, like, for example, someWebApp.war, on the Glassfish server, you have several options, as follows:

- You can use the web administration console. Open http:// localhost:4848 while the Glassfish server is running, then navigate to the Applications entry in the menu. Click the "Deploy..." button. On the page that appears make sure "Packaged File to Be Uploaded to the Server" is checked. In the corresponding field, select the WAR file to upload. Make sure as "Type" the entry "Web Application" is selected. Also make sure the checkboxes at "Status" and "Implicit CDI" are both selected. Fill in the other fields according to your needs. See Figure 12-1. If the deployment using the web administration console does not work as expected, see the following caution note. You can also undeploy applications using the Applications page in the web administration console.

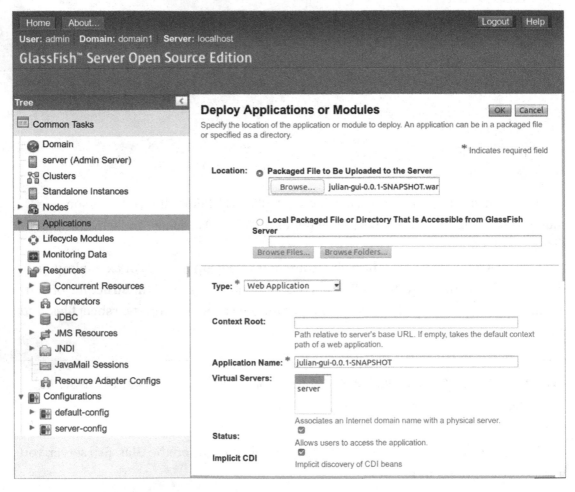

Figure 12-1. *WAR file Installation*

- The `asadmin` command from `GLASSFISH_INST/bin` allows for the
  deployment and undeployment of WARs via the following:

```
./asadmin deploy /path/to/the/war/someWebApp.war
```

```
./asadmin list-applications
# -> someWebApp
# -> [others]
```

```
./asadmin undeploy someWebApp
```

- To use the REST interface and some REST client program, like, for
  example, CURL, you can deploy a WAR application via the following:

```
curl -X POST \
  -u admin:<PASSWORD> \
  -F 'id=@/path/to/the/war/someWebApp.war' \
  -H 'Accept: application/json' \
  -H 'X-Requested-By: dummy' \
  http://localhost:4848/management/
      domain/applications/application
```

(keep the `http://...` URL in one line) where `<PASSWORD>` is the
password of the `admin` user. The "@" is a special construct for `curl` that
allows the passing of files. To undeploy you instead write the following:

```
curl -X DELETE \
  -u admin:PASSWORD8 \
  -H 'Accept: application/json' \
  -H 'X-Requested-By: dummy' \
  http://localhost:4848/management/
      domain/applications/application/
      someWebApp
```

(with the `http://...` URL in one line). The name used for the
application by default is the name of the WAR file without the `.war`
suffix. You can override this and use a different name if you add
`-F 'name=someName'` to the `CURL POST`. For the last URL path
element in the `DELETE` command you then use this new name.

301

- If you put a WAR file into the "GLASSFISH_INST/glassfish/domains/
domain1/autodeploy" folder it will be deployed immediately. Once
you remove it from there, it gets undeployed in turn.

Caution   For Glassfish 5.1, if you try to deploy an application using the web
administration console, you might get an error message "GUI internal error: Archive
Path is NULL." You should then use one of the other deployment procedures. If you
still want to use the web administration console, a workaround is to use Firefox as
the browser, open the developer tools by pressing F12, and then use the Inspector
to change the form attribute from

```
enctype = "application/x-www-form-urlencoded"
```

to

```
enctype = "multipart/form-data"
```

before pressing the "OK" button.

Creating WARs with Maven

There is no requirement to use a special tool to create WAR files. Nobody prevents you
from assembling WAR files manually using some ZIP tool. In this book, we didn't use
WAR archives so far, because we relied on Eclipse to do the right thing when we deployed
applications, and the Glassfish plugin of Eclipse actually creates directories from the
development files and then deploys these directories instead of WAR files.

But even if we want to create WAR files, Eclipse can help us, and the requirements for
this to work are low. The reason is simple: because all web projects we have described
in this book are Maven projects, and Maven actually is able to create WAR archives via
some plugin, we are already close to being able to create WAR files for all our projects.
Do you remember the `<packaging>` tag we had to provide in the Maven configuration file
`pom.xml`? For all our web projects we wrote the following:

```
<packaging>war</packaging>
```

This gives Maven a hint as to which kind of artifact to produce for the project.

With "war" specified as Maven packaging, there is basically one step left for creating WAR files from Eclipse. Right-click on the project, then navigate to Run As ➤ Maven build.... In the dialog that then appears enter "package" in the "Goals" field, then press the "Run" button. The final WAR file will show up in the "target" folder (maybe you have to update the folder view in Eclipse by pressing F5 on it).

You can try this for the `julian-gui` project we developed for Chapter 3. The WAR file created is named `julian-gui-0.0.1-SNAPSHOT.war`, but you are free to rename it first before it gets deployed on the Glassfish server.

The story can become more complex if we need to fulfill project dependencies. Let us have a look at the `julian-gui-secure` project we created in Chapter 11.

We first make a small adaptation so the WAR can be deployed separately and so there is no need to pack everything into an enterprise application archive. This is easy; open the `Julian` class from that project and change the `private NameEjbLocal nameEjb;` field to `private NameEjbRemote nameEjb;`

If you now start a Maven build with goals of "clean packaging," which means the same thing as first doing a cleanup and then a packaging, we get the following error message:

```
[ERROR] Failed to execute goal org.apache.maven.plugins:
    maven-compiler-plugin:3.1:compile (default-compile)
    on project julian-gui-secure: Compilation failure:
    Compilation failure:
[ERROR] /home/peter/Dokumente/GESCHAEFT/Apress/
    JakartaEE8/Eclipse/e/julian-gui-secure/src/main/java/
    book/jakarta8/julianguisecure/Julian.java:[14,52]
    package book.jakarta8.juliansecureejb.ejb.interfaces
    does not exist
[ERROR] /home/peter/Dokumente/GESCHAEFT/Apress/JakartaEE8/
    Eclipse/e/julian-gui-secure/src/main/java/book/
    jakarta8/julianguisecure/Julian.java:[31,17] cannot
    find symbol
[ERROR]   symbol:   class NameEjbLocal
[ERROR]   location: class book.jakarta8.julianguisecure.
    Julian
```

The reason for this is that the `clean` goal removes the compiled classes, and the `package` goal tries to recompile the classes. This fails because Maven doesn't know how to address the EJB classes that are referred to from the project. This wasn't a problem until now, because for the deployment plugin to work properly it was sufficient to let the Eclipse project depend on the EJB project.

To fix this for the Maven project, we first install the `julian-secure-ejb` project. To do so, right-click on the `julian-secure-ejb` project and navigate to Run As ➤ Maven install. This adds the EJB project JAR and the client JAR to your local Maven repository.

As a next step, deploy the EJB module on the server. Right-click on the `julian-secure-ejb` and select Run As ➤ Maven build.... At "Goals" enter "package" and click on the "Run" button. Fetch the EJB module JAR `julian-secure-ejb-0.0.1-SNAPSHOT.jar` from the "target" folder (maybe you have to press F5 on the "target" folder first to update the view). Use

```
cd GLASSFISH_INST
bin/asadmin deploy path/to/ejb/jar
```

to deploy the EJB module. The `GLASSFISH_INST` as usual is the installation folder of the Glassfish server.

We can now refer to the EJB client JAR from the WAR project. In the `pom.xml` file of the `julian-gui-secure` project add the following as a dependency:

```
<dependency>
    <groupId>book.jakarta8</groupId>
    <artifactId>julian-secure-ejb</artifactId>
    <version>0.0.1-SNAPSHOT</version>
    <classifier>client</classifier>
</dependency>
```

We have never used the `<classifier>` tag before. It just makes sure we will have only the client classes included within the WAR file.

If you now run the `clean package` Maven goal, everything should work, and you will have the finished WAR file placed inside the project's "target" folder (maybe you need to press F5 on the "target" folder to update the view). Fetch the WAR file, rename it according to your needs, and deploy it on the Glassfish server as follows to see it running:

```
cd GLASSFISH_INST
bin/asadmin deploy path/to/the/war
```

Exercise 1

Create a WAR file for the household accounting application from Chapter 4. Deploy it on the Glassfish server using the `asadmin` command-line tool. Hint: Specify `-name hacc` and `-contextroot hacc` to simplify handling. Which URL do you have to enter in the browser to access the web application once deployed?

Enterprise Application Archives

An Enterprise Application Archive (EAR) is a ZIP file with the ending `.ear` instead of `.zip`. EARs serve as containers for the following types of modules and libraries:

- Zero, one, or more web applications as WAR files (yes, as archive files inside the EAR archive file).

- Zero, one, or more EJB jars.

- Zero, one, or more resource adapters (`.rar`) files. We don't talk about resource adapters in this beginner's book.

- Zero, one, or more application clients. These are client components running in the server environment. They usually provide a GUI, like, for example, a Java Swing interface or a command-line interface. We don't talk about application clients in this beginner's book.

- Any number of libraries as JAR files. The Jakarta EE server makes sure only modules within the same EAR see these libraries. This is important because it means that one EAR may use one particular version of some library while another EAR uses a different version of the same library. You will usually also add EJB client interfaces (see the EJB chapter for details) as library JARs.

As a descriptor file, you may also add an `application.xml` file inside a top-level folder, "META-INF." We will talk about this descriptor file's contents shortly.

With all possible child elements and a single descriptor file inside "META-INF," the overall structure of an EAR file reads as follows:

```
webApplication1.war
webApplication2.war
...
```

```
ejbJar1.jar
ejbJar2.jar
...
applicationClient1.jar
applicationClient2.jar
...
resourceAdapter1.rar
resourceAdapter2.rar
...
lib/
    lib1.jar
    lib2.jar
    ...
META-INF/
    application.xml
```

The `application.xml` file may be used to specify the contents of the EAR file and define additional application-wide properties. This file is optional, and if you omit it then sensible defaults apply. The full specification of this file is part of JSR-000366 Java Platform, Enterprise Edition 8 Specification, downloadable from `http://jcp.org`, and the relevant section is EE.8.6. The following example shows a couple of settings you can specify in this file:

```
<!DOCTYPE application PUBLIC "-//Sun Microsystems,
  Inc.//DTD J2EE Application 1.2//EN"
  "http://java.sun.com/j2ee/dtds/application_1_2.dtd">
<application
  xmlns="http://xmlns.jcp.org/xml/ns/javaee"
  xmlns:xsi="http://www.w3.org/2001/XMLSchema-instance"
  xsi:schemaLocation="http://xmlns.jcp.org/xml/ns/javaee
      http://xmlns.jcp.org/xml/ns/javaee/application_8.xsd"
  version="8">

<icon>
  <small-icon>small.ico</small-icon>
  <large-icon>large.ico</large-icon>
</icon>
```

```
<application-name>The Application</application-name>
<display-name>Application-42</display-name>

<description>This application ...</description>

<module>
  <ejb>someEjb.jar</ejb>
</module>
<module>
  <java>someApplicationClient.jar</java>
</module>
<module>
  <connector>someResourceAdapter.jar</connector>
</module>
<module>
  <web>
    <web-uri>someWebApp.jar</web-uri>
    <context-root>web-app</context-root>
  </web>
</module>

<library-directory>lib</library-directory>
</application>
```

The "META-INF" folder may also contain an implementation-dependent or Glassfish-specific descriptor file, `glassfish-application.xml`:

```
    ...
META-INF/
    application.xml
    glassfish-application.xml
```

This file gets used for settings that cannot be specified in the `application.xml` file but play a role for the Glassfish server's functioning. You won't use this very often; for the details please see the "GlassFish Server Open Source Edition, Application Deployment Guide" you can find for download on the internet.

To deploy an EAR file, like, for example, `someApp.ear`, on the Glassfish server, you basically have the same options as for WAR applications:

- Use the Applications menu entry of the web administration console at `http://localhost:4848`. If the deployment using the web administration console does not work, see the caution note from the earlier WAR section.

- Use the `asadmin` command from `GLASSFISH_INST/bin` as follows:

```
./asadmin deploy /path/to/the/ear/someApp.ear

./asadmin list-applications
# -> someApp
# -> [others]

./asadmin undeploy someApp
```

- Use the REST interface and some REST client program, like, for example, CURL:

```
curl -X POST \
  -u admin:<PASSWORD> \
  -F 'id=@/path/to/the/ear/someApp.ear' \
  -H 'Accept: application/json' \
  -H 'X-Requested-By: dummy' \
  http://localhost:4848/management/
      domain/applications/application
```

(with the `http://...` URL on one line), where `<PASSWORD>` is the password of the `admin` user. To undeploy you instead write the following:

```
curl -X DELETE \
  -u admin:PASSWORD8 \
  -H 'Accept: application/json' \
  -H 'X-Requested-By: dummy' \
  http://localhost:4848/management/
      domain/applications/application/
      someApp
```

(with the `http://...` URL on one line). The name used for the application by default is the name of the EAR file without the `.ear` suffix. You can override this and use a different name if you add `-F 'name=someName'` to the CURL POST. For the last URL path element in the `DELETE` command, you use this new name.

- You can put an EAR file into the "GLASSFISH_INST/glassfish/domains/ domain1/autodeploy" folder and it will be deployed immediately. Once you remove it from there, it gets undeployed in turn.

Creating EARs with Maven

To create EAR files, you can assemble a directory, structure it like just described, zip it, and then change the ending to `.ear`. But you can also use Maven to create an EAR file.

We are going to try that with the Enterprise Application Project "MyDateTimeEar" from Chapter 7. We have already introduced enterprise applications in the narrow sense, meaning a bundle of an EJB and a library JAR. In that chapter, we relied on Eclipse's capability to deploy the project on Glassfish, but we can use the same project to also create an EAR archive, which we can deploy manually on the Glassfish server.

To do so, we first convert the "MyDateTimeEar" project to a Maven project. Right-click on the project, then navigate to Configure ➤ Convert to Maven Project. In the dialog that then appears, enter the following:

```
Group Id:    book.jakarta8
Artifact Id: date-time-ear
Version:     0.0.1-SNAPSHOT
Packaging:   ear
Name:        date-time-ear
Description: An EAR project for date/time retrieval
```

Click the "Finish" button. Eclipse now provides us with a `pom.xml` build file similar to the following:

```
<project
  xmlns="http://maven.apache.org/POM/4.0.0"
  xmlns:xsi="http://www.w3.org/2001/XMLSchema-instance"
  xsi:schemaLocation="http://maven.apache.org/POM/4.0.0
    http://maven.apache.org/xsd/maven-4.0.0.xsd">
<modelVersion>4.0.0</modelVersion>
```

```
<groupId>book.jakarta8</groupId>
<artifactId>date-time-ear</artifactId>
<version>0.0.1-SNAPSHOT</version>
<packaging>ear</packaging>

<name>date-time-ear</name>

<description>
  An EAR project for date/time retrieval
</description>
<build>
  <plugins>
    <plugin>
      <artifactId>maven-ear-plugin</artifactId>
      <version>3.0.1</version>
      <configuration>
        <earSourceDirectory>
          EarContent
        </earSourceDirectory>
        <version>8</version>
        <defaultLibBundleDir>lib</defaultLibBundleDir>
      </configuration>
    </plugin>
  </plugins>
</build>
</project>
```

We need to add the EJB project dependency to the "MyDateTimeEar" project. For this, open this project's pom.xml file again and add the following in front of the <build> tag:

```
<dependencies>
  <dependency>
    <groupId>book.jakarta8</groupId>
    <artifactId>MyDateTimeEjb</artifactId>
    <version>0.0.1-SNAPSHOT</version>
     <type>ejb</type>
  </dependency>
</dependencies>
```

If you now invoke Run As ➤ Maven build... on the "MyDateTimeEar" project and enter "package" in the "Goals:" field, Maven will create an EAR file `date-time-ear-0.0.1-SNAPSHOT.ear` in the "target" folder (press F5 on the folder to update the view). You can inspect this file; unzipping it (maybe temporarily change the suffix to ".zip" for your ZIP program to recognize it) gives us the following structure:

```
book.jakarta8-MyDateTimeEjb-0.0.1-SNAPSHOT.jar
lib/
  com.sun.mail-javax.mail-1.6.0.jar
  javax-javaee-api-8.0.jar
  javax.activation-activation-1.1.jar
  book.jakarta8-MyDateTime-0.0.1-SNAPSHOT.jar
  MyDateTime-0.0.1-SNAPSHOT.jar
META-INF/
  maven/
  application.xml
  MANIFEST.MF
```

Note   The "maven/" folder inside "META-INF" only contains build-related files; the Glassfish Jakarta EE server will ignore it.

This is almost correct, but you can see the MyDateTime library shows up twice in the "lib" folder. This happens because in the build file we refer to both the EJB project, which has MyDateTime as a transitive dependency, and the JAR we copied into the "EarContent/lib" folder. To avoid this we should remove the latter reference, because the only reason it exists is that we wanted to be able to let Eclipse deploy the project for us. Because we added the EJB dependency to the Maven build file, we can now remove the file `MyDateTime-0.0.1-SNAPSHOT.jar` from the "lib" folder. Eclipse knows how to handle the transitive dependency on the library. Remove it, and to then make sure the configuration is correct, right-click on the project, select "Properties," navigate to Deployment Assembly, and remove the `lib/MyDateTime-0.0.1-SNAPSHOT.jar` file from the list. Add the project dependency to the assembly by pressing "Add..." in the same dialog, and then add the MyDateTimeEjb project. See Figure 12-2. Click "Apply and Close."

For now, building the EAR file with the updated configuration, it is better to enter "clean package" in the "Goals:" field of the Maven runner. This avoids having excluded files be taken into account in the new build.

The cleaned-up structure of the EAR file should now show the library just once, as follows:

```
book.jakarta8-MyDateTimeEjb-0.0.1-SNAPSHOT.jar
lib/
  com.sun.mail-javax.mail-1.6.0.jar
  javax-javaee-api-8.0.jar
  javax.activation-activation-1.1.jar
  book.jakarta8-MyDateTime-0.0.1-SNAPSHOT.jar
META-INF/
  maven/
  application.xml
  MANIFEST.MF
```

You can deploy the EAR file as described earlier.

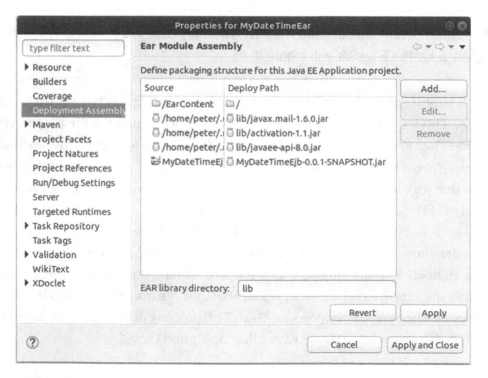

Figure 12-2. *Updating the EAR assembly*

Deploying Applications from Directories

Jakarta EE 8 applications can also be deployed from directories. This removes the advantages we assigned to using archive files, but it makes dealing with applications during development a little easier. You can, for example, change configuration files and JSF pages in place without having to repackage them. Another disadvantage is that there is no specification for deploying applications from directories, so each Jakarta EE server product has its own idea as to whether it can be done and how it needs to be done.

The Glassfish server allows for deployment from directories, and their structure must be as follows:

- For enterprise applications that normally end up in an EAR archive, you provide a folder that has the same structure as an EAR archive, but you extract child containers as well, renaming them to BASENAME_SUFFIX. This means you, for example, extract an included web archive (WAR) with name someWebApp.war and rename the resulting folder to "someWebApp_war." The structure of the folder thus reads as follows:

```
webApplication1_war/
   [extracted contents]
webApplication2_war/
   [extracted contents]
...
ejbJar1_jar
   [extracted contents]
ejbJar2_jar
   [extracted contents]
...
applicationClient1_jar
   [extracted contents]
applicationClient2_jar
   [extracted contents]
...
resourceAdapter1_rar
   [extracted contents]
resourceAdapter2_rar
```

```
        [extracted contents]
    ...
lib/
    lib1.jar
    lib2.jar
    ...
META-INF/
    application.xml
```

- For all other types of applications, you use the same folder structure
  as for the corresponding archive. So for a web application, for
  example, the folder structure reads as follows:

```
WEB-INF/
    classes/
        [Java classes]
    lib/
        [Libraries / JARs]
    web.xml
    [more configuration]
[web resources]
```

To deploy such directories, you can use the `asadmin` command-line tool, as follows:

```
./asadmin deploy --name NameOfTheApp \
    /path/to/the/folder
```

If you omit the `--name` parameter the name of the folder will be used as the
application's name.

You can also use the web administration console at `http://localhost:4848`. Use
the Applications option in the menu and then click the "Deploy…" button. Select the
checkbox for "Local Packaged File or Directory That Is Accessible from GlassFish Server"
and enter the full path to the directory in the field. Do not press the "Browse Folders…"
button, as it does not work on Glassfish 5.1. At "Type" select the type of the application,
and in the fields that then appear enter at least a decent name for the application in the
"Application Name" field. Make sure the checkboxes for "Status" and "Implicit CDI"
are checked. Fill in the other fields according to your needs. See Figure 12-3. Click the

"OK" button to finish the deployment. The new application should now show up in the applications listing (see Figure 12-4).

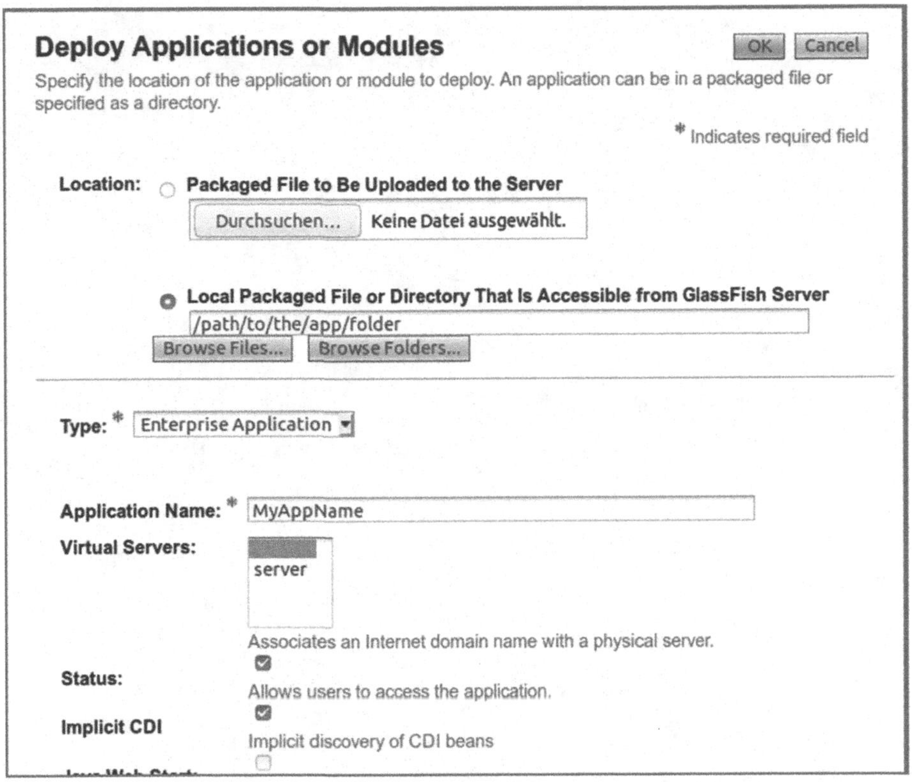

Figure 12-3. *Deploying from directories*

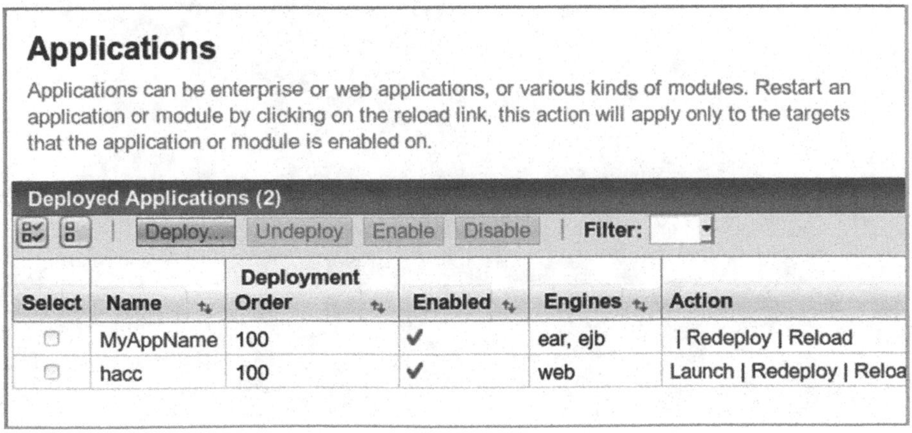

Figure 12-4. *New applications list*

## CHAPTER 13

Logging Jakarta EE Applications

Logging is a vital part of any application of mid- to high-level complexity. While the program runs through its execution paths, several logging statements describe what the program is doing, which parameters get passed to method calls, which values local variables and class fields have and how they change, which decisions are made, and so on. This logging information gets collected and sent to a file, a database, a message queue, or whatever, and the developer and the operations team may investigate program flows for bug-fixing or auditing purposes.

This chapter is about the various options you have to add logging to your programs or to investigate existing server logging.

System Streams

The Java Standard Environment (JSE) on which Jakarta EE builds its server technologies provides well-known standard output and error output streams, which you address as follows:

```
System.out.println("Some information: ...");
System.err.println("Some error: ...");
```

While at first sight it seems easy to generate diagnostic information using these streams, it is not recommended to use this procedure. The primary reason for this is that what happens with these stream data is highly operating-system and server-product dependent. We will very shortly introduce superior methods, but just in case you are temporarily tempted to use the system streams for diagnostic output, it is important to know that most Jakarta EE servers fetch the streams and redirect them to some file.

© Peter Späth 2019

P. Späth, *Beginning Jakarta EE*, https://doi.org/10.1007/978-1-4842-5079-2_13

> **Note**   Until now we have used the output and error output streams for diagnostic output. We did that just for simplicity. In any serious project, you should not do that, and the subsequent sections will show you how to avoid it.

The Jakarta EE 8 Glassfish server version 5.1 adds the output and error output stream to the `server.log` file you will find at

```
GLASSFISH_INST/glassfish/domains/domain1/logs
```

In this usually verbose listing you will recognize the `System.out` and `System.err` output as the following lines containing a `[SEVERE]` (for `System.err`) and `[INFO]` (for `System.out`):

```
...
[2019-05-20T14:42:03.791+0200] [glassfish 5.1] [SEVERE]
    [] [] [tid: _ThreadID=28 _ThreadName=Thread-9]
    [timeMillis: 1558356123791] [levelValue: 1000] [[
    The System.err message ]]
...
[2019-05-20T14:42:03.796+0200] [glassfish 5.1] [INFO]
    [NCLS-CORE-00022] [javax.enterprise.system.core]
    [tid: _ThreadID=28
    _ThreadName=RunLevelControllerThread-1558356114688]
    [timeMillis: 1558356123796] [levelValue: 800] [[
    The System.out message ]]
...
```

We will later learn how to change the verbosity level and the format of these logging lines.

JDK Logging in Glassfish

The logging API specification JSR 47 is part of Java and can be used by any Java program, including Jakarta EE server applications. You can download the specification from `https://jcp.org/en/jsr/detail?id=47`.

Glassfish Log Files

Glassfish uses the platform standard API JSR 47 for its logging. Unless you change the configuration, you can find the logging file at

```
GLASSFISH_INST/glassfish/domains/domain1/logs/server.log
```

In the same folder, you will also find archived logs with file names server.log_TS, where TS is a timestamp like 2019-05-08T15-45-58.

The standard logging format is defined as a combination of various information snippets, of course including the actual logging message, as follows:

```
[Timestamp] [Product-ID] [Message-Type]
        [Message-ID] [Logger-Name] [Thread-ID]
        [Raw-Timestamp] [Log-Level]
        [[Message]]
```

like in the following:

```
[2019-05-20T14:42:03.796+0200] [glassfish 5.1] [INFO]
        [NCLS-CORE-00022] [javax.enterprise.system.core]
        [tid: _ThreadID-28
        _ThreadName=RunLevelControllerThread-1558356114688]
        [timeMillis: 1558356123796]
        [levelValue: 800]
        [[Loading application xmlProcessing done in 742 ms]]
```

Adding Logging Output to the Console

If you want to have the logging output also appear in the terminal where you start the Glassfish server, use the following:

```
cd GLASSFISH_INST
bin/asadmin start-domain --verbose
```

This will show the complete logging output. It will also not put the server process into the background, as an asadmin start-domain without –verbose does, so the server will be stopped when you close the terminal, and you won't be able to enter more commands into this terminal after the server has started (for new commands you can of course enter a second terminal). To stop this foreground server process, press CTRL+C.

Note   The logging showed in the Eclipse console view uses a different format for the logging lines. An example would be

`2019-05-21T09:00:54.333+0200|Info: <the message>`

This is because Eclipse starts the server directly and is not mediated by `asadmin`.

Using the Standard Logging API for Your Own Projects

To add diagnostic output to your own classes and use the JSR 47 methodology, you write something like the following in your classes:

```
...
import java.util.logging.Logger;

public class MyClass {
  private final static Logger LOG =
        Logger.getLogger(MyClass.class.toString());

  public void someMethod() {
    LOG.entering(this.getClass().toString(),"someMethod");
    ...
    // different logging levels:
    LOG.finest("Finest: ...");
    LOG.finer("Finer: ...");
    LOG.fine("Fine: ...");
    LOG.info("Some info: ...");
    LOG.warning("Some warning: ...");
    LOG.severe("Severe: ...");
    ...
    LOG.exiting(this.getClass().toString(),"someMethod");
  }
  ...
}
```

For `LOG.entering()` there exists a variant where you can add method parameters to the logging statement. Likewise, for `LOG.exiting()` a variant allows us to add a returned value to the logging statement, as follows:

```
...
public String someMethod(String p1, int p2) {
  LOG.entering(this.getClass().toString(),"someMethod",
      new Object[]{ p1, p2 });
  ...
  String res = ...;
  LOG.exiting(this.getClass().toString(),"someMethod",
      res);
  return res;
}
...
}
```

Exercise 1

Change the `App` class from Chapter 8 to use INFO-level JSR 47 logging instead of `System.out` or `System.err` print statements.

Logging Levels

From the preceding samples you can see there are several levels you can use to indicate the severity of logging output. For standard logging the levels are, in order, *severe > warning > info > fine > finer > finest*. This greatly improves the usability of logging. At an early stage of a project you can set the logging threshold to a low value—for example, fine—and you will see all "fine"-level logging and all higher levels up to "severe" in the logging file.

If you lower the threshold (to `finest`, for example) the logging shows more details, but the logging file will be larger, of course. This is why you do that for bug-fixing purposes—more details help you to more easily identify problematic code. Later in the project, when the maturity rises, you apply a higher threshold (like `warning`, for example). This way the logging file does not get too big, but you still see important issues in the logging.

The special `Logger` methods `entering()` and `exiting()` belong to the log level `finer`. All the other methods we showed here match literally to the equally named level, so a `LOG.severe()` belongs to level `severe`, a `LOG.warning()` belongs to level `warning`, and so on.

The Logger Hierarchy and Thresholds

If you create a logger like

```
Logger.getLogger("com.example.projxyz.domain.Person");
```

you actually span up a hierarchy com ➤ com.example ➤ com.example.projxyz ➤ com.example.projxyz.domain ➤ com.example.projxyz.domain.Person.

This plays a role if you assign logging thresholds. This assignment happens in the configuration, via `asadmin`, or in the web administration console. We will see shortly how to do that. It is important to know that the threshold setting follows the logger hierarchy. If you assign a level LEV1 (severe, warning, info, . . .) to "com" this means the complete sub-tree at "com" gets threshold LEV1, unless you also specify levels for elements deeper in the hierarchy. So, if you also assign a level LEV2 to "com.example," LEV2 has precedence over LEV1 for "com.example" and all elements deeper in the hierarchy. More precisely, the rules are as shown in Table 13-1.

Table 13-1. *Logging Hierarchy*

Hierarchy	Level	Logger	Description
com	FINE	com.ClassA	FINE applies, because com.ClassA is inside the com hierarchy.
com	FINE	org.ClassA	FINE does not apply, because org.ClassA is not inside the com hierarchy.
com.ClassA	FINER	com.ClassA	FINER applies, because com.ClassA is inside the com.ClassA hierarchy. FINE no longer applies, because the hierarchy specification com.ClassA is more specific compared to just com.

(continued)

Table 13-1. (*continued*)

Hierarchy	Level	Logger	Description
com.example	WARNING	com.ClassA	WARNING does not apply, because com.ClassA is not inside the com.example hierarchy.
com.example	WARNING	com.example. ClassA	WARNING applies, because com.example. ClassA is inside the com.example hierarchy. The level specified for com no longer applies, because com.example is more specific compared to com.
com.example	WARNING	org.example. ClassA	WARNING does not apply, because org is not inside the com.example hierarchy.

The Logging Configuration

The logging configuration of JSR 47 standard logging relies on a configuration file, logging.properties. Normally this file resides in the JDK installation directory, but the Glassfish server overrules the standard logging configuration and uses the following file instead:

```
GLASSFISH_INST/glassfish/domains/domain1/
        config/logging.properties
```

Here, the various logging properties get specified. We don't talk about all of them—the specification for JSR 47 and the Glassfish server documentation will give you more ideas. The most important settings are the level thresholds, which you will find underneath the following #All log level details line:

```
...
#All log level details
com.sun.enterprise.server.logging.GFFileHandler.level=ALL
javax.enterprise.system.tools.admin.level=INFO
org.apache.jasper.level=INFO
javax.enterprise.system.core.level=INFO
javax.enterprise.system.core.classloading.level=INFO
java.util.logging.ConsoleHandler.level=FINEST
```

```
javax.enterprise.system.tools.deployment.level=INFO
javax.enterprise.system.core.transaction.level=INFO
org.apache.catalina.level=INFO
org.apache.coyote.level=INFO
javax.level=INFO
...
```

Here, we have an example for the hierarchic-level assignment: if you change the level at `javax.enterprise.system.core.level` to "FINE," any `javax.` logger will use the threshold INFO because of the `javax.level = INFO` line, but a logger `javax.enterprise.system.core.Main` logger will use FINE, because it matches the level we just entered and is more specific.

A setting of the form `.level=INFO` later in the `logging.properties` file makes sure all loggers not specified in the logging properties will have the threshold INFO applied. That is why in the standard configuration variant of Glassfish no `fine`, `finer`, or `finest` messages appear.

Instead of changing the file you can also use the web administration console at `http://localhost:4848`. Navigate to Configurations ➤ server-config ➤ Logger Settings. Changes here will be directly written to the `logging.properties` file.

As a third possibility to change the logging configuration, the `asadmin` command-line utility provides us with various logging-related sub-commands. The following shows some examples:

```
./asadmin list-log-levels
# -> A list of all log levels, like
# javax                          <INFO>
# javax.mail                     <INFO>
# javax.org.glassfish.persistence  <INFO>
# org.apache.catalina            <INFO>
# org.apache.coyote              <INFO>
# org.apache.jasper              <INFO>
# ...

./asadmin delete-log-levels javax.mail
# -> Deletes a level specification

./asadmin set-log-levels javax.mail=WARNING
```

```
# -> Setting a specific log level

./asadmin list-log-attributes
# -> Shows all log attributes (not the levels)

./asadmin set-log-attributes \
    com.sun.enterprise.server.logging.
    GFFileHandler.rotationLimitInBytes=2000000
# (discard the line break after "logging.")
# -> Sets an attribute. Attribute names are the same
# as in the logging.properties file

./asadmin rotate-log
# -> Manually rotates the log file. Takes the current
# server.log file, archives it, and starts a fresh
# empty server.log file.
```

Logging-level changes are dynamic, so you can change logging levels while the server is running.

The Logging Format

For JSR 47 standard logging, the logging format is prescribed by the logging handler. So in order to change the logging format you have to develop a new logging handler. This is not particularly hard to achieve, but we leave it to your discretion if you need to change the format and want to stick to Java platform logging.

Otherwise, you can easily switch to using a logging library. Most of the candidates for such a choice allow for changing the logging format by adjusting a configuration property. We will shortly talk about the Log4j logging framework and also handle the logging formatting options Log4js provides.

Using JDK Standard Logging for Other Servers

Although most developers prefer to use a logging library like Apache Commons Logging, Log4j, or Logback, you can use the JSR 47 logging for servers other than Glassfish as well. Just make sure you provide a customized logging.properties file. Do not change the logging.properties file in the JDK installation folder, though—changing the configuration there is highly discouraged.

Instead, provide a new `logging.properties` file and add (one line, remove the line break and the spaces after "=") the following to the server startup parameters:

```
-Djava.util.logging.config.file=
    /path/to/logging.properties
```

Your server documentation will tell you how to do that.

Adding Log4j Logging to Your Application

Log4j is a logging framework often used for any kind of Java application. Its features include the following:

- Clear separation of API and implementation. In a server environment you install the Log4j implementation on the server itself, while on the clients you only refer to a small-footprint Log4j API library.

- High performance. Log4j has lambda support included, so message calculations can be avoided if a corresponding log level will not be logged. For example, in `LOG.info("Error", () -> expensiveOperation())` the method call will not happen if info-level messages are disabled for the logger.

- Automatic configuration reloading. For Log4j it is easy to enable automatic configuration reloading. Any change in the logging configuration will then be applied immediately without a server restart.

- The logging format and various other logging properties can be set in the configuration.

- The Log4j configuration files can be formatted in either XML, Java properties, JSON, or YAML.

- Log4j can easily be extended by plugins.

Log4j can be downloaded from `http://logging.apache.org/log4j/2.x/`. The still widely used Log4j version 1.x is deprecated, and we will not talk about Log4j version 1.x in this book.

Log4j needs a couple of additional permissions in order to pass security checks. Open the following file:

```
GLASSFISH_INST/glassfish/domains/domain1/
      config/server.policy
```

and add the following at the end:

```
// Added for Log4j2
grant {
    permission
        java.lang.reflect.ReflectPermission
        "suppressAccessChecks";
    permission
        javax.management.MBeanServerPermission "*";
    permission
        javax.management.MBeanPermission "*", "*";
    permission
        java.lang.RuntimePermission "getenv.*";
};
```

Caution   This is a Glassfish server–specific requirement. For other servers, different settings might be necessary.

Adding Log4j Server-Wide

Adding Log4j server-wide means you put the Log4j implementation into a common libraries folder, write one Log4j configuration file that serves all Jakarta EE applications running on that server at once, and let all applications and application modules just use the Log4j API. Because this is a setting that needs to be configured only once and then all current and future applications on the server can easily use Log4j for their logging purposes, this way of including Log4j is probably used most often. Only if you have important reasons to encapsulate Log4j with the applications—for example, if you are also running legacy applications that use old Log4j 1.x versions—should you add Log4j on a per-application basis, as described a little bit later.

To add Log4j server-wide, you first download the Log4j distribution from `https://logging.apache.org/log4j/2.x/`. Then, copy the `log4j-core-2.11.2.jar`, `log4j-api--2.11.2.jar`, and `log4j-appserver-2.11.2` files (or whatever version you downloaded) to the "GLASSFISH_INST/glassfish/domains/domain1/modules/autostart" folder.

Note   The Log4j JAR files are implemented as OSGi bundles. This is why we put them into the "modules" folder. If you don't know OSGi, consider it an advanced library management framework.

Then, add a new file, `log4j2.json`, to the "GLASSFISH_INST/glassfish/domains/domain1/lib/classes" folder. As the basic contents of this file use the following:

```
{
"configuration": {
  "name": "Default",
  "appenders": {
    "RollingFile": {
      "name":"File",
      "fileName":
          "${sys:com.sun.aas.instanceRoot}/logs/log4j.log",
      "filePattern":
          "${sys:com.sun.aas.instanceRoot}/
          logs/log4j-backup-%d{MM-dd-yy-HH-mm-ss}-%i.gz",
      "PatternLayout": {
        "pattern":
            "%d{yyyy-MM-dd HH:mm:ss} %-5p %c{1}:%L - %m%n"
      },
      "Policies": {
        "SizeBasedTriggeringPolicy": {
          "size":"10 MB"
        }
      },
      "DefaultRolloverStrategy": {
        "max":"10"
      }
    }
```

```
    },
    "loggers": {
      "logger" : [
        {
          "name" : "book.jakarta8",
          "level":"debug",
          "appender-ref": {
            "ref":"File"
          }
        },{
          "name" : "some.other.logger",
          "level":"info",
          "appender-ref": {
            "ref":"File"
          }
        }
      ],
      "root": {
        "level":"error",
        "appender-ref": {
          "ref":"File"
        }
      }
    }
  }
}
```

This adds a root logger with level "error" and two more loggers, "book.jakarta8" and "some.other.logger," with levels "debug" and "info" threshold, respectively. The logger names inside the "logger" array correspond to logger hierarchy specifications. They work the same way as we described for the standard JDK logging (JSR 47). So, the "book.jakarta8" logger applies to logging statements for "book.jakarta8.SomeClass" and "book.jakarta8.pckg.OtherClass," but not to "book.jakarta99.FooClass." The special "root" logger serves as a default and matches all loggers for which no explicit logger specification can be found.

This file gives you a starting point—you can add more appenders and loggers. Please see the Log4j2 documentation you can find in the internet to learn how to extend the configuration.

Note   Log4j allows for configuration files using different formats. We choose the JSON format because of its conciseness.

If the server is running, restart it. This needs to be done because of the global nature of adding Log4j this way. You can now start using Log4j in your applications, as described later at "Using Log4j in the Coding."

Note   Add -Dlog4j2.debug as a server startup JVM parameter to get more output for what Log4j is doing. This meta-diagnostic information gets printed out to the standard server.log file.

Changing the Logging Format

In the Log4j configuration file we already specified the following logging pattern:

```
...
"pattern":
      "%d{yyyy-MM-dd HH:mm:ss} %-5p %c{1}:%L - %m%n"
...
```

This prints out a timestamp as specified by %d{yyyy-MM-dd HH:mm:ss}, the logging level as specified by %p (the −5 adds a padding to the output), the last path element of the logger name as specified by %c{1}, the line number because of the %L, and the message because of the %m. The %n finally adds a line break at the end.

You can change this at will. The online Log4j2 manual, "Layouts" section, lists all the options. Table 13-2 shows the most important options.

Table 13-2. *Logging Patterns*

Pattern	Description
m	The message.
c	The name of the logger.
c[N]	Only the last N path parts of the logger name. So with a logger org.example. memory.Main a %c{1} creates "Main" as output, a %{2} creates "memory. Main," and so on.
c[-N]	Remove the first N path parts of the logger name. So with a logger org. example.memory.Main a %c{-1} creates "example.memory.Main," and so on.
c[1.]	Replaces all but the last part of the logger name with a dot ".". So with a logger org.example.memory.Main a %c{1.} creates "o.e.m.Main."
p	The log level.
-5p	The log level, right-padded with spaces to five characters.
d	Outputs a timestamp like "2019-09-23 07:23:45.123."
d[DEFAULT_ MICROS]	Same as plain %d, but adds the microseconds: "2019-09-23 07:23:45.123456."
d[ISO8601]	Output like: "2019-09-23T07:23:45.123."
d[UNIX_ MILLIS]	Milliseconds since 1970-01-01 00:00:00 UTC.
highlight{p}	Add ANSI colors to the enclosed pattern p. For example: highlight{%d %-5p %c{1.}:%m}%n.
L	The line number. This is an expensive operation—use with care.
M	The method name. This is an expensive operation—use with care.
n	Line break.
t	The name of the thread.
T	The ID of the thread.

Log4j2 also allows for logging output in CSV format, in GELF format, embedded in a HTML page, as JSON, XML or YAML. Please see the Log4j2 manual for details.

Adding Log4j to Jakarta EE Web Applications

If you think you should add Log4j on a per-application basis and leave other applications running on the server unaffected, you can add the Log4j implementation to your web application (WAR).

Note   Running Log4j in such an isolated way might, for example, be necessary if your server is also running legacy applications that use the old Log4j 1.x.

To add the Log4j implementation we update the dependencies in our Maven build file. Open the pom.xml file and add the following inside the <dependencies> section:

```
<dependency>
  <groupId>org.apache.logging.log4j</groupId>
  <artifactId>log4j-core</artifactId>
  <version>2.11.2</version>
</dependency>
<dependency>
  <groupId>com.fasterxml.jackson.core</groupId>
  <artifactId>jackson-core</artifactId>
  <version>2.7.4</version>
</dependency>
<dependency>
  <groupId>com.fasterxml.jackson.core</groupId>
  <artifactId>jackson-databind</artifactId>
  <version>2.7.4</version>
</dependency>
<dependency>
  <groupId>com.fasterxml.jackson.core</groupId>
  <artifactId>jackson-annotations</artifactId>
  <version>2.7.4</version>
</dependency>
```

Here, the central part is the dependency on log4j-core; the dependencies on jackson are needed because we will be using JSON-formatted configuration files, and Log4j needs jackson to parse them.

The configuration file for Log4j needs to have the name `log4j2.json` and it must go to the "src/main/resources" folder for web applications (WARs). As a simplistic configuration, set the contents of `log4j2.json` to the following:

```
{
"configuration": {
  "name": "Default",
  "appenders": {
    "RollingFile": {
      "name":"File",
      "fileName":
          "${sys:com.sun.aas.instanceRoot}/logs/log4j.log",
      "filePattern":
          "${sys:com.sun.aas.instanceRoot}/
          logs/log4j-backup-%d{MM-dd-yy-HH-mm-ss}-%i.gz",
      "PatternLayout": {
        "pattern":
            "%d{yyyy-MM-dd HH:mm:ss} %-5p %c{1}:%L - %m%n"
      },
      "Policies": {
        "SizeBasedTriggeringPolicy": {
          "size":"10 MB"
        }
      },
      "DefaultRolloverStrategy": {
        "max":"10"
      }
    }
  },
  "loggers": {
    "logger" : [
      {
        "name" : "book.jakarta8",
        "level":"debug",
```

```
      "appender-ref": {
         "ref":"File"
      }
    },{
      "name" : "some.other.logger",
      "level":"debug",
      "appender-ref": {
         "ref":"File"
      }
    }
  ],
  "root": {
    "level":"debug",
    "appender-ref": {
      "ref":"File"
    }
  }
 }
}
}
```

Adding Log4j to Jakarta EE EAR Applications

Adding Log4j to enterprise applications (EARs) is not as straightforward as you might think it should be. Upon initialization, Log4j looks in several places for its configuration file, but it does not automatically look into containers that do not contain code. EARs contain EJBs, WARs, and libraries in the form of `.jar` files, but no genuine code of their own.

What we can do is pack the configuration file into a dummy EJB, which then gets added to the EAR. For this purpose, create an EJB project in Eclipse via New ➤ EJB Project. Use something like "TheEarProjectLog4j" as a project name, and make sure the "EJB module version" reads "3.2." In the wizard, uncheck the "EJB Client JAR" feature—we don't need that. In the project settings, navigate to Java Build Path ➤ Source, remove the "ejbModule" source folder, and add "src/main/java" instead (you have to create it). Remove the "ejbModule" folder from the Project Explorer view. Click

Configure ➤ Convert to Maven Project, and in the wizard that then appears enter the following coordinates:

```
Group Id:    book.jakarta8
Artifact Id: TheEarProjectLog4j
Version:     0.0.1-SNAPSHOT
Packaging:   ejb
```

What's important is the "ejb" packaging; the other coordinates can be adapted according to your needs. Click the "Finish" button. In the pom.xml file that the wizard generates, remove the <build> ... </build> section and instead enter the following:

```xml
<dependencies>
  <dependency>
    <groupId>javax</groupId>
    <artifactId>javaee-api</artifactId>
    <version>8.0</version>
  </dependency>
</dependencies>

<build>
  <plugins>
    <plugin>
      <artifactId>maven-compiler-plugin</artifactId>
      <configuration>
        <source>1.8</source>
        <target>1.8</target>
      </configuration>
    </plugin>
    <plugin>
      <groupId>org.apache.maven.plugins</groupId>
      <artifactId>maven-ejb-plugin</artifactId>
      <version>3.0.1</version>
      <configuration>
        <generateClient>false</generateClient>
        <ejbVersion>3.2</ejbVersion>
      </configuration>
```

```
      </plugin>
    </plugins>
  </build>
```

In order to comply with the specifications, we must add at least one EJB class to the EJB project. We write a dummy EJB as follows:

```
@Singleton
public class MyDateTimeEarLog4j {
}
```

The name and package are free for you to choose.

Add a log4j2.json file to the "src/main/resources" folder. As the contents you can use the same JSON text as we used for the preceding sections, or a more elaborate version, according to your needs.

Add the new EJB to the EAR by right-clicking on Properties ➤ Deployment Assembly ➤ Add... ➤ Project ➤ [Name of the dummy EJB project].

What is left for the EAR project is to add the Maven dependencies. Convert the EAR project to a Maven project if not done already, and insert the following into the <dependencies> section:

```
<dependency>
  <groupId>org.apache.logging.log4j</groupId>
  <artifactId>log4j-core</artifactId>
  <version>2.11.2</version>
</dependency>
<dependency>
  <groupId>com.fasterxml.jackson.core</groupId>
  <artifactId>jackson-core</artifactId>
  <version>2.7.4</version>
</dependency>
<dependency>
  <groupId>com.fasterxml.jackson.core</groupId>
  <artifactId>jackson-databind</artifactId>
  <version>2.7.4</version>
</dependency>
```

```
<dependency>
    <groupId>com.fasterxml.jackson.core</groupId>
    <artifactId>jackson-annotations</artifactId>
    <version>2.7.4</version>
</dependency>
```

Using Log4j in the Coding

To use Log4j in your Jakarta EE 8 application, make sure each project in question has the following Maven dependency added:

```
<dependency>
    <groupId>org.apache.logging.log4j</groupId>
    <artifactId>log4j-api</artifactId>
    <version>2.11.2</version>
</dependency>
```

In the classes, you then import Logger and LogManager and use a static logger field as follows:

```
import org.apache.logging.log4j.*;

public class SomeClass {
  private final static Logger LOG =
        LogManager.getLogger(SomeClass.class);
  ...
  public void someMethod() {
    ...
    // different logging levels:
    LOG.trace("Trace: ...");
    LOG.debug("Debug: ...");
    LOG.info("Some info: ...");
    LOG.warn("Some warning: ...");
    LOG.error("Some error: ...");
    LOG.fatal("Some fatal error: ...");
    ...
```

```
    // Logging in try-catch clauses
    try {
        ...
    } catch(Exception e) {
        ...
        LOG.error("Some error", e);
    }
  }
}
```

Inside the `log4j2.json` configuration file the `"level"` inside each logger then declares a logging threshold, as follows:

```
"loggers": {
  "logger": [
    {
        "name":"book.jakarta8",
        "level":"debug",
        "appender-ref": {
          "ref":"appenderName"
        }
    }
    ...
  ]
  ...
}
```

This can be any of the following: "trace," "debug," "info," "warn," "error," or "fatal."

Exercise 2

Add server-wide Log4j logging to your Glassfish server. Choose any of your projects and add Log4j logging to it.

## CHAPTER 14

Monitoring Jakarta EE Applications

In a project's development stage, the correct functioning of a Jakarta EE 8 server and the applications it hosts gets measured by checking whether the functional requirements are being fulfilled. This gets verified by tests and an investigation of the logs the server and the applications produce.

In a production environment, correct functioning is, of course, important as well, but issues like throughput, elapsed time for method invocations, memory usage, and the general stability of a server gain more importance. This is what monitoring is for—the server provides a monitoring interface that client programs can use to gain insight into such non-functional aspects. In this chapter, we will talk about monitoring and cover both monitoring of the Glassfish server and monitoring that our own applications can provide.

Monitoring over the Admin Console

The `asadmin` command-line utility allows access to various Glassfish server monitoring modules. The following monitoring modules are available:

- **jvm**

  This module includes the server uptime, the initial amount of memory used, the maximum available amount for memory management, and the current memory usage.

© Peter Späth 2019
P. Späth, *Beginning Jakarta EE*, https://doi.org/10.1007/978-1-4842-5079-2_14

- **httplistener**

    This module includes the number of HTTP requests, the number
    of erroneous HTTP requests, the maximum HTTP request
    processing time, and the total time spent for all HTTP requests.

- **webmodule**

    This module provides figures for HTTP sessions: the total number
    of sessions that have been created, the number of active sessions,
    the total number of session activations, and the number of
    rejected sessions. In addition, the current, maximum, and total
    number of JSPs get shown, and the module also gives the number
    of currently active servlets, the maximum number of activated
    servlets, and the total number of servlets that have been loaded.
    Note that we don't use JSPs in this book, so the associated figures
    are not of much use for us here.

Do not confuse the term "module" used here with the module notion used
elsewhere—a *monitoring module* is a set of monitorable objects subject to investigation,
and it applies only to the Glassfish server. You can enter `./asadmin help monitor` to
learn more about these monitoring modules (the Glassfish server must be running for
this to work).

You must enable the monitoring for each module in question to actually see the
monitoring data. You either enter the Configurations ➤ serverconfig ➤ Monitoring
section in the web administration console at `http://localhost:4848` (see Figure 14-1)
or enter one of the following:

```
cd GLASSFISH_INST/bin
./asadmin set \
    server.monitoring-service.
    module-monitoring-levels.<key>=<level>
```

(with no line break and no spaces after `service`) in a terminal, where the `<level>` reads
LOW for simple statistics, HIGH for additional method statistics, and OFF for disabling the
monitoring. The GLASSFISH_INST must as usual be substituted with the installation
folder of the Glassfish server. For the possible `<key>` values, see Table 14-1 at the
"Asadmin Key" column.

Table 14-1. *Monitoring Keys*

Name	Web Admin Key	Asadmin Key
jvm	Jvm	jvm
httplistener	Http Service	http-service
webmodule	Web Container	web-container

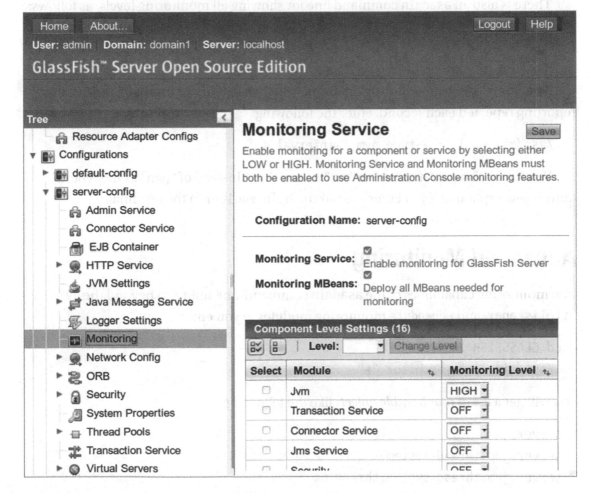

Figure 14-1. *Monitoring administration*

For the rest of this chapter, we will assume that the JVM monitoring is switched on, as follows:

```
cd GLASSFISH_INST/bin
./asadmin set \
    server.monitoring-service.
    module-monitoring-levels.jvm=HIGH
```

There is also an `asadmin` command line for showing all monitoring levels, as follows:

```
./asadmin get \
  server.monitoring-service.module-monitoring-levels.*
```

To actually see the monitoring figures in CSV format and, for example, to have this reporting repeated each second, enter the following:

```
./asadmin monitor --type jvm --interval 1
```

You could also put "httplistener" or "webmodule" instead of "jvm" as the type. The output gets explained if you enter `./asadmin help monitor` in the terminal.

Advanced Monitoring

The monitoring capabilities of the `asadmin` command-line utility go beyond the `jvm`, `httplistener`, and `webmodule` monitoring modules. If you enter

```
cd GLASSFISH_INST/bin
./asadmin list --monitor "*"
```

you will get a list of *monitorable objects* like the following:

```
server.jvm
server.jvm.thread-system
server.jvm.thread-system.thread-64
...
server.jvm.memory
server.jvm.class-loading-system
server.jvm.compilation-system
server.jvm.operating-system
server.jvm.runtime
```

```
server.jvm.garbage-collectors
server.jvm.garbage-collectors.PS MarkSweep
server.jvm.garbage-collectors.PS Scavenge
server.http-service
...
```

The extent of this list depends on which monitoring object categories have been enabled and whether they were configured with a LOW or HIGH monitoring level. We can use the get sub-command to see a list of all monitoring object categories, like so:

```
./asadmin get \
    server.monitoring-service.module-monitoring-levels.*
```

And we can use

```
./asadmin set <key>=<level>
```

to enable the monitoring for a category from that list, with <level> being one of "HIGH," "LOW," or "OFF." To, for example, see the class loading statistics, we first have to know that it is part of the "jvm" category. So, with the "jvm" category monitoring enabled (we already did that in the preceding section), the preceding list sub-command gives us the key for the class loading system: server.jvm.class-loading-system. To see the actual figures, we can now use the get sub-command as follows:

```
./asadmin get --monitor server.jvm.class-loading-system.*
```

The output will be something like this:

```
server.jvm.class-loading-system.dotted-name =
    server.jvm.class-loading-system
sjc.loadedclass-count-count = 19405
sjc.loadedclass-count-description =
    Number of classes currently loaded in the
    Java virtual machine
sjc.loadedclass-count-lastsampletime = 1558858266471
sjc.loadedclass-count-name = LoadedClassCount
sjc.loadedclass-count-starttime = 1558856758543
sjc.loadedclass-count-unit = count
sjc.totalloadedclass-count-count = 19411
sjc.totalloadedclass-count-description =
```

```
    Total number of classes that have been loaded since
    the Java virtual machine has started execution
sjc.totalloadedclass-count-lastsampletime = 1558858266471
sjc.totalloadedclass-count-name = TotalLoadedClassCount
sjc.totalloadedclass-count-starttime = 1558856758543
sjc.totalloadedclass-count-unit = count
sjc.unloadedclass-count-count = 6
sjc.unloadedclass-count-description = Total number of
    classes unloaded since the Java virtual machine has
    started execution
sjc.unloadedclass-count-lastsampletime = 1558858266471
sjc.unloadedclass-count-name = UnLoadedClassCount
sjc.unloadedclass-count-starttime = 1558856758543
sjc.unloadedclass-count-unit = count
```

For the sake of brevity I replaced `server.jvm.class-loading-system` with `sjc` in the listing. You can see that the figures come with a description, which is a nice feature and helps us to understand the numbers.

There is a large number of valuable statistics we can retrieve this way using the `asadmin` utility: EJB statistics, HTTP service statistics, Jersey statistics, JMS/connector service statistics, JVM statistics, network statistics, ORB statistics (connection manager), resource statistics (connection pool), security statistics, thread pool statistics, transaction service statistics, and web statistics. The Glassfish Server Administration Guide chapter on "Viewing Comprehensive Monitoring Data" gives you more information about it.

Using REST to Access Monitoring Data

We can also use the RESTful administrative interface to see the monitoring data. If we have a monitorable object like, for example, "server.jvm.class-loading-system," and monitoring is enabled for the object (we did that in the preceding sections), a REST client like CURL can be used to obtain the monitoring figures by adding the object name to `monitoring/domain/` and replacing the dots "." with slashes "/", as follows:

```
curl -u admin:PASSWORD -X GET \
    -H "Accept: application/json" \
    http://localhost:4848/monitoring/domain/
    server/jvm/class-loading-system \
| jq .
```

(with no line break and no spaces after domain/), where we also use the jq command to prettify the output (you have to install jq on your system). For PASSWORD enter the admin user's password. This gives us something like the following:

```
{
  "message": "",
  "command": "Monitoring Data",
  "exit_code": "SUCCESS",
  "extraProperties": {
    "entity": {
      "loadedclass-count": {
        "unit": "count",
        "lastsampletime": 1558862718603,
        "name": "LoadedClassCount",
        "count": 19022,
        "description": "Number of classes currently
            loaded in the Java virtual machine",
        "starttime": 1558856758543
      },
      "totalloadedclass-count": {
        "unit": "count",
        "lastsampletime": 1558862718603,
        "name": "TotalLoadedClassCount",
        "count": 19453,
        "description": "Total number of classes that
            have been loaded since the Java virtual
            machine has started execution",
        "starttime": 1558856758543
      },
```

```
      "unloadedclass-count": {
        "unit": "count",
        "lastsampletime": 1558862718603,
        "name": "UnLoadedClassCount",
        "count": 431,
        "description": "Total number of classes unloaded
            since the Java virtual machine has started
            execution",
        "starttime": 1558856758543
      }
    },
    "childResources": {}
  }
}
```

From there, we can dig deeper using the various options the jq command offers. For example:

```
curl -s -u admin:PASSWORD -X GET \
    -H "Accept: application/json" \
    http://localhost:4848/monitoring/domain/server/
    jvm/class-loading-system \
  | jq '.extraProperties.entity["loadedclass-count"].count'
```

(with no line break and no spaces after server/). This suppresses the progress meter (because of the -s) and directly gives us the loaded classes count figure.

Note   Enter man jq to learn all about filters in jq. The dot notation for a jq filter is self-explanatory. The ["..."] has to be used because of the hyphen "-" inside the name.

Exercise 1

Create a similar curl/jq script for reading the used heap space (current memory usage).

JMX Monitoring

So far we have used the `asadmin` tool and the admin REST interface for monitoring. These are Glassfish-specific features—obviously for other Jakarta EE servers monitoring won't work this way. To learn about the monitoring capabilities for your server product you will have to read its administration manuals.

There is, however, one technology that is situated halfway between proprietary monitoring features and an unfortunately non-existent full monitoring standard. It is called Java Management Extensions (JMX), and it can be used for any Java software, including all Java servers. Basically, you can use JMX monitoring for any Jakarta EE server product, although sometimes it is not very straightforward to set up the interface. Describing such a setup procedure for all possible Jakarta EE 8 servers is out of scope for this book, but we will describe it for Glassfish 5.1 so you can get an idea of how to use it and what you can do with it.

Glassfish's JMX Interface

If you look into the server logs, at `GLASSFISH_INST/glassfish/domains/domain1/ logs/server.log` you will find an entry containing something like "JMXStartupService has started JMXConnector on JMXService URL service:jmx:rmi://talenos:8686/jndi/ rmi://talenos:8686/jmxrmi]]" (*talenos* is my computer's name, so if searching inside the file, don't use it). This basically says that the JMX interface is already running; in fact, Glassfish starts it by default.

This JMX interface works for local connections only, though, with JMX clients running on the same machine as the Glassfish server does. For development this is a suitable restriction, but obviously this won't work for integration tests and production setups. For this reason, we must enable remote JMX connectivity, which happens by adding a couple of JVM parameters: open the web administration console at `http://localhost:4848`. Navigate to Configurations ➤ server-config ➤ JVM Settings ➤ "JVM Options" tab. See Figure 14-2. Add the following options:

```
-Djava.rmi.server.hostname=<yourhost>
-Dcom.sun.management.jmxremote.port=8686
-Dcom.sun.management.jmxremote.ssl=false
-Dcom.sun.management.jmxremote.authenticate=false
```

For <yourhost> you must enter the IP address or DNS name of the network node with Glassfish running on it. With Glassfish restarted, a remote connection to JMX now should work.

Caution   The access is not secured—use this setup only behind a firewall.

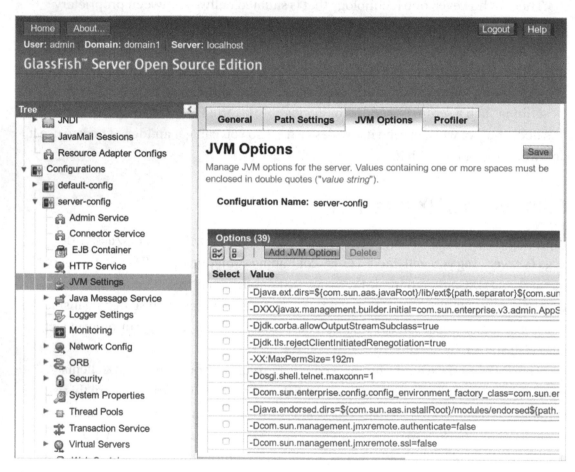

Figure 14-2. *JVM parameters*

To check whether the remote JMX connectivity works, you can use a simple Groovy client on any accessible network node. For example, you can connect from your development PC to a network node with Glassfish running and remote JMX enabled. The Groovy code reads as follows:

```
import javax.management.remote.JMXConnectorFactory as
  JmxFactory
import javax.management.remote.JMXServiceURL as
  JmxUrl

def glassfishServer = "192.168.1.100"
def serverUrl = "service:jmx:rmi://${glassfishServer}:" +
    "8686/jndi/rmi://${glassfishServer}:8686/jmxrmi"
def server = JmxFactory.connect(new JmxUrl(serverUrl)).
    MBeanServerConnection

def memInfo =
    new GroovyMBean(server, 'java.lang:type=Memory').
    HeapMemoryUsage.contents
println(memInfo)
```

For `glassfishServer` you must enter the IP or DNS name of the network node where Glassfish is running. This must also match the server's JVM property `java.rmi.server.hostname` as described earlier. The output should look like this:

```
[
  committed:316669952,
  init:197132288,
  max:477626368,
  used:182012688
]
```

A JMX GUI Client

There are several JMX GUI clients you can use to access JMX data. An open source software I often use for this purpose is VisualVM. You can download it from `https://visualvm.github.io/`. After you start it, add a JMX plugin via Tools ➤ Plugins ➤ Available Plugins. Select "VisualVM-MBeans" and install it.

Note JMX objects get called "MBeans" for *manageable beans*.

Create a new remote host by right-clicking on "Remote" ➤ Add Remote Host.... Enter
the IP address or the DNS name of the network node where Glassfish is running. This
must also match the server's JVM property `java.rmi.server.hostname` as described
earlier. Right-click on the new entry and click "Add JMX Connection." Enter

```
service:jmx:rmi://<HOST>:8686/jndi/
    rmi://<HOST>:8686/jmxrmi
```

(one line) at "Connection" and check "Do not require SSL connection." See Figure 14-3.

Caution   VisualVM automatically adds local servers. Adding remote connections
only makes sense if VisualVM and the Jakarta EE server are running on different
network nodes.

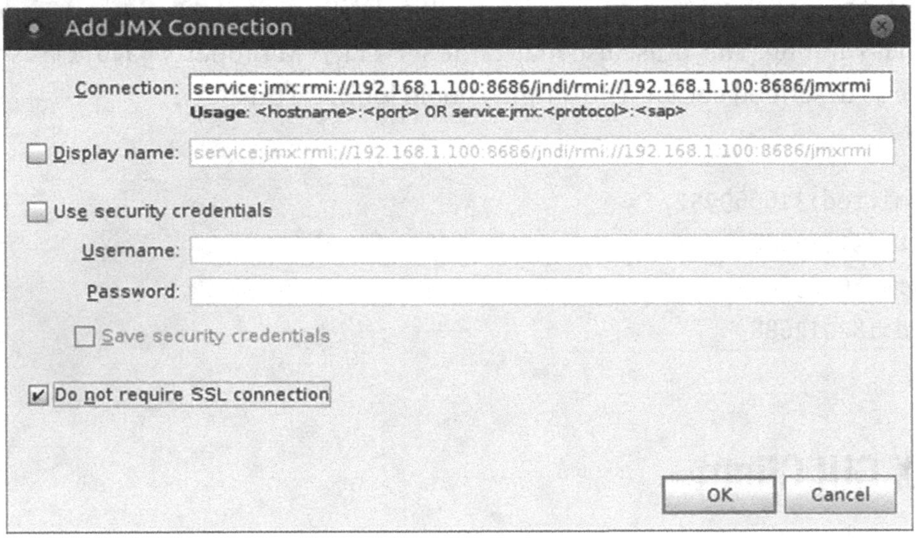

Figure 14-3.   *VisualVM: Adding a connection*

You can now establish the connection by double-clicking on it (in VisualVM,
details for objects often are available by double-clicking on them). The JMX interface is
available at the "MBeans" tab. See Figure 14-4.

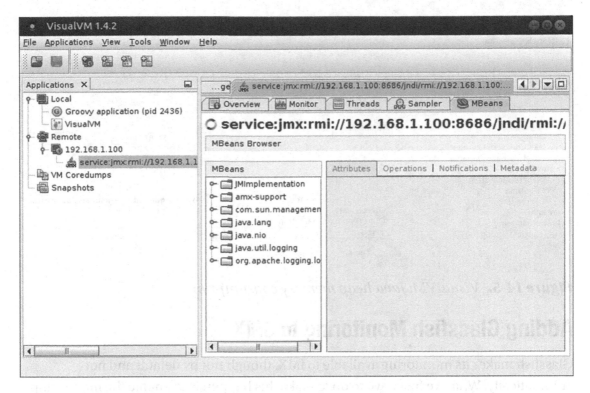

Figure 14-4. *VisualVM: JMX view*

To see, for example, the memory consumption figures, open java.lang ➤ Memory and double-click on the "Value" field of the HeapMemoryUsage row. This will show the heap memory consumption details (see Figure 14-5).

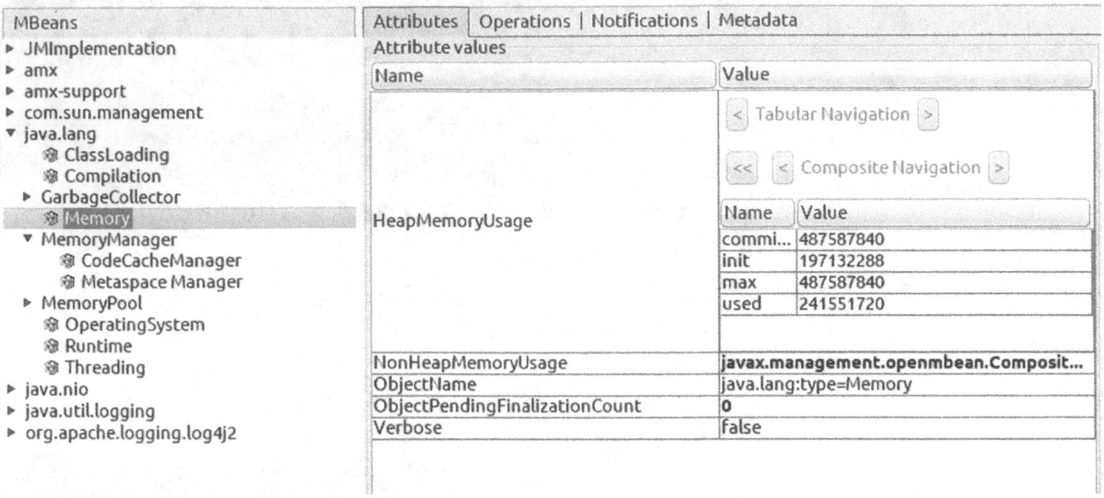

Figure 14-5. *VisualVM: Java heap memory consumption*

Adding Glassfish Monitoring to JMX

Glassfish makes its monitoring available to JMX, though not by default and not automatically. What we first have to do to make this happen is to enable the monitoring MBeans. Open the web administration console at `http://localhost:4848` and navigate to Configurations ➤ server-config ➤ Monitoring. Make sure the checkbox at "Monitoring MBeans" is enabled. See Figure 14-1. You have to restart the server if you change the value of this checkbox.

With this prerequisite fulfilled, the Glassfish monitoring still needs to be told to forward its figures to the MBeans. You have to do this manually, and you have to do it every time you start the server. To switch this on, enter VisualVM as described in the preceding section and navigate to amx-support ➤ boot-amx. Select the "Operations" tab and click on the "bootAMX" button. A new entry, "amx," should appear in the MBeans list, and it will contain all JMX monitoring that has been enabled for Glassfish. See Figure 14-6.

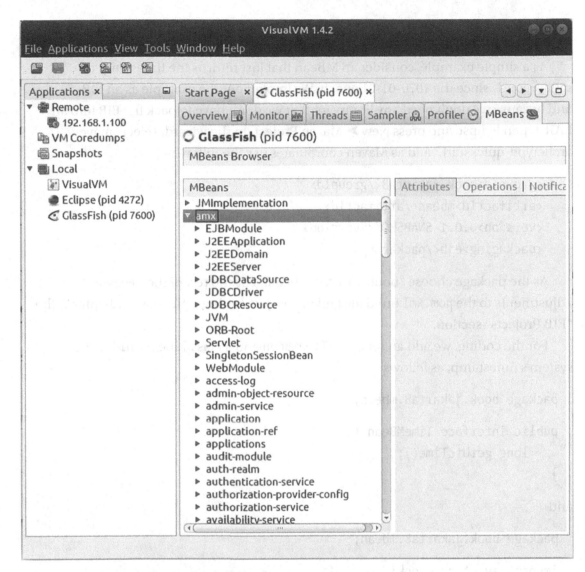

Figure 14-6. *Glassfish AMX monitoring extension*

Implementing Custom JMX Modules

You can create your own MBeans for monitoring classes of your Jakarta EE 8 application.
It is not complicated. You must define an interface MyMbeanMBean, where the "MBean"
at the end is mandatory, and an implementing class, MyMbean. It is important that
the names match, so if you have an MBean interface DatabaseAccessMBean the
implementing class must have the name DatabaseAccess. You then use the platform's

MBean server to register an instance of the MBean. As interface methods for MBean attributes, you add any number of getSomething() methods; see the following example.

As a simple example, consider an MBean that just returns the timestamp in milliseconds since the 1070-01-01 epoch. We implement the example as an EJB, and because we don't need any library for that we don't have to pack the EJB into an EAR. Open Eclipse and press New ➤ Maven Project. In the wizard, select "maven-archetype-quickstart," and as Maven coordinates use the following:

```
<groupId>book.jakarta8</groupId>
<artifactId>mbean</artifactId>
<version>0.0.1-SNAPSHOT</version>
<packaging>ejb</packaging>
```

As the package choose "book.jakarta8.mbean." For the rest of the necessary adjustments to the pom.xml build file and the project settings, please see Chapter 7, the "EJB Projects" section.

For the coding, we add an interface TimeMBean and a class Time returning the system's timestamp, as follows:

```
package book.jakarta8.mbean;

public interface TimeMBean {
    long getUtcTime();
}
```

and

```
package book.jakarta8.mbean;

import java.time.Clock;

public class Time implements TimeMBean {
    @Override
    public long getUtcTime() {
        return Clock.systemUTC().millis();
    }
}
```

The method must be marked as a getter method, and hence must start with a "get."

We learned in Chapter 7 that we can create an EJB that gets constructed reliably upon application startup and as a singleton if we add the two annotations @Startup and @Singleton to the EJB. The Maven project wizard we used created a class App for us. For simplicity's sake, we replace it with the EJB code, but in a larger project you can register the MBean at any suitable other place. Open class App and replace its contents with the following:

```
package book.jakarta8.mbean;

import java.lang.management.ManagementFactory;

import javax.annotation.PostConstruct;
import javax.annotation.PreDestroy;
import javax.ejb.Singleton;
import javax.ejb.Startup;
import javax.management.MBeanServer;
import javax.management.ObjectName;

@Singleton
@Startup
public class App {
    private final static String OBJECT_NAME =
            "book.jakarta8:type=Time";

    @PostConstruct
    public void postConstruct() {
        System.err.println("!!!!!!!!!!!!!!!!!!!!!!!!!!!");
        System.err.println("!!!!!!!!!!!!!!!!!!!!!!!!!!!");
        System.err.println("!!!!!!!!!!!!!!!!!!!!!!!!!!!");

        try {
            MBeanServer mbs = ManagementFactory.
                getPlatformMBeanServer();
            ObjectName name = new ObjectName(OBJECT_NAME);
            TimeMBean mbean = new Time();
            mbs.registerMBean(mbean, name);
```

```
        }catch(Exception e) {
            e.printStackTrace(Systm.err);
        }
    }

    @PreDestroy
    public void preDestroy() {
        try {
          MBeanServer mbs = ManagementFactory.
                getPlatformMBeanServer();
          ObjectName name = new ObjectName(OBJECT_NAME);
          mbs.unregisterMBean(name);
        }catch(Exception e) {
            e.printStackTrace(Systm.err);
        }
    }
}
```

Because of the @Startup annotation, the method marked with @PostConstruct gets called whenever the EJB gets deployed, redeployed, or the Jakarta EE 8 server starts. In preDestroy() we unregister the MBean.

You can now deploy the EJB project. In the console text like the following will appear:

```
2019-05-29T09:22:41.881+0200|
    Severe: !!!!!!!!!!!!!!!!!!!!!!!!!!!!!
2019-05-29T09:22:41.881+0200|
    Severe: !!!!!!!!!!!!!!!!!!!!!!!!!!!!!
2019-05-29T09:22:41.881+0200|
    Severe: !!!!!!!!!!!!!!!!!!!!!!!!!!!!!
2019-05-29T09:22:41.916+0200|
    Info: Loading application mbean done in 934 ms
```

If you now open VisualVM again, a new entry, "book.jakarta8," with sub-item "Time," will appear. If you click on it, a new attribute, "UtcTime," will be shown. The platform MBean server deduced this attribute from the MBeans method name getUtcTime. See Figure 14-7.

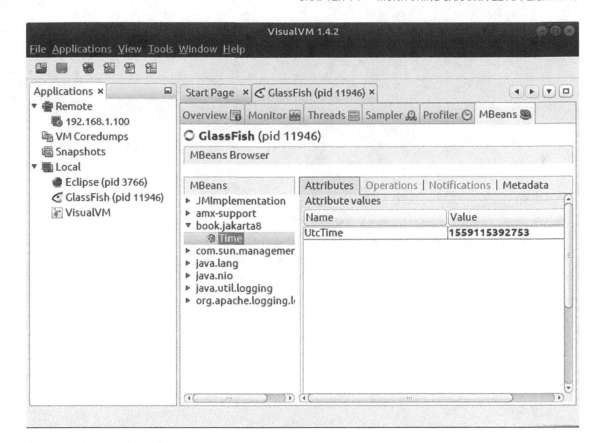

Figure 14-7.   Time MBean

Exercise 2

Add Log4j logging to the project and replace all `System.err.println()` statements with logging statements.

Appendix

Standard HTML RenderKit Tags
HTML Tag Attribute Classes

The Standard HTML RenderKit Tags, especially the HTML RenderKit tags, usually have a lot of possible attributes, like in the following:

```
<h:outputText id="name"
    rendered="#{person.nameRendered}"
    value="#{person.name}"
    converter="#{person.nameConverter}"
    escape="true"
    lang="en"
    style="color:red"
    styleClass="ot"
    [and more...] />
```

Fortunately for many tags, there are common attribute sets that mean the same thing. For this reason, I introduce a number of attribute shortcuts and classes in Table A-1.

© Peter Späth 2019

P. Späth, *Beginning Jakarta EE*, https://doi.org/10.1007/978-1-4842-5079-2

Table A-1. *Tag Attribute Classes*

Class	Attributes
[0]	Basic attributes. These are attributes used by almost all HTML RenderKit tags. `id`: An elements ID. Corresponds to an HTML "id" attribute, but the rendered ID on the target HTML page may look different, so you, for example, cannot use this ID in JavaScript code without further adaption. However, whenever an ID is requested for an attribute of a JSF tag, this is the ID meant. To distinguish between this ID and the rendered ID, the latter often gets called *client ID*. For this ID attribute a value expression is not allowed. `rendered`: Whether or not this element gets rendered. If you write a value expression like `rendered = #{someClass.prop}` you can connect the attribute to a Boolean-valued getter of an injected Java class, but you can also use the literals "true" and "false" here.
[H]	Typical HTML-related attributes. Same as [0], plus the following: `style`: Apply a CSS style declaration. Corresponds directly to the HTML "style" attribute. For example, `<h:outputText value="Hello" style="color:red; font-weight: bold;" />`. You can, of course, also use a value expression like `style = "#{person.style}"`. `styleClass`: Apply a CSS style class. Corresponds directly to the HTML "class" attribute. For example, `<h:outputText value="Hello" styleClass="myLabel" />`. You can also use a value expression here. `title`: Advisory title information. Corresponds directly to the HTML "title" attribute. You can also use a value expression here. `role`: Space-separated tokens according to WAI-ARIA. Directly passed through to the HTML "role" attribute. You can also use a value expression here.
[R]	The "required" flag for input elements. `required`: Whether or not the element is required. One of: `true`, `false`, or a Boolean value expression. Defaults to `false`. `requiredMessage`: A string or a `String` value expression indicating the message to be shown if `required` was set `true` and no value was submitted.
[T]	Tab index for input elements. Designates the position of the element in the tabbing order of the whole document. A number between 0 and `32767`, as a string, or a `String` value expression.

(continued)

Table A-1. (*continued*)

Class	Attributes
[RO]	Read-only flag for input elements. `readonly`: Whether or not the element is a read-only element. One of: `true`, `false`, or a `Boolean` value expression. Defaults to `false`.
[V]	Value and converter. Many tags have a value and use a converter to translate between this value's representation in an injected Java class and the textual representation in the generated HTML. `value`: The current value of the component. Usually you'll write a value expression like `#{person.name}` to connect the value to a property of an injected Java class, but you can also use literal strings like "John Smith," "27," "true," or "false" if it fits your needs. If the value is not of type `String`, the type gets specified in round brackets, as in `[V(Boolean)]`. `converter`: Use a value expression evaluating to `javax.faces.convert.Converter` for specifying a converter. Converters are for transforming the value to a `String` and vice versa. If you use a converter, a value expression for the `value` attribute can have other types than the originally specified one. It is generally not recommended to use this attribute—some tags even do not allow it, and instead specify `<f:converter>` sub-elements from the core tag library.
[V+]	Same as [V], but added the following: `converterMessage`: A converter message to be shown if the conversion fails. You can use a `String` value expression here.
[?]	A validator. Validators are for checking if the user's input complies with some rule. Validators can also be specified as sub-elements using the `<f:validator>` tag. `validator`: A method expression pointing to a method with signature void `methodName(FacesContext, UIComponent, Object)` for validating the input. `validatorMessage`: A validator message to be shown if the validation fails. Can be a value expression.

(*continued*)

Table A-1. (*continued*)

Class	Attributes
[-]	A Boolean attribute that allows for shortcutting an element's lifecycle. See section "Overview of the JSF chapter." immediate: Indicates whether the elements shortcut the normal JSF lifecycle. Either "true" or "false," but may also be a value expression evaluating to Boolean.
[K]	JavaScript keyboard control. Any of the following: onkeydown: Corresponds directly to the HTML "onkeydown" handler. Here, you specify any JavaScript code that needs to be executed while a key is pressed. You can use a value expression here. onkeyup: Corresponds directly to the HTML "onkeyup" handler. Here, you specify any JavaScript code that needs to be executed while a key is released. You can use a value expression here. onkeypress: Corresponds directly to the HTML "onkeypress" handler. Here, you specify any JavaScript code that needs to be executed after a key has been pressed and released. You can use a value expression here.
[C]	JavaScript clicking control. Any of the following: onclick: Corresponds directly to the HTML "onclick" handler. JavaScript code that needs to be executed when the mouse has clicked on the element. You can use a value expression here. ondblclick: Corresponds directly to the HTML "ondblclick" handler. JavaScript code that needs to be executed when the mouse has double-clicked on the element. You can use a value expression here.

(*continued*)

Table A-1. (*continued*)

Class	Attributes
[M]	JavaScript mouse-handling attributes. Any of the following: onmousedown: Corresponds directly to the HTML "onmousedown" handler. JavaScript code that needs to be executed when the mouse has been pressed. You can use a value expression here. onmouseup: Corresponds directly to the HTML "onmouseup" handler. JavaScript code that needs to be executed when the mouse has been released. You can use a value expression here. onmousemove: Corresponds directly to the HTML "onmousemove" handler. JavaScript code that needs to be executed when the mouse has been moved. You can use a value expression here. onmouseover: Corresponds directly to the HTML "onmouseover" handler. JavaScript code that needs to be executed when the mouse has entered the element. You can use a value expression here. onmouseout: Corresponds directly to the HTML "onmouseout" handler. JavaScript code that needs to be executed when the mouse has exited the element. You can use a value expression here.
[F]	JavaScript handling for the input focus that was gained or lost. onfocus: Corresponds directly to the HTML "onfocus" handler. JavaScript code that needs to be executed when the element receives the focus. You can use a value expression here. onblur: Corresponds directly to the HTML "onblur" handler. JavaScript code that needs to be executed when the element loses the focus. You can use a value expression here.
[L]	Language specifier. lang: Corresponds directly to the HTML "lang" attribute. Can also be a value expression evaluating to String.

(*continued*)

Table A-1. (*continued*)

Class	Attributes
[B]	A direct binding.
	binding: If you specify this and add a binding, like binding = "#{person.binding1}", the *component* that handles the tag gets controlled by the getter and setter corresponding to the value expression. This is for increased control over the component's behavior, although it perhaps moves too much presentation logic to the view. We don't use it in this book.
[D]	Text-direction indication.
	dir: One of LTR and RTL for left-to-right and right-to-left. You can use a String value expression here.

HTML Top-Level Tags

In Table A-2 you can see the top-level tags to be used in template files.

Table A-2. *HTML Top-Level Tags*

Tag	Translates to	Description
<h:doctype>	<!DOCTYPE>	Renders a <!DOCTYPE>. The implementation seems to be buggy, so don't use it. Usually it will be OK to just start your template files with a line <!DOCTYPE html> (for HTML 5).
<h:head>	<head>	Use this instead of <head>.
<h:body>	<body>	Use this instead of <body>.

The possible attributes of these elements get shown in Table A-3. Elements in square brackets denote attributes as shown in Table A-1. If the "Val-Expr" contains a type, you can use value expressions for this attribute that evaluate to the indicated type.

Table A-3. *HTML Top-Level Tags Attributes*

Tag	Attributes	Val-Expr	Description
`<h:doctype>`	`[O,B]` `[V(Object)]`		Attribute classes from Table A-1
	`public`	String	The PUBLIC part.
	`rootElement`	String	(required) The root XML element.
	`system`	String	The SYSTEM part.
`<h:head>`	`[L,B,D]`		Attribute classes from Table A-1
	`id`	-	An elements ID. For an explanation, see the corresponding entry inside the [O] class of Table A-1.
	`xmlns`	String	Gets passed through as an XML namespace.
`<h:body>`	`[H without "rendered"]` `[L,C,K,M,B,D]`		Attribute classes from Table A-1
	`onload`	String	JavaScript code to be executed when the document gets loaded.
	`onunload`	String	JavaScript code to be executed when the document gets unloaded.
	`xmlns`	String	Gets passed through as an XML namespace.

HTML Header Elements

In Table A-4, you can see the tags to be used inside `<h:head>` elements.

Table A-4. *HTML RenderKit Tags*

Tag	Translates to	Description
`<h:outputScript>`	`<script>`	Renders a `<script>` tag. If the attributes `library = "js"` and `name = "theName.js"` are specified, it refers to a file named `theName.js` inside folder "js" in "src/main/webapp/resources." Otherwise, you can also omit the `name` attribute—in this case, specify whatever has to go inside `<script>` as child elements (for example, a `<h:outputText>`).
`<h:outputStylesheet>`	`<link>`	Creates a `<link rel="stylesheet">` element. If the attributes `library = "css"` and `name = "theName.css"` are specified, it refers to a file named `theName.css` inside folder "css" in "src/main/webapp/resources."

The possible attributes of the header elements are shown in Table A-5. Elements in square brackets denote attributes as shown in Table A-1. If the "Val-Expr" contains a type, you can use value expressions for this attribute that evaluate to the indicated type.

Table A-5. *HTML Header Tags Attributes*

Tag	Attributes	Val-Expr	Description
`<h:outputScript>`	`[O,V,B]`		Attribute classes from Table A-1
	`library`	String	Gets used as a folder inside "src/main/webapp/resources" to use for loading a script file.
	`name`	String	(required) Gets used as the file name of the script to load.
	`target`	String	Where in the HTML to put the script-loading declaration. One of head, body, or form. If unspecified, use the current location.

(continued)

Table A-5. (*continued*)

Tag	Attributes	Val-Expr	Description
`<h:outputStylesheet>`	`[O,V,B]`		Attribute classes from Table A-1
	`library`	String	Gets used as a folder inside "src/main/webapp/resources" to use for loading a style file.
	`name`	String	(required) Gets used as the file name of a style file to load.
	`media`	String	The media type. For example, "screen."

HTML Form

Forms get used for transmitting user data from the front end (browser) to the server. As is usually the case for input elements in the target HTML, for JSF too all input elements must be placed somewhere inside a `<h:form>` element. See Table A-6 for the `<h:form>` tag itself.

Table A-6. *HTML Form Tag*

Tag	Translates to	Description
`<h:form>`	`<form>`	Creates a `<form>` element that you use to send values to the server. Contrary to the HTML `<form>` elements, you don't specify a target here—this is left to the "Submit" button or submit link elements inside the form.

The possible attributes of `<h:form>` elements are shown in Table A-7. Elements in square brackets denote attributes, as shown in Table A-1. If the "Val-Expr" contains a type, you can use value expressions for this attribute that evaluate to the indicated type.

367

Table A-7. *HTML Form Tag Attributes*

Tag	Attributes	Val-Expr	Description
`<h:form>`	`[H,D,C,K,M,L,B]`		Attribute classes from Table A-1
	`prependId`	Boolean	Indicates whether the form ID gets prepended to the descendants' IDs for calculating the client ID. If unspecified, defaults to `true`. To avoid confusion, in most cases you will go with the default behavior and don't specify this attribute.
	`accept`	String	A comma-separated list of content types the server is able to handle. Except for some corner cases, you don't have to specify this attribute.
	`acceptcharset`	String	A comma-separated list of character encodings the server is able to handle. Except for some corner cases, you don't have to specify this attribute.
	`enctype`	String	The content type used to submit the form. If unspecified, "application/x-www-form-urlencoded" will be used. Except for some corner cases, you don't have to specify this attribute.
	`onreset`	String	Denotes the JavaScript code to be executed when the form gets reset.
	`onsubmit`	String	Denotes the JavaScript code to be executed when the form gets submitted.
	`target`	String	The name of the frame where the response is to be sent. Frames don't get used often nowadays, so you probably won't use this attribute.

HTML Text Input and Output

Table A-8 shows the tags you can use for text input and output.

Table A-8. *HTML Text Input and Output Tags*

Tag	Translates to	Description
`<h:outputText>`	text	Outputs some text, specified by the `value` attribute. Depending on other attributes like `styleClass` the text might be wrapped in a `<span>` element in the generated HTML. This is probably the tag used most often in any JSF page because any static text passages should be rendered by this tag to allow for localized texts.
`<h:outputFormat>`	text	This is for parameterized text output. Use its `value` attribute to specify a format string with {0}, {1}, {2}, … as placeholders. You then fill the parameters via `<f:param value = "THE_VALUE" />` child elements.
`<h:outputLabel>`	`<label>`	Creates a `<label>` element. Use the contents of the `value` attribute for the label text, and use the `for` attribute to determine the `for` attribute of the generated element. Inside `for` you use the `id` attribute's value of the referred-to element.
`<h:inputText>`	`<input>`	Creates an `<input type = "text">` element that gets used for a text-input field in forms. Use the `value` attribute to hold the text (both input and output).
`<h:inputTextarea>`	`<input>`	Creates an `<input type = "textarea">` element that gets used for a multi-line text-input field in forms. The attributes are similar to `<h:inputText>`, but additionally support `cols` and `rows` attributes for the number of columns and rows.

(continued)

369

Table A-8. (*continued*)

Tag	Translates to	Description
`<h:inputHidden>`	`<input>`	Creates an `<input type = "hidden">` element that you can use to send values to the server that the front end doesn't render. Use the `value` attribute to hold the text (both input and output).
`<h:inputSecret>`	`<input>`	Creates an `<input type = "password">` element for a password-input field. Use the `value` attribute to hold the text (both input and output).
`<h:message>`	`text or` `<span>`	A `FacesContext` allows for adding messages to particular components of a page, or to the page in general. Messages can, for example, be error messages the application or a validator has generated. This tag shows the first message for a particular component, which you have to specify using its ID attribute. If you, for example, have `<h:inputText id="lastName" value="..."/>` you can output this component's message *anywhere* in the document via `<h:message for="lastName">`
`<h:messages>`	`various`	Same as `<h:message>`, but allows for the output of all messages of some component or all messages of all components of a page.

The possible attributes of the text input and output elements are shown in Table A-9. Elements in square brackets denote attributes as shown in Table A-1. If the "Val-Expr" contains a type, you can use value expressions for this attribute that evaluate to the indicated type. Naturally, the value expressions for the input fields denote input and output attributes.

Table A-9. *HTML Text Input/Output Tag Attributes*

Tag	Attributes	Val-Expr	Description
`<h:outputText>`	[H,V,L,T,B,D]		Attribute classes from Table A-1
	`escape`	Boolean	A Boolean flag indicating whether characters that are sensitive to HTML and XML are to be escaped. Defaults to `true`.
`<h:outputFormat>`	[H,V,L,B,D]		Attribute classes from Table A-1
	`escape`	Boolean	A Boolean flag indicating whether characters that are sensitive to HTML and XML are to be escaped. Defaults to `true`.
`<h:outputLabel>`	[H,V,C,K,M,F,L,B,D]		Attribute classes from Table A-1
	`for`	String	Evaluates to the ID of the referred-to element.
	`escape`	Boolean	A Boolean flag indicating whether characters that are sensitive to HTML and XML are to be escaped. Defaults to `true`.
	`accesskey`	String	A key that, once pressed, leads to the label's getting the focus.
`<h:inputText>`	[H,R,V+,RO,?,-,C,K, M,F,L,T,B,D]		Attribute classes from Table A-1
	`valueChangeListener`		A method expression pointing to a method with signature `void` `methodName(Valuechange` `Event)` for sending an event when the value has changed. You can also use appropriate sub-elements instead to listen to this event.

(continued)

Table A-9. (*continued*)

Tag	Attributes	Val-Expr	Description
	accesskey	String	A key that, once pressed, leads to the label's getting the focus.
	alt	String	The alternate textual description; passes through to the HTML "alt" attribute.
	autocomplete	String	Only if it reads "off," disables the browser's autocomplete functionality. The value "on" means: render nothing. Defaults to "on."
	disabled	Boolean	Indicates whether the element must be disabled.
	label	String	A user-presentable name for this element. Does not directly influence the rendered output, but goes to a property of the component class, so you can use it for development purposes, or you can use it indirectly.
	maxlength	int	The maximum number of characters for this field.
	onchange	String	JavaScript code to be executed when this element loses focus and has been changed.
	onselect	String	JavaScript code to be executed when text inside this element is selected by the user.
	size	int	Number of characters used to determine the visible length of the field. This is not the same as maxlength!

(*continued*)

Table A-9. (*continued*)

Tag	Attributes	Val-Expr	Description
`<h:inputTextarea>`			Same as `<h:inputText>`, but in addition:
	cols	int	Number of columns used to determine the visible width of the field.
	rows	int	Number of rows used to determine the visible height of the field.
`<h:inputSecret>`			Same as `<h:inputText>`, but in addition:
	redisplay	Boolean	Indicates whether previously entered values should be redisplayed. The value is not actually shown to the user in cleartext, but it will be sent to the server on submit.
`<h:inputHidden>`	[O,R,V+,?,-,B]		Attribute classes from Table A-1
	valueChangeListener		A method expression pointing to a method with signature void methodName(Valuechange Event) for sending an event when the value has changed. You can also use appropriate sub-elements instead to listen to this event.

(*continued*)

Table A-9. (*continued*)

Tag	Attributes	Val-Expr	Description
<h:message>	[H,L,B,D]		Attribute classes from Table A-1
	for	String	(required) Evaluating to the ID of the referred-to element.
	showDetail	Boolean	Indicates whether the detail portion of the message should be included. Defaults to true.
	showSummary	Boolean	Indicates whether the summary portion of the message should be included. Defaults to true.
	tooltip	Boolean	Indicates whether the detail portion of the message should be shown as a tooltip.
	infoClass	String	The style class attribute for "info"-level messages.
	infoStyle	String	The style attribute for "info"-level messages.
	warnClass	String	The style class attribute for "warning"-level messages.
	warnStyle	String	The style attribute for "warning"-level messages.
	errorClass	String	The style class attribute for "error"-level messages.
	errorStyle	String	The style attribute for "error"-level messages.
	fatalClass	String	The style class attribute for "fatal"-level messages.
	fatalStyle	String	The style attribute for "fatal"-level messages.

(*continued*)

Table A-9. (*continued*)

Tag	Attributes	Val-Expr	Description
<h:messages>			Same as <h:message>, but the for attribute is not required, and it has two more attributes:
	globalOnly	Boolean	Indicates whether only messages not associated with dedicated fields should be shown. Default is false.
	layout	String	Declares the layout of the messages. One of: table and list. Default is list.

HTML Selectables

Table A-10 shows the tags you can use for selectables style input and output fields. As is usually the case for input elements in HTML, selectables input elements must be placed somewhere inside a <h:form> element for JSF too.

Table A-10. *HTML Selectables Tags*

Tag	Translates to	Description
<h:selectBoolean Checkbox>	<input>	Creates an <input type = "checkbox"> element that gets used for checkbox input fields in forms. Use attribute value to specify whether the checkbox is checked or not. This can be a value expression like #{TheClass.chk1} pointing to a Boolean type getter and setter for input and output value.

(*continued*)

Table A-10. (*continued*)

Tag	Translates to	Description
`<h:selectMany Checkbox>`	`<input>`	Use this to render a set of interrelated checkboxes. Take its `value` attribute to connect it to getters and setters (type `String[]`, or a collection type holding strings) of a class, like in `value = "#{theClass.chkb}"`. Inside the tag, specify child elements, like `<f:selectItem itemValue = "v" itemLabel = "Item x" />`, for the various checkboxes—the `itemValue` must then correspond to the string values returned by `#{theClass.chkb}`. To use a more dynamic setup with the checkbox list controlled by a Java class, use `<f:selectItems>` as a child element.
`<h:selectMany Listbox>`	`<select>`	This is used to generate an HTML option list. Take its `value` attribute to connect it to getters and setters (type `String[]`, or a collection type holding strings) of a class, like in `value = "#{theClass.opts}"`. Inside the tag, specify child elements like `<f:selectItem itemValue = "v" itemLabel = "Item x" />` for the various options. The `itemValue` must then correspond to the string values returned by `#{theClass.opts}`. You can also use a single `<f:selectItems>` child and let the application control the option list.
`<h:selectMany Menu>`	`<select>`	Same as `<h:selectManyListbox>` but with the `size` attribute set to 1.
`<h:selectOne Listbox>`	`<select>`	Same as `<h:selectManyListbox>` but with at most one element selected. The `value` attribute gets connected to a `String` type getter and setter.

(*continued*)

Table A-10. (*continued*)

Tag	Translates to	Description
`<h:selectOneMenu>`	`<select>`	Same as `<h:selectManyMenu>` but with at most one element selected. The `value` attribute gets connected to a `String` type getter and setter.
`<h:selectOneRadio>`	`<input>`	Renders a set of radio buttons. Take its `value` attribute to connect it to getters and setters (type `String`, or a collection type holding strings) of a class, like in `value = "#{theClass.radio}"`. Inside the tag, specify child elements, like `<f:selectItem itemValue = "v" itemLabel = "Item x" />`, for the various options. The `itemValue` must then correspond to the string value returned by `#{theClass.radio}`. You can also use a single `<f:selectItems>` child and let the application control the option list.

The possible attributes of the selectables elements are shown in Table A-11. Elements in square brackets denote attributes, as shown in Table A-1. If the "Val-Expr" contains a type, you can use value expressions for this attribute that evaluate to the indicated type. Naturally, the value expressions for the input fields denote input and output attributes.

Table A-11. *HTML Selectables Tag Attributes*

Tag	Attributes	Val-Expr	Description
<h:selectBoolean Checkbox>	[H,R,V+(boolean),RO,?,-, D,L,F, C,K,M,T,B]		Attribute classes from Table A-1
	valueChangeListener		A method expression pointing to a method with signature void methodName(ValuechangeEvent) for sending an event when the value has changed. You can also use appropriate sub-elements instead to listen to this event.
	accesskey	String	A key that, once pressed, leads to the label's getting the focus.
	disabled	Boolean	Indicates whether the element must be disabled.
	label	String	A user-presentable name for this element. Does not directly influence the rendered output, but goes to a property of the component class, so you can use it for development purposes, or you can use it indirectly.
	onchange	String	JavaScript code to be executed when this element loses focus and was changed.
	onselect	String	JavaScript code to be executed when this element is selected by the user.

Element	Attribute	Type	Description
`<h:selectMany Checkbox>`	`[H,R,V+(Object),RO,?,-, D,L,F, C,K,M,T,B]`		Attribute classes from Table A-1. The value can be a `String[]` or a collection of strings.
	valueChangeListener		A method expression pointing to a method with signature void methodName(ValuechangeEvent) for sending an event when the value has changed. You can also use appropriate sub-elements instead to listen to this event.
	accesskey	String	A key that, once pressed, leads to the label's getting the focus.
	border	int	Border width in pixels.
	collectionType	String	The class implementing java.util.Collection to be used. The fully qualified class name as a string, or a value expression evaluating to the Class object. Optional.
	disabled	Boolean	Indicates whether the element must be disabled.
	disabledClass	String	Style class for disabled options.
	enabledClass	String	Style class for enabled options.
	selectedClass	String	Style class for selected options.
	unselectedClass	String	Style class for unselected options.
	hideNo-SelectionOption	Boolean	If "true," the "no selection option" must be hidden.

(continued)

Table A-11. (*continued*)

Tag	Attributes	Val–Expr	Description
	label	String	A user-presentable name for this element. Does not directly influence the rendered output, but goes to a property of the component class, so you can use for development purposes, or you can use it indirectly.
	layout	String	The layout. One of: pageDirection (list is laid out vertically) or lineDirection (list is laid out horizontally). Default is the latter.
	onchange	String	JavaScript code to be executed when this element loses focus and has been changed.
	onselect	String	JavaScript code to be executed when this element is selected by the user.
<h:selectMany Listbox>	[H,R,V+(Object),RO, ?,-,D,L,F,C,K,M,T,B]		Attribute classes from Table A-1. The value can be a String[] or a collection of strings.
	valueChangeListener		A method expression pointing to a method with signature void methodName(ValuechangeEvent) for sending an event when the value has changed. You can also use appropriate sub-elements instead to listen to this event.
	accesskey	String	A key that, once pressed, leads to the label's getting the focus.

collectionType	String	The class implementing java.util.Collection to be used. The fully qualified class name as a string, or a value expression that evaluates to the Class object. Optional.
disabled	Boolean	Indicates whether the element must be disabled.
disabledClass	String	Style class for disabled options.
enabledClass	String	Style class for enabled options.
hideNo-SelectionOption	Boolean	If "true," the "no selection option" must be hidden.
label	String	A user-presentable name for this element. Does not directly influence the rendered output, but goes to a property of the component class, so you can use for development purposes, or you can use it indirectly.
onchange	String	JavaScript code to be executed when this element loses focus and has been changed.
onselect	String	JavaScript code to be executed when this element is selected by the user.
size	int	Number of available options to be shown. Defaults to no limit.

(continued)

Table A-11. (*continued*)

Tag	Attributes	Val-Expr	Description
`<h:selectOne Listbox>`			Like `<h:selectManyListbox>`, but without the "collectionType" attribute.
`<h:selectManyMenu>`			Like `<h:selectManyListbox>`.
`<h:selectOneMenu>`			Like `<h:selectManyMenu>`, but without the "collectionType" attribute.
`<h:selectOneRadio>`			Like `<h:selectManyCheckbox>`, but without the "collectionType," "selectedClass," and "unselectedClass" attributes.

HTML Images

Table A-12 describes the image tag you can use to add images to a page.

Table A-12. *HTML Images*

Tag	Translates to	Description
<h:graphicImage>	<img>	Creates an <img> element, which represents an image. Image files can go to the folder specified by the library attribute inside "src/main/webapp/resources." In addition, images can be represented by URLs.

The possible attributes of the image element are shown in Table A-13. Elements in square brackets denote attributes, as shown in Table A-1. If the "Val-Expr" contains a type, you can use value expressions for this attribute that evaluate to the indicated type.

Table A-13. *HTML Image Attributes*

Tag	Attributes	Val-Expr	Description
<h:graphic Image>	[H,D,L,C,K,M,B]		Attribute classes from Table A-1
	url	String	The URL pointing to the image.
	value	Object	Same as "url."
	alt	String	Alternate textual representation of the image.
	height	String	Override the height of the image.
	width	String	Override the width of the image.
	ismap	Boolean	Whether the image represents a server-side image map. If true, the mage must be enclosed inside an <a>. Default is false.
	usemap	String	The name of a client-side image map.
	library	String	Gets used as a folder inside "src/main/webapp/resources" to use for loading the image file.
	name	String	Gets used as the file name of the image file to load.
	longdesc	String	URI to a long description of the image.

HTML Buttons and Links

Buttons and links are something a user can click on to submit a form or initiate other actions, like reloading a page or advancing to another page.

Table A-14 describes the button and link tags.

Table A-14. *HTML Buttons and Links*

Tag	Translates to	Description
`<h:commandButton>`	`<input>`	Creates a button `<input type = "submit>"` for submitting a form. May contain an `action` attribute that holds a method expression pointing to a method of a connected class. The `value` attribute holds the button text. Or you can use an `image` attribute pointing to the URL of an image to be used as the button.
`<h:commandLink>`	`<a>`	Creates a link that acts like a `<h:commandButton>` inside a form. May contain an `action` attribute that holds a method expression pointing to a method of a connected class. The `value` attribute holds the link text.
`<h:link>`	`<a>`	Creates a link. The `value` attribute specifies the link text, the `outcome` attribute designates a value expression that gets evaluated to produce the logical link destination (for example, "xyz" if "xyz.xhtml" is an existing template).
`<h:outputLink>`	`<a>`	Creates a link. The `value` attribute specifies the generated link's `href` attribute. Use any number of child elements to define the link's contents.

(*continued*)

Table A-14. (*continued*)

Tag	Translates to	Description
`<h:button>`	`<button>`	Creates a `<button>` element that does not strictly correspond to a form-submit action. Instead, the button might be placed outside a `<h:form>` tag, and it might perform some calculation via JavaScript. Nevertheless, a click on the button will lead to reloading the page or loading a different page via setting `window.location.href`. The `value` attribute specifies the link text. The `outcome` attribute designates a method expression invoked *before* the page gets loaded (not when the button gets pressed!), and points to a new page that gets navigated to when the button gets pressed.

The possible attributes of the buttons and links are shown in Table A-15. Elements in square brackets denote attributes, as shown in Table A-1. If the "Val-Expr" contains a type, you can use value expressions for this attribute that evaluate to the indicated type.

Table A-15. *HTML Buttons and Links*

Tag	Attributes	Val-Expr	Description
`<h:command Button>`	`[H,RO,D,L,-,C, K,M,F,T,B]`		Attribute classes from Table A-1
	`value`	Object	The button text.
	`action`	-	A method expression. Must point to a method without parameters returning an `Object`. The `toString()` method of this object represents the navigation case. If the object equals `null`, the button press will lead to reloading the page.
	`action-Listener`	String	A method expression of signature `void methodName()` or `void methodName(javax.faces.event.ActionEvent)`. Will be called when this button gets activated by the user.
	`type`	String	The type. One of: `submit`, `reset`, `button`. Default is `submit`.
	`accesskey`	String	A key that, once pressed, leads to the button's getting the focus.
	`alt`	String	Alternate textual representation of the button.
	`disabled`	Boolean	Indicates whether the element must be disabled.
	`image`	String	URL of the image to be loaded for the button.
	`label`	String	A user-presentable name for this element. Does not directly influence the rendered output, but goes to a property of the component class, so you can use for development purposes, or you can use it indirectly.
	`onchange`	String	JavaScript code to be executed when this element loses focus and has been changed.
	`onselect`	String	JavaScript code to be executed when text inside this element is selected by the user.

`<h:command` `[H,D,L,-,C,K,` `Link>` `M,F,T,B]`		Attribute classes from Table A-1
value	Object	The link text.
action	-	A method expression. Must point to a method without parameters returning an `Object`. The `toString()` method of this object represents the navigation case. If the object equals `null`, the button press will lead to reloading the page.
action-Listener	String	A method expression of signature `void methodName()` or `void methodName(javax.faces.event.ActionEvent)`. Will be called when this button gets activated by the user.
type	String	The content type of the resource the link points to.
charset	String	The character encoding of the resource the link points to.
hreflang	String	The language of the resource the link points to.
accesskey	String	A key that, once pressed, leads to the link's getting the focus.
disabled	Boolean	Indicates whether the element must be disabled.
coords	String	Position and shape of the hot spot for client-side image maps.
shape	String	Shape of the hot spot for client-side image maps.
rel	String	Passes through as the "rel" attribute of the link.
rev	String	Passes through as the "rev" attribute of the link.
target	String	Same as the generated `<a>` element's `target` attribute. One of: `_blank`, `_parent`, `_self`, `_top`, or the name of the frame to which the response is to be sent.

(continued)

387

Table A-15. (*continued*)

Tag	Attributes	Val-Expr	Description
<h:link>	[H,D,L,C,K,M, F,T,B]		Attribute classes from Table A-1
	value	Object	The link text.
	includeView-Params	Boolean	Whether to include page parameters in the target URI.
	outcome	String	A navigation target, used to determine the URL written in the HTML "href" attribute. Because JSF knows we use XHTML as a template page ending, an outcome = "page2", for example, will resolve to href = "[CONTEXT]/page2.xhtml".
	type	String	The content type of the resource the link points to.
	charset	String	The character encoding of the resource the link points to.
	hreflang	String	The language of the resource the link points to.
	accesskey	String	A key that, once pressed, leads to the link's getting the focus.
	disabled	Boolean	Indicates whether the element must be disabled.
	coords	String	Position and shape of the hot spot for client-side image maps.
	shape	String	Shape of the hot spot for client-side image maps.
	rel	String	Passes through as the "rel" attribute of the link.
	rev	String	Passes through as the "rev" attribute of the link.
	target	String	Same as the generated <a> element's target attribute. One of: _blank, _parent, _self, _top, or the name of the frame to which the response is to be sent.
	fragment	String	Added as a URL fragment ("#" + fragment ID) to the link.

			Attribute classes from Table A-1
<h:output Link>	[H,V,D,L,C, K,M,F,T,B]		
	value	Object	The link URL. Ends up in the href attribute of the generated <a> element. Can also be a relative URL.
	target	String	Same as the generated <a> element's target attribute. One of: _blank, _parent, _self, _top, or the name of the frame to which the response is to be sent.
	type	String	The content type of the resource the link points to.
	charset	String	The character encoding of the resource the link points to.
	hreflang	String	The language of the resource the link points to.
	accesskey	String	A key that, once pressed, leads to the link's getting the focus.
	disabled	Boolean	Indicates whether the element must be disabled.
	coords	String	Position and shape of the hot spot for client-side image maps.
	shape	String	Shape of the hot spot for client-side image maps.
	rel	String	Passes through as the rel attribute of the link.
	rev	String	Passes through as the rev attribute of the link.

(continued)

Table A-15. (*continued*)

Tag	Attributes	Val-Expr	Description
<h:button>	[H,V(no converter), D,L,C,K, M,F,T,B]		Attribute classes from Table A-1
	value	Object	The button text.
	includeView-Params	Boolean	Whether to include page parameters in the target URI.
	outcome	String	A navigation target, used to determine the URL written in the HTML href attribute. Because JSF knows we use XHTML as a template page ending, an outcome = "page2", for example, will resolve to href = "[CONTEXT]/page2.xhtml".
	accesskey	String	A key that, once pressed, leads to the link's getting the focus.
	alt	String	Alternate textual representation of the button.
	fragment	String	Added as a URL fragment ("#" + fragment ID) to the link.
	image	String	URL of the image to be loaded for the button.

HTML File Upload

The <h:inputFile> tag can be used to let the user upload a file from the browser to the server. See Table A-16 for more details.

Table A-16. *HTML File Upload*

Tag	Translates to	Description
<h:inputFile>	<input>	Creates an <input type = "file"> element that gets used to send complete files from the client (browser) to the server. The value attribute corresponds to a setter with parameter type javax.servlet.http.Part in a connected class.

The possible attributes of the file-upload element are shown in Table A-17. Elements in square brackets denote attributes, as shown in Table A-1. If the "Val-Expr" contains a type, you can use value expressions for this attribute that evaluate to the indicated type.

Table A-17. *HTML File-Upload Attributes*

Tag	Attributes	Val-Expr	Description
`<h:input File>`	[H,RO,D,L,C, K,M,F,T,B]		Attribute classes from Table A-1
	`value`	Part	The file data. The fully qualified class reads `javax.servlet.http.Part`. See below for how to read the file data.
	`accesskey`	String	A key that, once pressed, leads to the button's getting the focus.
	`alt`	String	Alternate textual representation of the button.
	`autocomplete`	String	If set to "off," the autocomplete function of the browser will be disabled.
	`disabled`	Boolean	Indicates whether the element must be disabled.
	`label`	String	A user-presentable name for this element. Does not directly influence the rendered output, but goes to a property of the component class, so you can use it for development purposes, or you can use it indirectly.
	`maxlength`	int	The maximum number of characters allowed for this field.
	`size`	int	The number of characters used to calculate the visual width of the field.
	`onchange`	String	JavaScript code to be executed when this element loses focus and is changed.
	`onselect`	String	JavaScript code to be executed when text inside this element is selected by the user.

HTML Grouping

In case you need a component that just draws a bracket around its children, you can use the `<h:panelGroup>` tag. This comes in handy if you use a component that allows for just one child, but you need more-complex contents. A `<f:facet>` is such a case (will come in the appendix). Another use case is a grouping you need for styling purposes. See Table A-18 for more details.

Table A-18. *HTML Grouping*

Tag	Translates to	Description
`<h:panelGroup>`	`<span>` or `<div>`	Gathers its children in its own element serving as a container. Depending on which "layout" gets chosen and whether "style" or "styleClass" is specified, renders a `<div>` or a `<span>` HTML element.

The possible attributes of the grouping element are shown in Table A-19. If the "Val-Expr" contains a type, you can use value expressions for this attribute that evaluate to the indicated type.

Table A-19. *HTML Grouping Attributes*

Tag	Attributes	Val-Expr	Description
`<h:panelGroup>`	`id`	-	A `String`, not a value expression, denoting the ID of the element.
	`rendered`	Boolean	Whether or not the group gets rendered. Defaults to `true`.
	`layout`	String	Which layout to choose. If it evaluates to `block`, render a `<div>`. Otherwise renders a `<span>`.
	`style`	String	Passes through as the HTML `style` attribute.
	`styleClass`	String	A space-separated list of CSS style classes; passes through as the HTML `class` attribute.
	`binding`	UIComponent	A binding, see shortcut [B] in Table A-17

HTML Tables

Especially for enterprise web applications, the rendering of data tables given a list of items is an important task. In addition, tables sometimes get used for the laying out of a fixed number of elements. Table A-20 lists the corresponding tags.

Table A-20. *HTML Tables Tags*

Tag	Translates to	Description
`<h:dataTable>`	`<table>`	Creates a `<table>` element. A standard usage pattern is: specify the list or array as a value expression inside the `value` attribute: `<h:dataTable value = "#{injectedClass.fieldName}" ... >`. As another attribute, tell the component which formal variable to use for each row: `<h:dataTable ... var = "row" ... >`. As children, specify one `<h:column>` per table column. For the contents of each `<h:column>`, see below.
`<h:column>`	-	A column specification inside `<h:dataTable>`. Inside each `<column>`, you write an output statement for an element of a row, as follows: `<h:column>` `#{row.something}` `</h:column>` To specify a column header, add a `<f:facet>`, as follows: `<h:column>` `<f:facet name="header">` `Header Title` `</f:facet>` `#{row.something}` `</h:column>`
`<h:panelGrid>`	`<table>`	An alternative way of specifying a table. Contrary to the `<dataTable>` tag, no `<h:column>` elements get used. Instead, you tell the tag how many columns you want to have, and as children you just give all table elements one after another. This element thus can serve as both a data table and a mere layout component.

The possible attributes of the table tags are shown in Table A-21. Elements in square brackets denote attributes, as shown in Table A-1. If the "Val-Expr" contains a type, you can use value expressions for this attribute that evaluate to the indicated type.

Table A-21. HTML Table Tags Attributes

Tag	Attributes	Val-Expr	Description
`<h:dataTable>`	`[H,D,L,C,K,M,B]`		Attribute classes from Table A-1
	`value`	coll. or array	The table data.
	`var`	–	Name of the formal variable to use for each row.
	`cellpadding`	String	A CSS style padding between cells. You want to use this! Example: 0.5em
	`cellspacing`	String	A CSS style spacing between the left-most, bottom-most, top-most, and right-most cells and the table border. Example: 0.5em
	`columnClasses`	String	A comma-delimited list of CSS classes applied to the columns. You want to use this if columns should look different from each other.
	`rowClasses`	String	A comma-delimited list of CSS classes applied to the rows in round-robin fashion. You want to use this if rows should look different from each other. Each row may also have a space-separated list of CSS classes assigned to it. Examples: "even,odd" or "even one, odd two, even three, odd four"
	`border`	int	Width in pixels for an outer table border. Default is 0.
	`rules`	String	Specifies which rules will appear between cells. Possible values: none (no rules; this is the default), groups (between row groups), rows (between rows), cols (between columns), and all (all).
	`first`	int	If specified, the index of first element used from the list or array. Default is 0.

(continued)

Table A-21. (*continued*)

Tag	Attributes	Val-Expr	Description
	`rows`	int	The number of rows to use from the list or array. Starting from the index given by the `first` attribute, if this one is specified. A value of 0 means to show all data starting at `first`.
	`bgcolor`	String	The background color to use for the table. Use an HTML color name or #RRGGBB color specification.
	`bodyrows`	String	While not used very often, tables can have more than one `<tbody>` element. If you use this attribute, write a comma-separated list of row indices for which new `<tbody>` elements should be started.
	`captionClass`	String	Space-separated CSS style classes applied to the table caption.
	`captionStyle`	String	CSS style applied to the table caption.
	`footerClass`	String	Space-separated CSS style classes applied to the table footer.
	`headerClass`	String	Space-separated CSS style classes applied to the table header.
	`frame`	String	Specifies which sides of the table border should be visible. Possible values: none, above (top side only), below (bottom side only), lhs (left side only), rhs (right side only), hsides (top and bottom), vside (left and right), box (all sides), border (all sides)
	`summary`	String	A summary for agent rendering to non-visual media (speech, Braille)
	`width`	String	Table width. For example: "80%" or "27em."

Element	Attribute	Type	Description
`<h:column>`	[O,B]		Attribute classes from Table A-1
	footerClass	String	Space-separated list of CSS style classes applied to any table footer.
	headerClass	String	Space-separated list of CSS style classes applied to any table header.
	rowHeader	Boolean	If true, treat the column as a header-only column to be rendered with `<th>` instead of `<td>`. Default is false.
`<h:panelGrid>`	[H,D,L,C,K,M,B]		Attribute classes from Table A-1
	columns	int	The number of columns.
	bgcolor	String	The background color to use for the table. Use an HTML color name or #RRGGBB color specification.
	bodyrows	String	While not used very often, tables can have more than one `<tbody>` element. If you use this attribute, write a comma-separated list of row indices for which new `<tbody>` elements should be started.
	border	int	Width in pixels for an outer table border. Default is 0.
	captionClass	String	Space-separated CSS style classes applied to the table caption.
	captionStyle	String	CSS style applied to the table caption.
	footerClass	String	Space-separated CSS style classes applied to the table footer.
	headerClass	String	Space-separated CSS style classes applied to the table header.
	cellpadding	String	A CSS style padding between cells. You want to use this! Example: 0.5em
	cellspacing	String	A CSS style spacing between the left-most, bottom-most, top-most, and right-most cells and the table border. Example: 0.5em

(continued)

Table A-21. (*continued*)

Tag	Attributes	Val-Expr	Description
	columnClasses	String	A comma-delimited list of CSS classes applied to the columns. You want to use this if columns should look different from each other.
	rowClasses	String	A comma-delimited list of CSS classes applied to the rows in round-robin fashion. You want to use this if rows should look different from each other. Each row may also have a space-separated list of CSS classes assigned to it. Examples: "even,odd" or "even one, odd two, even three, odd four."
	frame	String	Specifies which sides of the table border should be visible. Possible values: none, above (top side only), below (bottom side only), lhs (left side only), rhs (right side only), hsides (top and bottom), vside (left and right), box (all sides), border (all sides)
	rules	String	Specifies which rules will appear between cells. Possible values: none (no rules, this is the default), groups (between row groups), rows (between rows), cols (between columns), and all (all).
	summary	String	A summary for agent rendering to non-visual media (speech, Braille)
	width	String	Table width. For example: "80%" or "27em."

Solutions to the Exercises

The following are the solutions to the exercises given in the chapters.

Chapter 1

- **Exercise 1:**

  (1.) is not true. Jakarta EE 8, while running under the umbrella of the Eclipse Foundation, gets maintained by a community process. (2.) is not true. The Java standard edition is an integral part of Jakarta EE. (3.) is not true, as the predecessor of Jakarta EE 8 was JEE 7 (4.) is not true; layers are stacked and layers other than the bottom layer depend on the layer underneath them. (5.) is true.

- **Exercise 2:**

  Both are not true. Jakarta EE 8 applications *could* follow microservices paradigms, but they don't need to. Jakarta EE 8 might access cloud services, but using cloud technologies is utterly optional.

- **Exercise 3:**

  (1.) No. Java as a runtime platform is obligatory. (2.) True. (3.) True, but the language must be able to generate code that runs on the Java platform (Kotlin and Scala are able to do so).

Chapter 4

- **Exercise 1:**

  The tag reads:

```
<h:outputText
  value="The list contains #{b.list.size()}
      #{b.list.size() == 1 ?
      'item' : 'items'}"/>
```

(shown split here; in your template file, don't use line breaks inside the value)

– **Exercise 2:**

In file src/main/webapp/WEB-INF/faces-config.xml add a new child element to <locale-config> and let it read as follows:

```
<locale-config>
  <default-locale>en</default-locale>
  <supported-locale>es</supported-locale>
</locale-config>
```

Add a file src/main/resources/hacc/web/WebMessages_es. properties and let it read as follows:

```
label_enterYourName = Inserte su nombre:
label_enterTheDate = Inserte el día (yyyy-MM-dd):
submit = Enviar
label_noExpenses = No expensas
```

Note For development purposes you can check the new language in Firefox if you change the key intl.accept_languages in about:config (enter as URL). Prepend "es" to the list.

– **Exercise 3:**

Inside <h:form> in file main.xhtml add the following:

```
<p/>
<h:selectManyListbox
    value="#{accounting.expenseTypes}">
  <f:selectItem itemValue="Food"
      itemLabel="Food" />
  <f:selectItem itemValue="Clothing"
      itemLabel="Clothing" />
```

```
<f:selectItem itemValue="Car"
    itemLabel="Car" />
<f:selectItem itemValue="Fun"
    itemLabel="Fun" />
<f:selectItem itemValue="Other"
    itemLabel="Other" />
</h:selectManyListbox>
```

Inside class Accounting add the following:

```
...
public class Accounting {
 ...
 private List<String> expenseTypes =
   new ArrayList<>();
 public List<String> getExpenseTypes() {
  return expenseTypes;
 }
 public void setExpenseTypes(
    List<String> expenseTypes) {
  this.expenseTypes = expenseTypes;
 }
 ...
 }
```

– **Exercise 4:**

The adapted part inside <h:form> reads as follows:

```
<h:selectManyListbox
  value="#{accounting.expenseTypes}">
 <f:selectItems
  value="#{accounting.expenseTypeOptions}"/>
</h:selectManyListbox>
```

In class Accounting add the following:

```
...
import javax.faces.model.SelectItem;
...
public class Accounting {
 ...
 private SelectItem[] expenseTypeOptions;

 public Accounting() {
  ...
  setExpenseTypeOptions(new SelectItem[] {
   new SelectItem("Food", "Food"),
   new SelectItem("Clothing", "Clothing"),
   new SelectItem("Car", "Car"),
   new SelectItem("Fun", "Fun"),
   new SelectItem("Other", "Other")
  });
 }
 ...
 public SelectItem[] getExpenseTypeOptions() {
  return expenseTypeOptions;
 }
 public void setExpenseTypeOptions(
   SelectItem[] expenseTypeOptions) {
  this.expenseTypeOptions = expenseTypeOptions;
 }
 ...
}
```

– **Exercise 5:**

(A) is true.

- **Exercise 6:**

In the `Accounting` class, add the following:

```
private double value;
public double getValue() {
  return value;
}
public void setValue(double value) {
  this.value = value;
}
```

In file `WebMessages.properties` add the following:

```
label_value = Value (#.##):
```

In file `main.xhtml` add the following inside `<h:form>`:

```
<h:outputText value="#{bundle.label_value}"
  style="float:left" />
<h:inputText value="#{accounting.value}">
 <f:convertNumber type="number"
   minFractionDigits="2"
   maxFractionDigits="2"/>
 <f:validateDoubleRange
   minimum="0.0" />
</h:inputText>
<div class="clearfloat" />
```

Note, the `style` attribute and the `clearfloat` are for styling purposes only.

- **Exercise 7:**

On page `main.xhtml`, write the following as the attribute `action` of the "Submit Command" button:

```
<h:commandButton value="#{bundle.submit}"
  action="response" />
```

This is an auto-navigation case. We can do that because the
submit() method of class Accounting does not do interesting
things. Later, we want to add access to a database, so, anticipating
further elaboration, you could just as well leave the command
button unaltered, with action = "#{accounting.register}",
and let the register() method return response instead of null.

Create a file src/main/webapp/response.xhtml and let it read
as follows:

```
<!DOCTYPE html>
<html xmlns:h="http://xmlns.jcp.org/jsf/html"
 xmlns:f="http://xmlns.jcp.org/jsf/core"
 xmlns:ui="http://java.sun.com/jsf/facelets"
 xmlns:pt="http://xmlns.jcp.org/jsf/passthrough">
<h:head>
 <title>Household Accounting</title>
 <h:outputStylesheet library = "css"
  name = "style.css" />
</h:head>
<h:body>
 <h1>
 <h:outputText
   value="#{bundle.response_title}" />
 </h1>
 <h:outputText
   value="#{bundle.response_label_name}
   #{accounting.name}" />
 <div class="clearfloat" />
 <h:outputText
   value="#{bundle.response_label_date}
   #{accounting.date}" />
 <div class="clearfloat" />
 <h:outputText
   value="#{bundle.response_label_types}
   #{accounting.expenseTypes}" />
 <div class="clearfloat" />
```

```
<h:outputText
    value="#{bundle.response_label_value}
    #{accounting.value}" />

<div class="clearfloat" />
<h:button
    value="#{bundle.response_btn_back}"
    outcome="main" />
```

```
</h:body>
</html>
```

The formatting/styling is up to you; what's important is the access to the properties of the injected `Accounting` bean via `#{accounting.someThing}`. This is possible because the bean is session scoped and survives the advancing to the response page. The back button can go without an enclosing `<h:form>` because the button's `outcome` attribute takes care of properly navigating to other pages.

Because we are using language resource bundle identifiers, add the following to `src/main/resourceshaccwebWebMessages.properties`:

```
response_title = You entered
response_label_name = Your name:
response_label_date = The date:
response_label_types = Types:
response_label_value = Value:
response_btn_back = Back
```

- **Exercise 8:**

The listener class reads, for example:

```
package book.jakarta8.hacc.jsfgui.listeners;

import javax.faces.event.PhaseEvent;
import javax.faces.event.PhaseId;
import javax.faces.event.PhaseListener;
```

```java
public class MyPhaseListener
  implements PhaseListener{

 @Override
 public void
 afterPhase(PhaseEvent event) {
   System.err.println("AFTER PHASE - " +
   event.getPhaseId().getName());
 }

 @Override
 public void
 beforePhase(PhaseEvent event) {
   System.err.println("BEFORE PHASE - " +
   event.getPhaseId().getName());
 }

 @Override
 public PhaseId getPhaseId() {
   return PhaseId.ANY_PHASE;
 }
}
```

Class name and package are up to you—this is just an example.

On the template page, add the following as a first child to the
<h:body> element:

```xml
<f:phaseListener
 type="book.jakarta8.hacc.jsfgui.
   listeners.MyPhaseListener" />
```

(remove the line break in the attribute value).

Chapter 5

- **Exercise 1:**

  The JSON representation reads as follows:

  ```
  {
    "title":"Somewhere over the Rainbow",
    "composers": [
     {
      "firstName":"Harold",
      "lastName":"Arlen"
     },
     {
      "firstName":"E. Y.",
      "lastName":"Harburg"
     }
    ],
    "performer":"Judy Garland",
    "makeYear":1939
   }
  ```

- **Exercise 2:**

  Say for editing you have downloaded an edit.png icon, and for deleting a delete.png icon. Create a folder, "src/main/webapp/static/images," and put edit.png and delete.png there. Inside the tableRow() JavaScript function, replace the <button> tags with the following:

  ```
  <button onclick="edit('+id+')">
   <img src="images/edit.png"/>
  </button>
  ```

  and

  ```
  <button onclick="del('+id+')">
   <img src="images/delete.png"/>
  </button>
  ```

For sizing or other styling purposes, you can add a class to the buttons, as in `<button class = "delBtn">` ... or `<button class = "edtBtn">`, and then add in your `styles.css` file as follows or similar:

```
button.delBtn img, button.edtButton img {
  height: 32px,
  width: 32px
}
```

Chapter 6

– **Exercise 1:**

(1.) No, although DAOs help to improve code quality. (2.) No, the entity manager will take care of that. (3.) No, this is the entity classes' responsibility. (4.) Yes. (5.) No, EJBs help to improve DAO handling, but you don't need to use them if it does not fit your needs.

– **Exercise 2:**

(1.) True. (2.) No, you can provide the table name inside the `@Table` annotation: `@Table( name = "TAB_NAME" )`. (3.) No, you can provide the column name inside the `@Column` annotation: `@Column( name = "COL_NAME" )`. (4.) True.

– **Exercise 3:**

The updated `script.js` file reads as follows:

```
function showEntry(entity) {
 $('#lastName').val(entity.lastName);
 $('#firstName').val(entity.firstName);
 $('#birthday').val(entity.birthday);
 $('#status').val(entity.status);
 $('#idView').html(
   (entity.id && entity.id !="")?
   'ID: ' + entity.id : ");
}
```

```
function clearEntry() {
 $('#lastName').val("");
 $('#firstName').val("");
 $('#birthday').val("");
 $('#status').val("");
 $('#idView').html("");
}

function makeForm() {
 ...

 $('#memberEntry').html(
  '<table><tbody> \
  ' + formLine("Last name", "lastName") + '\
  ' + formLine("First name", "firstName") + '\
  ' + formLine("Birthday", "birthday") + '\
  ' + formLine("Status", "status") + '\
  </tbody></table>'
 )
 .append(
 ...
}

function makeList(data) {
 clearList();

 function tableRow(lastName, firstName,
   birthday, status, id) {
  return '<tr id="tab-'+id+'"> \
   <td>'+lastName+'</td> \
   <td>'+firstName+'</td> \
   <td>'+birthday+'</td> \
   <td>'+status+'</td> \
   <td><button onclick="edit('+id+')"> \
     EDIT</button></td> \
```

```
      <td><button onclick="del('+id+')"> \
        DEL</button></td> \
      </tr>';
    }

  var tab = $('<table class="listTable"></table>');
  tab.html('<tbody>');
  $.each(data, function(ind,val) {
    tab.append(tableRow(
      val.lastName, val.firstName,
      val.birthday, val.status, val.id));
  });
  tab.append('</tbody>');
  $('#memberList').append(tab);
}

function submit() {
 var id = $('#idView').html();
 if(id.length > 4) id = id.substring(4);

 var lastName = $('#lastName').val();
 var firstName = $('#firstName').val();
 var birthday = $('#birthday').val();
 var status = $('#status').val();

 var url = (id == "") ?
  "../webapi/member" :
  "../webapi/member/" + id;
 var meth = (id == "") ?
  "POST" : "PUT";

 $.ajax({
  method: meth,
  url: url,
  data: { lastName:lastName,
   firstName:firstName,
   birthday:birthday,
```

```
     status:status }
  })
  .done(function(msg) {
   clearErr();
   loadList();
  })
  .fail(function(jqXHR, textStatus, errorThrown) {
   showErr("AJAX: " + errorThrown);
  });
}

$(function() {
 makeForm();
 loadList();
})
```

(unchanged functions not shown). The Calypso REST interface class gets updated to the following:

```
@Path("/member")
public class Calypso {
 @EJB private MemberDAO members;

 @GET
 @Path("/")
 @Produces("application/json")
 public Response list() {
  List<Member> memberList = members.allMembers();
  StringBuilder outStr = new StringBuilder();
  outStr.append("[");
  outStr.append(
   memberList.stream().sorted().
   map((Member itm) ->
    "{\"firstName\":\"" +
      itm.getFirstName() + "\"," +
    "\"lastName\":\"" +
      itm.getLastName() + "\"," +
```

```
        "\"birthday\":\"" +
          itm.getBirthday() + "\"," +
        "\"status\":\"" +
          itm.getStatus().stream().
         map(Status::getName).sorted().
         collect(Collectors.joining(", ")) +
         "\", " +
        "\"id\":" + itm.getId() + "}"
      ).collect(Collectors.joining(","))
    );
   outStr.append("]");
   return Response.ok().entity(
    outStr.toString()
   ).build();
  }

  @GET
  @Path("/{id}")
  @Produces("application/json")
  public Response entity(@PathParam("id") int id) {
   Member m = members.getMember(id);
   return Response.ok().entity(
    "{\"lastName\":\"" +
      m.getLastName() + "\", " +
    "\"firstName\":\"" +
      m.getFirstName() + "\", " +
    "\"birthday\":\"" +
      m.getBirthday() + "\", " +
    "\"status\":\"" +
      m.getStatus().stream().
      map(Status::getName).sorted().
      collect(Collectors.joining(", "))
     + "\", " +
    "\"id\":" + m.getId() + "}"
   ).build();
  }
```

```java
@POST
@Path("/")
@Produces("application/json")
public Response post(
    @FormParam("lastName") String lastName,
    @FormParam("firstName") String firstName,
    @FormParam("birthday") String birthday,
    @FormParam("status") String statusStr) {
  Set<String> statusSet =
    Stream.of(statusStr.split(",")).
    collect(Collectors.toSet());
  int newId = members.newMember(lastName,
    firstName, birthday, statusSet);
  return Response.ok().
    entity("{\"id\":"+ newId +"}").build();
}

@PUT
@Path("/{id}")
@Produces("application/json")
public Response put(
    @FormParam("lastName") String lastName,
    @FormParam("firstName") String firstName,
    @FormParam("birthday") String birthday,
    @FormParam("status") String statusStr,
    @PathParam("id") int id) {
  Set<String> statusSet =
   Stream.of(statusStr.split(",")).
   map(String::trim).collect(Collectors.toSet());
  members.updateMember(lastName, firstName,
    birthday, statusSet, id);
  return Response.ok().entity("{}").build();
}
```

```
@DELETE
@Path("/{id}")
@Produces("application/json")
public Response del(@PathParam("id") int id) {
 members.deleteMember(id);
 return Response.ok().entity("{}").build();
 }
}
```

Finally, the MemberDAO needs to be rewritten to the following:

```
@Singleton
public class MemberDAO {
 @PersistenceContext
 private EntityManager em;

 public List<Member> allMembers() {
  TypedQuery<Member> q =
    em.createQuery("SELECT m FROM Member m",
      Member.class);
  List<Member> l = q.getResultList();
  return l;
 }

 public Member getMember(int id) {
  return em.find(Member.class, id);
 }

 public int newMember(String lastName,
    String firstName, String birthday,
    Set<String> status) {
  Member m = new Member();
  m.setFirstName(firstName);
  m.setLastName(lastName);
  m.setBirthday(birthday);
  m.setStatus(status.stream().map(String::trim).
    map(Status::new).
    collect(Collectors.toSet()));
```

```java
    em.persist(m);
    em.flush();
    return m.getId();
}

public void updateMember(String lastName,
    String firstName, String birthday,
    Set<String> status, int id) {
  Member m = em.find(Member.class, id);
  m.setLastName(lastName);
  m.setFirstName(firstName);
  m.setBirthday(birthday);

  // Add new status members that are not
  // already in the STATUS table
  Set<Status> currentStatus = m.getStatus();
  status.stream().forEach( st -> {
   if(! currentStatus.stream().
      anyMatch(
       st2 -> st2.getName().equals(st) )) {
    m.getStatus().add(new Status(st));
   }
  });

  // Remove status members that are not part
  // of the parameter
  new ArrayList<Status>(currentStatus).
    stream().forEach(st -> {
   if(!status.contains(st.getName())) {
    m.getStatus().remove(st);
   }
  });

  em.persist(m);
}
```

```
public void deleteMember(int id) {
 Member m = em.find(Member.class, id);
 em.remove(m);
}
}
```

Chapter 7

- **Exercise 1:**

  (1.) No, an EJB can have only a local interface, only a remote interface, or both. (2.) No, a no-interface EJB means it can only be used for local access. (3.) No, a remote EJB can be accessed from the same application, a different application on the same Jakarta EE server, or applications from other servers on the same machine or anywhere in the network. (4.) No, a stateful EJB *can* maintain a state. (5.) No, at least a singleton EJB never gets instantiated more often than just once. (6.) No, for local EJBs you can also use injection via the @EJB annotation. (7.) No, only the remote interfaces must be exported if EJBs get used remotely.

- **Exercise 2:**

  The pom.xml file of the library (JSE, plain Java) project reads, for example, as follows:

```
<project xmlns="http://maven.apache.org/POM/4.0.0"
 xmlns:xsi=
  "http://www.w3.org/2001/XMLSchema-instance"
 xsi:schemaLocation=
  "http://maven.apache.org/POM/4.0.0
   http://maven.apache.org/xsd/maven-4.0.0.xsd">
<modelVersion>4.0.0</modelVersion>

<groupId>book.jakarta8</groupId>
<artifactId>MyDateTime</artifactId>
<version>0.0.1-SNAPSHOT</version>
<packaging>jar</packaging>
```

```xml
<name>MyDateTime</name>
<url>http://maven.apache.org</url>

<properties>
 <project.build.sourceEncoding>UTF-8
 </project.build.sourceEncoding>
</properties>

<dependencies>
 <dependency>
  <groupId>junit</groupId>
  <artifactId>junit</artifactId>
  <version>3.8.1</version>
  <scope>test</scope>
 </dependency>
</dependencies>

<build>
 <plugins>
  <plugin>
   <artifactId>maven-compiler-plugin
   </artifactId>
   <configuration>
    <source>1.8</source>
    <target>1.8</target>
   </configuration>
  </plugin>
 </plugins>
</build>
</project>
```

The class reads as follows:

```java
package book.jakarta8.mydatetime;

import java.time.ZonedDateTime;
import java.time.format.DateTimeFormatter;
```

```java
public class MyDateTime {
 public String date(String format) {
  ZonedDateTime zdt = ZonedDateTime.now();
  String outStr = "";
  try {
   outStr = (format == null || "".equals(format) ?
     zdt.toString() :
     zdt.format(DateTimeFormatter.
       ofPattern(format)));
  } catch(Exception e) {
   e.printStackTrace(System.err);
  }
  return outStr;
 }
}
```

The pom.xml file of the EJB project reads as follows:

```xml
<project xmlns="http://maven.apache.org/POM/4.0.0"
 xmlns:xsi=
  "http://www.w3.org/2001/XMLSchema-instance"
 xsi:schemaLocation=
  "http://maven.apache.org/POM/4.0.0
   http://maven.apache.org/xsd/maven-4.0.0.xsd">
<modelVersion>4.0.0</modelVersion>

<groupId>book.jakarta8</groupId>
<artifactId>MyDateTimeEjb</artifactId>
<version>0.0.1-SNAPSHOT</version>
<packaging>ejb</packaging>

<name>MyDateTimeEjb</name>
<url>http://maven.apache.org</url>
```

```
<properties>
 <project.build.sourceEncoding>UTF-8
 </project.build.sourceEncoding>
 <failOnMissingWebXml>false
 </failOnMissingWebXml>
</properties>

<dependencies>
 <dependency>
  <groupId>book.jakarta8</groupId>
  <artifactId>MyDateTime</artifactId>
  <version>0.0.1-SNAPSHOT</version>
 </dependency>
 <dependency>
  <groupId>javax</groupId>
  <artifactId>javaee-api</artifactId>
  <version>8.0</version>
 </dependency>
 <dependency>
  <groupId>junit</groupId>
  <artifactId>junit</artifactId>
  <version>3.8.1</version>
  <scope>test</scope>
 </dependency>
</dependencies>

<build>
 <plugins>
  <plugin>
   <artifactId>maven-compiler-plugin
   </artifactId>
   <configuration>
    <source>1.8</source>
    <target>1.8</target>
   </configuration>
  </plugin>
```

```
        <plugin>
         <groupId>org.apache.maven.plugins</groupId>
         <artifactId>maven-ejb-plugin</artifactId>
         <version>3.0.1</version>
         <configuration>
          <generateClient>true</generateClient>
          <ejbVersion>3.2</ejbVersion>
          <clientExcludes>
           <clientExclude>
             book/jakarta8/mydatetimeejb/ejb/*
           </clientExclude>
          </clientExcludes>
         </configuration>
        </plugin>
       </plugins>
      </build>
    </project>
```

The classes and interfaces read as follows:

```
package book.jakarta8.mydatetimeejb.ejb;

import javax.ejb.Local;
import javax.ejb.Remote;
import javax.ejb.Singleton;

import book.jakarta8.mydatetime.MyDateTime;
import book.jakarta8.mydatetimeejb.ejb.
   interfaces.MyDateTimeLocal;
import book.jakarta8.mydatetimeejb.ejb.
   interfaces.MyDateTimeRemote;

@Singleton
@Local(MyDateTimeLocal.class)
@Remote(MyDateTimeRemote.class)
public class MyDateTimeEjb
    implements MyDateTimeLocal,
        MyDateTimeRemote {
```

```
  public String date(String format) {
   return new MyDateTime().date(format);
  }
}
-
package book.jakarta8.mydatetimeejb.ejb.
     interfaces;

public interface MyDateTimeLocal {
 String date(String format);
}
-
package book.jakarta8.mydatetimeejb.ejb.
     interfaces;

public interface MyDateTimeRemote {
 String date(String format);
}
```

For the EAR project, create it via New → Java EE → Enterprise
Application Project. Make sure that it includes the EJB project
as a dependency, and also copy the library JAR [Project-
MyDateTime]/target/MyDateTime-0.0.1-SNAPSHOT.jar to the
EAR project's "Ear-Content/lib" folder (you have to create that
folder). You can now deploy the EAR project on the server.

The client class reads as follows:

```
import java.util.Properties;

import javax.naming.InitialContext;
import javax.naming.NameClassPair;
import javax.naming.NamingEnumeration;

import book.jakarta8.mydatetimeejb.ejb.
     interfaces.MyDateTimeRemote;
```

```
public class Client {
 public static void main(String[] args) {
  String remoteServerHost = "localhost";
  String remoteServerPort = "3700";
  Properties props = new Properties();
  props.setProperty("java.naming.factory.initial",
    "com.sun.enterprise.naming." +
    "SerialInitContextFactory");
  props.setProperty("java.naming.factory.url.pkgs",
    "com.sun.enterprise.naming");
  props.setProperty("java.naming.factory.state",
    "com.sun.corba.ee.impl.presentation.rmi." +
    "JNDIStateFactoryImpl");
  props.setProperty("org.omg.CORBA.ORBInitialHost",
   remoteServerHost);
  props.setProperty("org.omg.CORBA.ORBInitialPort",
   remoteServerPort);
  try {
   InitialContext ic = new InitialContext(props);
   MyDateTimeRemote testEJB = (MyDateTimeRemote)
    ic.lookup("book.jakarta8.mydatetimeejb.ejb."+
        "interfaces.MyDateTimeRemote");
   System.out.println(testEJB.date(
      "yyyy-MM-dd HH:mm:ss"));
  } catch (Exception e) {
   e.printStackTrace(System.err);
  }
 }
}
```

Make sure you've added the MyDateTimeEjb-0.0.1-SNAPSHOT-client.jar file from the EJB project and the gf-client.jar file from Glassfish's "lib" folder as library dependencies.

Chapter 8

– **Exercise 1:**

JAX-WS web service methods are allowed to return string arrays.
The new method thus reads as follows:

```
@WebMethod
public String[] date2(String dateFormat) {
 ZonedDateTime zdt = ZonedDateTime.now();
 String outStr = "";
 String errMsg = "";
 try {
  outStr = ("".equals(dateFormat) ?
    zdt.toString() :
    zdt.format(DateTimeFormatter.
         ofPattern(dateFormat)));
  errMsg = "";
 } catch(Exception e) {
  errMsg = e.getMessage();
 }
 return new String[] { outStr, errMsg };
}
```

– **Exercise 2:**

Run the `jaxws:wsimport` maven goal again to rebuild the interface
artifacts, reflecting the new web method. In the servlet, replace

```
out.println("<p>" +
  date("yyyy-MM-dd HH:mm:ss") +
  "</p>");
```

with

```
String[] wsRes = date2("yyyy-MM-dd HH:mm:ss");
out.println("<p>" +
  wsRes[0] + "</p>");
out.println("<p style=\"color:red\">" +
  wsRes[1] + "</p>");
```

Try date("rubbish") to see the error message.

Chapter 9

- **Exercise 1:**

  Create a topic and a queue as described in the chapter. Create an
  EJB-only Maven project with the following coordinates:

  ```
  <groupId>book.jakarta8</groupId>
  <artifactId>jmsexample</artifactId>
  <version>0.0.1-SNAPSHOT</version>
  <packaging>ejb</packaging>
  ```

  The whole pom.xml reads as follows:

  ```
  <project xmlns="http://maven.apache.org/POM/4.0.0"
   xmlns:xsi=
     "http://www.w3.org/2001/XMLSchema-instance"
   xsi:schemaLocation=
     "http://maven.apache.org/POM/4.0.0
     http://maven.apache.org/xsd/maven-4.0.0.xsd">
  <modelVersion>4.0.0</modelVersion>

  <groupId>book.jakarta8</groupId>
  <artifactId>jmsexample</artifactId>
  <version>0.0.1-SNAPSHOT</version>
  <packaging>ejb</packaging>

  <name>jmsexample</name>
  <url>http://maven.apache.org</url>
  ```

```xml
<properties>
 <project.build.sourceEncoding>UTF-8
 </project.build.sourceEncoding>
 <failOnMissingWebXml>false
 </failOnMissingWebXml>
</properties>

<dependencies>
 <dependency>
  <groupId>javax</groupId>
  <artifactId>javaee-api</artifactId>
  <version>8.0</version>
 </dependency>
 <dependency>
  <groupId>junit</groupId>
  <artifactId>junit</artifactId>
  <version>3.8.1</version>
  <scope>test</scope>
 </dependency>
</dependencies>
<build>
 <plugins>
  <plugin>
   <artifactId>maven-compiler-plugin
   </artifactId>
   <configuration>
    <source>1.8</source>
    <target>1.8</target>
   </configuration>
  </plugin>
  <plugin>
   <groupId>org.apache.maven.plugins</groupId>
   <artifactId>maven-ejb-plugin</artifactId>
   <version>3.0.1</version>
```

```
    <configuration>
     <generateClient>true</generateClient>
     <ejbVersion>3.2</ejbVersion>
    </configuration>
   </plugin>
  </plugins>
 </build>
</project>
```

The project facets are EJB Module 3.2 and Java 1.8. The classes read as follows:

```
package book.jakarta8.jmsexample;

import javax.annotation.PostConstruct;
import javax.annotation.Resource;
import javax.ejb.Singleton;
import javax.ejb.Startup;
import javax.inject.Inject;
import javax.jms.JMSContext;
import javax.jms.Queue;

@Singleton
@Startup
public class QueueSender {
 @Resource(lookup = "jms/TestQueue")
 private Queue queue;

 @Inject
 private JMSContext jmsContext;

 @PostConstruct
 public void go() {
  String msg = "My JMS Message";
  jmsContext.createProducer().send(queue, msg);
 }
}
-

package book.jakarta8.jmsexample;
```

```java
import javax.annotation.PostConstruct;
import javax.annotation.Resource;
import javax.ejb.SessionContext;
import javax.ejb.Singleton;
import javax.ejb.Startup;
import javax.ejb.Timeout;
import javax.ejb.Timer;
import javax.ejb.TimerConfig;
import javax.inject.Inject;
import javax.jms.JMSContext;
import javax.jms.Topic;

@Singleton
@Startup
public class TopicSender {
 @Resource(lookup = "jms/TestTopic")
 private Topic topic;

 @Inject
 private JMSContext jmsContext;

 @Resource
 private SessionContext context;

 @PostConstruct
 public void go() {
  context.getTimerService().
    createSingleActionTimer(5000,
            new TimerConfig());
 }

 @Timeout
 public void programmaticTimeout(Timer timer) {
  String msg = "My JMS Message";
  jmsContext.createProducer().send(topic, msg);
 }
}
```
—

```java
package book.jakarta8.jmsexample;

import javax.annotation.Resource;
import javax.ejb.ActivationConfigProperty;
import javax.ejb.MessageDriven;
import javax.ejb.MessageDrivenContext;
import javax.jms.JMSException;
import javax.jms.Message;
import javax.jms.MessageListener;
import javax.jms.TextMessage;

/**
 * Message-Driven Bean implementation class
 * for: TestQueueReceiverEJB
 */
@MessageDriven(
 activationConfig = {
  @ActivationConfigProperty(
   propertyName = "destinationType",
   propertyValue = "javax.jms.Queue")
 },
 mappedName = "jms/TestQueue")
public class TestQueueReceiverEJB
   implements MessageListener {
 @Resource
 private MessageDrivenContext mdc;

 public void onMessage(Message message) {
  try {
   System.err.println("!#!#!#! QUEUE " +
      ((TextMessage)message).getText());
  } catch (JMSException e) {
   e.printStackTrace(System.err);
  }
 }
}
```
_

```java
package book.jakarta8.jmsexample;

import javax.annotation.Resource;
import javax.ejb.ActivationConfigProperty;
import javax.ejb.MessageDriven;
import javax.ejb.MessageDrivenContext;
import javax.jms.JMSException;
import javax.jms.Message;
import javax.jms.MessageListener;
import javax.jms.TextMessage;

/**
 * Message-Driven Bean implementation class for:
 * TestQueueReceiverEJB
 */
@MessageDriven(
 activationConfig = {
  @ActivationConfigProperty(
   propertyName = "destinationType",
   propertyValue = "javax.jms.Topic")
 },
 mappedName = "jms/TestTopic")
public class TestTopicReceiverEJB
    implements MessageListener {
 @Resource
 private MessageDrivenContext mdc;

 public void onMessage(Message message) {
  try {
   System.err.println("!#!#!#! TOPIC " +
      ((TextMessage)message).getText());
  } catch (JMSException e) {
   e.printStackTrace(System.err);
  }
 }
}
```

Chapter 11

- **Exercise 1:**

  Proceed as described in the text: add user "user1" to the messaging provider and appropriately update the Glassfish configuration using the web administration console.

- **Exercise 2:**

  Proceed as described in Chapter 7. Create an EJB-only project with facets EJB Module 3.2 and Java 1.8. Make sure the Eclipse project correctly uses Java 8. Use a pom.xml file as described in Chapter 7 (watch the <failOnMissingWebXml> property, the <packaging> element, and the client-exclude setting for the EJB plugin).

- **Exercise 3:**

  The changed EJB reads as follows:

```
package book.jakarta8.juliansecureejb.ejb;

import javax.annotation.security.DeclareRoles;
import javax.annotation.security.RolesAllowed;
import javax.ejb.Local;
import javax.ejb.Remote;
import javax.ejb.Singleton;

import book.jakarta8.juliansecureejb.ejb.interfaces.
    NameEjbLocal;
import book.jakarta8.juliansecureejb.ejb.interfaces.
    NameEjbRemote;

@Singleton
@Local(NameEjbLocal.class)
@Remote(NameEjbRemote.class)
@DeclareRoles({"admin"})
public class NameEjb
  implements NameEjbLocal, NameEjbRemote {
  @RolesAllowed({"admin"})
```

```
public String hello(String name) {
 return "Hello " + name + " (admin)";
 }
}
```

For that "adminX" experiment, change @DeclareRoles({"admin"})
to @DeclareRoles({"adminX"}) and @RolesAllowed({"admin"})
to @RolesAllowed({"adminX"}). If you then redeploy the application,
even after you enter the correct password for the "AdminUser" login,
an error message appears on the screen. Obviously user "AdminUser"
does not map to role "adminX". See Figure A-1.

HTTP Status 500 - Internal Server Error

type Exception report

messageInternal Server Error

descriptionThe server encountered an internal error that prevented it from fulfilling this request.

exception

`javax.servlet.ServletException`

root cause

`javax.ejb.EJBAccessException`

root cause

`javax.ejb.AccessLocalException: Client not authorized for this invocation`

note The full stack traces of the exception and its root causes are available in the GlassFish Server Open Source Edition 5.1.0 logs.

GlassFish Server Open Source Edition 5.1.0

Figure A-1. *Security breach for the Julian day converter enterprise application project*

Chapter 12

- **Exercise 1:**

  In Eclipse, right-click on the hacc-jsf project, then Run As →
  Maven build.... Enter "package" at "Goals." Press the "Run" button.
  This will create the WAR file in project folder "target" (press F5
  on the folder to update the view). Fetch the WAR file, then in a
  terminal enter the following:

```
cd GLASSFISH_INST
bin/asadmin deploy \
    --name hacc \
    --contextroot hacc \
    /path/to/war/hacc-jsfgui-0.0.1-SNAPSHOT.war
```

As the URL you have to enter `http://localhost:8080/hacc/` in your browser.

Chapter 13

– **Exercise 1:**

The updated class starts with the following:

```
import java.util.logging.Logger;
...
@Singleton
@Startup
public class App {
  private final static Logger LOG =
    Logger.getLogger(App.class.toString());
  ...
```

Inside the class, replace each `System.err.println(...)` with `LOG.info(...)`. To convert `long` values to strings, write `Long.toString(...)`.

– **Exercise 2:**

Adapt the `server.policy` file as described in the text. Add the files `log4j-core-2.11.2.jar`, `log4j-api-2.11.2.jar`, and `log4j-appserver-2.11.2` (or whatever version you downloaded) from the Log4j2 distribution to folder "GLASSFISH_INST/glassfish/domains/domain1/modules/autostart." Add a `log4j2.json` file to "GLASSFISH_INST/glassfish/domains/domain1/lib/classes." Example configuration files are presented in the text.

To your project, add the following as a dependency:

```
<dependency>
  <groupId>org.apache.logging.log4j</groupId>
  <artifactId>log4j-api</artifactId>
  <version>2.11.2</version>
</dependency>
```

Add a static logger field to each class and use it as follows:

```
public class SomeClass {
 private final static Logger LOG =
    LogManager.getLogger(SomeClass.class);
 ...
 public void someMethod() {
  ...
  LOG.trace("Trace: ...");
  LOG.debug("Debug: ...");
  LOG.info("Some info: ...");
  LOG.warn("Some warning: ...");
  LOG.error("Some error: ...");
  LOG.fatal("Some fatal error: ...");
  ...
  try {
   ...
  } catch(Exception e) {
   ...
   LOG.error("Some error", e);
  }
 }
}
```

Chapter 14

– **Exercise 1:**

Enable JVM monitoring as follows if you haven't done so already:

```
cd GLASSFISH_INST/bin
./asadmin set \
  server.monitoring-service.
  module-monitoring-levels.jvm=HIGH
```

(no line break and no spaces after "service"). Now

```
cd GLASSFISH_INST/bin
./asadmin list --monitor "*"
```

gives us a list containing the monitorable object "server.jvm. memory." If we now enter

```
BASE_URL=http://localhost:4848/monitoring/domain
curl -s -u admin:PASSWORD -X GET \
 -H "Accept: application/json" \
 $BASE_URL/server/jvm/memory \
 | jq .
```

we get a JSON string containing

```
"usedheapsize-count": {
 "unit": "bytes",
 "lastsampletime": 1558877537635,
 "name": "UsedHeapSize",
 "count": 170636808,
 "description": "Amount of used memory
   in bytes",
 "starttime": 1558856758609
}
```

Adding a filter gives us the used heap space in bytes, as follows:

```
BASE_URL=http://localhost:4848/monitoring/domain
curl -s -u admin:PASSWORD -X GET \
 -H "Accept: application/json" \
 $BASE_URL/server/jvm/memory \
 | jq '.extraProperties.entity
    ["usedheapsize-count"].count'
```

(no line break and no spaces after the ".entity").

– **Exercise 2:**

Add the following to pom.xml inside the <dependencies> section:

```
<dependency>
   <groupId>org.apache.logging.log4j</groupId>
   <artifactId>log4j-api</artifactId>
   <version>2.11.2</version>
</dependency>
```

Add a static field as follows to class App:

```
...
import org.apache.logging.log4j.LogManager;
import org.apache.logging.log4j.Logger;
...
class App {
 private static Logger LOG =
    LogManager.getLogger(App.class);
 ...
}
```

and replace all `System.err.println()` instructions with `LOG.info()`. In the exception catch clauses, also add the following exception objects to the parameters:

```
...
}catch(Exception e) {
  LOG.error("Cannot register MBean", e);
}
...
}catch(Exception e) {
  LOG.error("Cannot unregister MBean", e);
}
```

Index

A

ACID Paradigm, 241
Action listener, 114–116
Advanced monitoring, 342–344
AJAX core tags
    attributes, 121, 122
    components, 117, 119, 120
    Java class, 117
    submit() method, 118
    template file, 119
Application clients, 298
Application, JSF
    development process, 55–58
    household accounting
        class, 64
        expression language, 59
        HTML 5 file, 59
        JSF template page, 60
        method expression, 61
        register(), 62
        template file, 58
        value expression, 61
asadmin command-line, 339, 342
ASADMIN tool, 257, 261, 296, 347

B

Batch processing, 4
Bean-managed transactions, 248–250
Bean validation, 4, 102
Boolean properties, 65

C

clearEntry() function, 154
clearErr() function, 154
clearList() function, 155
ComponentSystemEventListener, 123
Conditional rendering/repetitions, 98, 99
Container-managed transactions, 245–248
Context and Dependency Injection
    (CDI), 4
Core tags, JSF
    components, 99–101
    converter
        components, 107
        date and times, 109, 110
        ID, 107
        injected class, 106
        numbers, 108
    library, 83
    listeners, 114–116
    selection items, 110–114
    validator, 101–106
createSingleActionTimer()
    invocation, 202

D

Data access object (DAO)
    @EJB annotation, 174
    entity class member, 174
    package book.jakarta8.calypsojpa.ejb,
        174, 175

437

J, K

Jakarta EE
  applications and cloud, 10, 11
  servers and licensing, 8, 9
Java API for XML Processing (JAXP),
    5, 216, 217
JavaBean classes, 64–66
Java 8, 13
JavaMail, 4
Java Management Extensions
    (JMX), 6, 347, 352
Java Messaging Service (JMS), 3, 227
Java Naming and Directory Interface
    (JNDI), 5, 190
Java Persistence API (JPA)
  boolean indicators, 165
  DAO, 171–176
  database access, 165, 166
  EclipseLink, 169, 170
  entity, add, 176–179
  relations, add, 179–182
  SQL database, set up, 166, 167
    authentication mechanism, 168
    Glassfish server configuration, 168
    JDBC resource, 168
    unique ID generation, 169
JavaScript code, characteristics, 149
JavaScript object notation (JSON), 142
Java Server Faces (JSF), 2
  application (*see* Application, JSF)
  core tags (*see* Core tags, JSF)
  EL (*see* Expression language)
  FacesContext class, 129
  injected classes, 127, 128
  lifecycle, 130
  localized resources, 79–82
  namespace, 124, 125
  navigation case, 125–127

process validations, 129, 131
renderResponse(), 131
and servlets, 53, 54
tag library, 82, 83
view, 129
Java Server Pages (JSP), 2, 4, 340
Java Standard Edition (JSE 8)
  configurations, 12
  features, 13
  language, 12
  success, 12
Java Standard Environment (JSE), 317
Java Transaction API (JTA), 3, 239
Java XML Binding (JAXB), 6, 216
JDBC, 5, 242
JDK logging
  adding output to
    console, 319, 320
  Glassfish log files, 319
  hierarchy, 322, 323
  JSR 47 methodology, 320, 321
  levels, 321, 322
  thresholds, 322
JMS/connector service
    statistics, 344
JMS messaging, secure, 263
JMX GUI clients, 349, 350, 352
JMX monitoring
  custom JMX modules,
    implementation, 353–357
  Glassfish AMX monitoring
    extension, 352, 353
  Glassfish's JMX interface, 347–349
  JMX GUI clients, 349, 350, 352
JSON Binding (JSON-B), 3
JSON Processing (JSON-P), 3
JSP Standard Tag Library
    (JSTL), 5, 98

Printed in the United States
By Bookmasters